Democracy in Latin America

MANCHESTER
UNIVERSITY PRESS

PERSPECTIVES ON DEMOCRATIZATION

The series presents critical texts on democratization processes and democratic theory. Written in an accessible style, the books are theoretically informed and empirically rich, and examine issues critical to the establishment, extension and deepening of democracy in different political systems and contexts. Important examples of successful democratization processes, as well as reasons why experiments in democratic government fail, are some of the issues analyzed in the series. The books in the series make an important contribution to the ongoing debates about democracy, good governance and democratization.

SHIRIN M. RAI AND WYN GRANT series editors

already published

Funding democratization
PETER BURNELL AND ALAN WARE (editors)

Globalizing democracy
KATHERINE FIERLBECK

Democratization in the South
ROBIN LUCKHAM AND GORDON WHITE (editors)

Democracy in Latin America

Mobilization, power and the search for a new politics

GERALDINE LIEVESLEY

MANCHESTER UNIVERSITY PRESS
Manchester and New York

distributed exclusively in the USA by St. Martin's Press

Copyright © Geraldine Lievesley 1999

The right of Geraldine Lievesley to be identified as the author of
this work has been asserted by her in accordance with the Copyright,
Designs and Patents Act 1988.

Published by Manchester University Press
Oxford Road, Manchester M13 9NR, UK
and Room 400, 175 Fifth Avenue, New York, NY 10010, USA
http://www.man.ac.uk/mup

Distributed exclusively in the USA
by St. Martin's Press, Inc., 175 Fifth Avenue, New York,
NY 10010, USA

Distributed exclusively in Canada
by UBC Press, University of British Columbia, 6344 Memorial Road,
Vancouver, BC, Canada V6T 1Z2

British Library Cataloguing-in-Publication Data
A catalogue record for this book is available from the British Library

Library of Congress Cataloging-in-Publication Data applied for

ISBN 0 7190 4310 7 *hardback*
    0 7190 4311 5 *paperback*

First published 1999

06 05 04 03 02 01 00 99   10 9 8 7 6 5 4 3 2 1

Typeset in Trump Medieval
by Graphicraft Limited, Hong Kong
Printed in Great Britain
by Bell & Bain Ltd, Glasgow

Dedicated to the memory of
my father, Dennis Lievesley

Contents

Acknowledgements

I owe a number of debts of gratitude to many friends who have supported and encouraged me in the writing of this book. The first must be to my editors at Manchester University Press, Nicola Viinikka and Pippa Kenyon. The second is to my colleagues at Manchester Metropolitan University, including Frank Carr, Michael Tyldesley and Jules Townshend and, most particularly, Neill Nugent and Catherine Danks. The last is to my daughters, Claire and Kate, for their forbearance and, most importantly, to my husband David for his sustenance, caring and love.

G. L.

Introduction

When, on 1 January 1994, Zapatista guerrillas and peasants from the southern Mexican state of Chiapas rose in rebellion against the central government and the ruling Partido Revolucionaria Institucional (PRI, Institutional Revolutionary Party), it appeared a throwback to an earlier age of armed struggle and talk of revolution in Latin America. However, despite its armed stance, the Ejército Zapatista de Liberación Nacional (EZLN, Zapatista National Liberation Army) has persistently contended that political violence is not the solution to Mexico's socio-economic problems and has demanded a more inclusionary and representative system, whereas older insurrections, such as those in Colombia and Peru, continue to adhere to the conviction that military struggle is the answer. The Partido Comunista del Perú–Sendero Luminoso, PC del P–SL (Communist Party of Peru – Shining Path) has fought against the Peruvian state since 1980. In December 1996, the seizure of the Japanese embassy in Lima and the subsequent hostage siege undertaken by its rival organization, the Movimiento Revolucionario Túpac Amaru (MRTA, Túpac Amaru Revolutionary Movement) underlined the persistence of the armed option, but perhaps also its ultimate ineffectiveness (given that the embassy was stormed and all the guerrillas killed). Nevertheless, this type of political activity still appears anomalous in the 1990s, when the majority of left-wing parties have acknowledged the incapacity of insurrectionary strategies to challenge for state power, leading to their decision to engage in electoral politics. The ideological subtext here implies an acceptance by the Left of the pre-eminence of liberal democracy (albeit, it will be argued, of a narrow and elitist variety) and an acceptance of the historic defeat of Marxism.

The Chiapas rebellion combines traditional peasant demands for land and social justice – essentially for the goals of the Mexican Revolution to be honoured – with modernity; it can be described as the first revolution on the Internet, as well as exhibiting an astute management of international opinion. It has had a tremendous impact upon national politics, which have been in a state of seemingly constant crisis since the assassination of PRI Presidential candidate Donaldo Colosio in March 1994. Other assassinations, increasing political violence, corruption scandals, the growing electoral challenge of the centre-right Partido de Acción Nacional (PAN, National Action Party) and the left-leaning Partido de la Revolución Democratica (PRD, Party of the Democratic Revolution), and massive economic problems all challenge the long-established hegemony of the PRI. Mexico – long regarded as one of the most stable political systems of the subcontinent – appears to be entering a period of transformation (a similar situation of potential regime breakdown has characterized recent Venezuelan politics). The phenomenon of Chiapas introduces serious questions about the nature of both Mexican and, more generally, Latin and Central American politics, which this book seeks to address. It also challenges the 'end of ideology' triumphalism associated with writers such as Francis Fukuyama,[1] and articulated by Osvaldo Hurtado when he writes that 'ideology is no longer fundamental in Latin American political debate'.[2] Counterpoised to the prevailing idea of a political consensus existing between political actors of erstwhile left, right and centre and of a growing homogeneity of political processes across national borders – represented by the 'pacted' model of democracy – is the reality of the fundamental socio-economic problems which continue to beset Latin and Central American countries, the skewed distribution of political power, the unequal access to maintenance of elite politics and the attempted exclusion of the mass of people from citizenship which other authors remark upon.

This book is concerned with the nature of contemporary Latin American political culture. It does not adopt an institutional approach but rather attempts to define and situate actors, processes and perceptions in order to reach some evaluation of how democratic political systems are. It uses as a skeleton for its study an assessment of two broad and conflicting perspectives upon politics. One, which can be described as the official or established orthodoxy held by both practitioners of government and many academics, talks of politics as being consensual and of democracies as 'pacted'. In this it adheres to the tradition of the Western liberal democratic paradigm, which considers politics to be a compromise and repudiates ideological, holistic world-views.[3] Thus, in discussing countries which have experienced transitions to constitutional government following periods of military rule, Lawrence Whitehead describes the emergence of 'stalemate' politics: 'reformist, populist or socialist projects had been attempted and had failed; reactionary authoritarian projects had also been attempted and had also failed'.[4]

The other perspective is based upon a radical democratic model which is critical of the first approach and advocates popular empowerment. It projects the need for structural transformations of Latin American societies and economies (to avoid needless repetition, this umbrella term is to be understood as including Central America unless otherwise stated), the opening up of political systems and the end of mass marginalization. It thus continues in the Marxist and socialist tradition but searches for new methods and strategies, given the bankruptcy of earlier radical projects.

The first model is posited upon a non-participatory view of democracy, with politics being regarded as an elite occupation. Commentators have pointed to a general decline in partisan alignment and in party competition. Even relatively new parties – such as the Brazilian Partido dos Trabalhadores (PT, Workers' Party), Causa R (Radical Cause) and the Movimiento al Socialismo (MAS, Movement Towards Socialism) of Venezuela – are seen to be pragmatic, multi-class, catch-all organizations. Others have talked of the emergence of a social-democratic mainstream.[5] The logical consequence of an 'end of ideology' position may be demonstrated by the emergence of 'anti-politics' politicians. Alberto Fujimori, the President of Peru since 1990, is a clear example,[6] while other countries appear to be joining the trend.[7] Walter Little argues that old-style radical parties of the Left and Right have virtually disappeared or have no real influence, and that parties of the Left now accept neo-liberalism and adopt antistatist positions. Voters regard political parties as corrupt and ineffective and are increasingly apathetic.[8] He contends that in future, government will be confined to a technocratic approach to problem-solving. For Little, whilst partisan politics may be of dwindling importance, polit-ics as the 'effective and efficient delivery of services' remains central.[9] However, it might be argued that if this criterion is applied, the inability of Latin American states to deliver the most basic services – such as nutrition, health, housing and employment – to their populations suggests that this type of 'politics' is malfunctioning. Growing social polarization based upon extremes of income inequalities and the rolling back of state provision of services may produce what can be termed 'democratic fatigue'. I return to this possibility and its con-sequences with respect to the breakdown of stability and the loss of governmental legitimacy in subsequent chapters.

The radical model of democratic politics regards govern-ments resting upon the foundations of citizen passivity and disillusionment as systems which are not working and are, therefore, unable to claim democratic credentials. One influ-ential strand builds upon the experience of the new social movements,[10] indicating the important role that popular par-ticipatory mechanisms played in opposition to military rule, their efforts to maintain their independence from the corporatist intentions of governments and their relationship to revolu-tionary regimes. Such groups have also developed innovative survival strategies to help withstand the effects of economic restructuring, both in terms of the pursuit of neo-liberal projects and attempts to resolve the debt crisis. Petras and Morley have contested that when the neo-liberal economic policies of states are praised as 'economic miracles', the consequences for the poor are not included in the analysis.[11] They also challenge whether such policies are compatible with democracy. This critique has resonances with the debate concerning the negative impact neo-liberalism has had upon the possibilities for the growth and health of democratic institutions and practices in the former Eastern European countries.[12]

The radical perspective believes that ideological politics can-not be deemed to have ended – as the 'pacted' model wishes us to believe – so long as profound socio-economic and political cleavages persist within Latin American states. It maintains that the first model holds a narrow conception of politics (con-centrating upon voting and formal institutions) which ignores the fact that such – clearly desirable but not sufficient – rights cannot be effectively enjoyed within the context of the socio-economic marginalization of large sectors of populations. Indeed,

it accuses the 'pacted' model of being a self-serving justification of the continuance of elite rule of a deeply undemocratic
nature. Grassroots activism is presented as genuinely democratic whilst 'official' democracy is condemned as a sham.
However, the radical model has itself been criticized as naive
in overlooking the weakness in terms of organizational sustainability and political consciousness of the new social movements
and their capacity to influence local, national and transnational
power structures.

Radical writers additionally point to what they see as growing trends towards authoritarianism (the so – called *autogolpe*,
literally 'self-made coup', of President Fujimori of Peru is seen
as merely the most obvious example[13]). The transition from
military to civilian rule in many Latin American countries
since 1980 'has brought the introduction of electoral processes,
the establishment of elected parliaments or congresses and, in
some cases, greater individual freedom but these regimes have
continued to function within an authoritarian institutional
framework and to pursue policies totally at variance with democratic procedures'.[14] If this analysis were correct – and clearly
it would be contested by many – then it would be necessary to
start a debate which offered proposals for stemming the growth
of authoritarianism, such as the strengthening of the repres-
entativeness and accountability of public institutions and the
expansion of participatory mechanisms within both government
and civil society.

Different types of political system are discussed in the book.
One category will be those countries such as Mexico, Colombia
and Venezuela which have generally been regarded as consolidated, 'pacted' systems. Another is those consolidating systems
which have moved from military to civilian rule since the first
such transition in Peru in 1980. A third constitutes those emerging from civil war in Central America and a fourth the experience of the socialist systems of Cuba and Nicaragua under the
Frente Sandinista de Liberación (FSLN, Sandinista Liberation
Front) which have faced or may have to contend with profound
political transformations, although clearly the Cuban situation
must still be a matter of conjecture. Similarities abound as all
states wrestle with the question of democratic consolidation
and decide what form of democracy they will engage with –
elitist and restricted, or popular and participatory? However,
each individual state must also be placed within the historical

background and contemporary political context in which it operates as well as its position both within Latin America and the world order.

Clearly, a detailed history of Latin and Central America is outside the possibilities of a single volume, but I will attempt to indicate significant elements such as dictatorships, insurgencies, links with foreign powers, the impact of international financial institutions, previous levels of political participation, attitudes towards citizenship and what it entails, degrees of repression, government legitimacy and respect for legality. Thus, for example, the impact of the drugs wars upon contemporary Colombian politics cannot be understood without reference to the prolonged civil conflict of 1948–57 known as *la violencia*, the nature of its pacted settlement, and the degree and strength of institutionalization of its governmental structures, as well as their vulnerability to corruption. Also of relevance is the nature of the political culture of respective states, the political actors and processes which populate and characterize them and the rules and methods of the political game (what is known in Spanish as *hacer política*). Individual political cultures approach political activity differently in distinct historical periods. To return to military to civilian transitions, the evidence suggests that popular movements were involved to a greater or lesser degree in opposition to military rule. Their mobilization was used as a bargaining tool by traditional political parties of the centre-right in their negotiations with the generals. The tendency since the establishment of civilian 'pacted' democracies has, however, been for members of the political elite to pursue a demobilization of popular activism and the reinvigoration of clientelist relations and practices. This has not been the purpose solely of centre and right-wing politicians; left-wing parties may also be seen as culpable.[15] One must additionally explore the interactions between different political actors, be they politicians, the military, the churches, business or social movements, and the divisions of opinion between and within them with respect to the socio-economic strategies governments adopt.

A case in point is that of debt and the socio-economic and political implications it has had for Latin America. The major consequence has been the virtually universal application of neoliberal economic restructuring programmes (under considerable pressure from international governments and agencies). The debt crisis contributed to the collapse of military authoritarian regimes (who were responsible for its creation), debilitated already 'pacted' systems, and severely threatened the evolution and maturing of relatively newly 'pacted' ones. The decision of the FSLN to apply restructuring measures in Nicaragua after 1987 (although this was provoked by the costs of the *contra* war) was, arguably, an important factor in their electoral defeat in 1990. The fallout of the debt and its restructuring aftermath have dominated recent Latin American politics and have contributed to growing political instability (the 'democratic fatigue' which I referred to earlier). It is possible that incumbent regimes risk the alienation of large proportions of their citizens if they do not begin to address structural investment, income redistribution, tax reforms and efficient service provision by the state; that is, long- rather than short-term planning. It will be suggested that neo-liberal policies do not contribute to a country's present and future socio-economic health. If the vast majority of people are expected to face the negative consequences of economic policies they have had no part in deciding upon, and if stratification based upon class, gender and ethnicity continues to prevent the significant entry of large communities into 'official' politics, then the human resources of Latin America are being squandered and political instability and the drift towards authoritarianism are definite possibilities.

The body of the text is divided in the following manner. Chapter 1 offers a more substantial presentation of the two theoretical perspectives summarized in this introduction. While Chapter 2 looks at the political establishment, Chapter 3 examines how the Latin American Left has attempted to engage with contemporary political systems and the strategies it has devised to do so. Chapters 4 and 5 approach the question of popular mobilization, with the former analysing the insertion of new social movements into formal politics and the latter the role of women. Chapter 6 discusses the constraints upon further democratization of different types of system by addressing socio-economic and political issues which challenge the legitimacy of individual states. The Conclusion offers some final thoughts on the nature of *hacer política* within Latin America and the prospects for either greater authoritarianism or a deepening of participatory democracy.

Notes

1 F. Fukuyama, *The End of History and the Last Man* (Harmondsworth, Penguin, 1992).

2 Quoted in R. A. Pastor (ed.), *Democracy in the Americas: Stopping the Pendulum* (New York, Holmes & Meier, 1989), p. 99.

3 A classic example of this is to be found in B. Crick's *In Defence of Politics* (Harmondsworth, Penguin, 1964), pp. 54–5: 'Politics . . . cannot be reduced to a system of precise beliefs or to a set of fixed goals . . . ideology means an end to politics. . . . [It] is an activity – lively, adaptive, flexible and conciliatory.'

4 L. Whitehead, 'The Alternatives to Liberal Democracy: A Latin American Perspective', *Political Studies*, XL (1992), 148.

5 T. A. Vasconi and E. Peraza Martell, 'Social Democracy and Latin America', *Latin American Perspectives*, XXVII: 20: 1 (Winter 1993).

6 The 1995 presidential and congressional election results produced a 10 per cent share of the vote for all political parties (G. Rochabrun, 'Deciphering the Enigmas of Alberto Fujimori', *NACLA. Report on the Americas*, XXX: 1 (July–August 1996), 23, with commentators asking if this meant the end of partisan alignment in Peru.

7 Carlos Menem was elected President of Argentina in 1989 as a *peronista* but has displayed no distinctive political loyalties, rather, governing in a highly opportunistic manner. However, one might suggest that this merely reflects the long-standing populist seam running through Latin American politics in the twentieth century.

8 W. Little, 'Democracy in Latin America: Problems and Prospects', *Democratization*, 1: 2 (Summer 1994), 202–3.

9 *Ibid.*, 204.

10 The diverse nature of the new social movements is discussed in Chapter 4; influential contributions to the literature include S. Eckstein, *Power and Popular Protest: Latin American Social Movements* (Berkeley, University of California Press, 1989) and J. Foweraker, *Theorising Social Movements* (London, Pluto Press, 1995).

11 J. Petras and M. Morley, *Latin America in the Time of Cholera: Electoral Politics, Market Economics and Permanent Crisis* (New York, Routledge, 1992), pp. 12–15. The neoliberal agenda involves creating the most favourable climate for foreign investment, with an accompanying reduction in state intervention and protection of domestic industry and the shifting of the locus of economic decision-making to external agencies.

12 David Ost has suggested that, whereas 'political democracy hinges on co-operation, compromise and inclusion, market reform is best introduced by surprise, inflexibly, with initial brutality, and often conflicts with the short-term interests of the majority of the people'. 'Is Latin America the Future of Eastern Europe?', *Problems of Communism*, XLI: 3 (May–June 1992), 48.

13 On 5 April 1992, Fujimori closed down all institutions of representative government; although subsequently reopened, power remains concentrated in the Presidency, with the strong backing of the Peruvian army and the state security services.

14 J. Petras and S. Vieux, 'The Transition to Authoritarian Electoral Regimes in Latin America', *Latin American Perspectives*, 83: 21: 4 (Autumn 1994), 5. The authors identify the following elements of authoritarianism: (i) decision-making with respect to public spending cutbacks, investment, debt servicing and other

issues is shaped by external agencies; (ii) executive branches of government dominate legislatures; (iii) there has been a continuity of personnel – military, bureaucracy, judiciary – between military and civilian regimes; (iv) massive public corruption; (v) the continuation of a climate of fear with the violation of human rights, albeit on a reduced scale.

15 While the Izquierda Unida (IU, United Left) controlled the municipal government of Lima, in the period 1983–85, it attempted to rein in union and popular-sector demonstrations against the Peruvian government's economic policies, the explanation being that it sought respectability as a legitimate political actor; after the 1985 election of Alán García's Alianza Popular Revolucionaria Americana (APRA, American Popular Revolutionary Alliance), the government pursued an understanding with it which, eventually, produced a split within the IU. For discussion of this see P. Paredes, 'Las luchas del movimiento obrero y popular bajo el Belaundismo', *Sociedad y Política*, 12 (1981) and J. Crabtree, *Peru under García: An Opportunity Lost* (London, Macmillan, 1992), pp. 77–81.

1

Models of democracy

In this chapter, I elucidate and criticize the two models of the nature and consolidation of democratic politics in Latin America to which I referred in my introduction. These models will be a constant presence within the remainder of the text as various aspects of the political process are highlighted. I will return to an appreciation of their validity and viability in the concluding remarks.

The approaches originate from the broad schools of liberal democracy and socialism, albeit allowing for some cross-fertilization and acknowledging various interpretations which coexist within them. My concern is to explore the meaning of democracy and citizenship in contemporary Latin America. It may well be that, having scrutinized the multiple meanings of these two concepts, the conclusion reached will be that neither paradigm is adequate to the task. It may then be useful to entertain the replacement of these historically hidebound models with a new political culture, one which Juan Carlos Portantiero has described as a public sphere not 'bound by the logic of the market or the logic of the state', but rather characterized by the decentralization of decision-making and the realization of authentic participation.[1] Such a culture would focus upon a re-examination of the entrenched elite-mass dichotomy of Latin American political systems and the emergence of new forms of expression and organization; that is, an active and autonomous civil society.

However, I am running on too fast. First, we must examine already existing models of transition and consolidation of Latin American politics and their relationship to democracy. For simplicity's sake, I will refer to them henceforth as the liberal pacted and radical participatory schools of thought. Here I am being consciously diffuse: these are broad categories which I will attempt to make sharper as I proceed. The general features of the liberal model include elite pacts, limited change and top-down political relationships. The radical approach divides into several streams. One, which I will term the optimistic position, argues that the preconditions for a revolutionary socialist transformation still exist. More adherents adopt a second view, which is that there must be a major revision of the socialist model in the light of the historical experience of regimes such as Cuba under Castro and Nicaragua under the FSLN, the failure of insurrections, principally in Central America, to take state power and also with respect to the internal party structures and strategies and the relationship of the Left to the popular movement.

A useful entry point into the liberal, pacted model is O'Donnell, Schmitter and Whitehead's 1986 work, *Transitions from Authoritarian Rule*,[2] which has been a highly influential contribution to the debate on democratization with reference to regimes experiencing military to civilian transfers of power. Its basic tenets also correspond to much orthodox thinking about the nature of government in those consolidated states regarded as being based upon 'foundational pacts' (Colombia and Venezuela, for example). Karl and Schmitter characterize the latter as 'a series of accords that are interlocking and dependent upon each other' between civilians and the military, political parties and a 'social contract' between state agencies, business and trade unions.[3] Such pacts originate from negotiations between elites enjoying relative autonomy from popular pressure. In writing about Mexico's post-1928 political settlement, Alan Knight argues that it has resulted not in a consolidated democracy but rather in an 'inclusionary authoritarianism' and a consensus based 'not on equal, plural access to political power and still less on a functioning liberal democracy but, rather on a tacit bargain between incumbent political elites'.[4] I will be returning to the specifics of the Colombian, Venezuelan and Mexican examples in Chapter 2, but I now resume consideration of the *Transitions* argument, which is encapsulated by a comment in Part 4 entitled 'Tentative Conclusions about Uncertain Democracies': 'The only route to political democracy is a pacific and negotiated one based upon initial liberalisation and on the subsequent introduction of institutions of electoral competition, interest representation and executive accountability – with the trade-offs and uncertainties such a course . . . entails.'[5]

The key words here are 'negotiated', 'trade-offs' and 'uncertainties'. An underlying assumption of the editors is the need for system management through agreement between military and civilian elites in both transitional periods and consolidating/consolidated regimes. Pacts are negotiated between certain political actors, the inference being that they will share a consensus upon the nature of the political and socio-economic structures they desire and that the civilian elements will be constituted by those on the centre and centre-right of the political spectrum. Representatives of the political Left are excluded unless they are willing to accept the parameters chosen. Pacts are predicated upon the attempted systematic exclusion of mass movements from political influence. The process of negotiation is based upon an acknowledgement of mutual or at least non-antagonistic interests on the part of the elites (the latter meaning that there may be short-term disagreements over policies, but that these are not insuperable) and acceptance of procedural rules. Such a process can, thus, only survive so long as pact partners continue to honour the deal.

The second key word – 'trade-off' – follows logically from the notion of 'negotiation'. The *Transitions* perspective was tentatively optimistic about the prospects for democratization (in countries such as Brazil, Peru, Chile, Argentina and Uruguay, which experienced military to civilian transfers in the 1980s) but held a rather narrow conception of what this entailed. Arguing the necessity of respect for constitutional structures, rules pertaining to political activity, a legitimate role for opposition parties and open elections, it insisted that the latter must be monitored in order to obtain 'the proper balance'. This was explained in the following manner: 'parties of the Right-Centre must be "helped" to do well – and parties of the Left-Centre and Left should not win by an overwhelming majority'.[6] The rationale given for what appears to the observer as an undemocratic practice of electoral massage was that it was essential to assuage the anxieties of the military and civilian right in order to prevent them preparing a coup (and, implicitly, it was necessary in order to reassure interested external parties such as the USA and international financial institutions with a stated interest in what occurs in Latin America). In similar fashion, parties of the Left who wished to participate in the pacted political system had to be prepared to abandon far-reaching programmes of socio-economic change, as the latter were highly likely to stimulate military reaction. As Cammack puts it: 'radical challenges to an emerging elite consensus . . . can be depicted as foolhardy provocations threatening a further plunge into chaos'.[7] The 'end of ideology' thread, which as I have indicated runs through much of the literature, is evident here. The election of centre-right parties will benefit the moderate Left who, so long as they repudiate radical groups on their flanks, will finally be allowed to engage with the political game, but transformative strategies – such as income redistribution or the expansion of participatory mechanisms – will be kept off the political agenda. Thus for the pacted settlement to continue, there will have to be a moratorium on structural reforms of either a political or socio-economic nature. The liberal democratic model does not accept the – radical – contention that democracy is fundamentally flawed unless it involves major socio-economic change. Indeed, the pursuit of political stability 'may have the effect of freezing existing social and economic arrangements',[8] which will undoubtedly be to the advantage of existing privileged sectors. Profound social change is likely to destroy fragile democratic transitions; therefore the Left – and the masses – must accept limited progress for an undetermined future until consolidation is achieved.

The notion of compromise – the 'trade-off' – substituting for ideological discourse is an intrinsic constant of this model. However, the compromise is predicated upon decisions made by elites whilst the poor – those huge sections of Latin American societies who need socio-economic change – are its non-consulted recipients. This inequality of experience is reflected in the virtually universal adoption by both post-military civilian and already existing elite settlement governments of neo-liberal economic programmes. The selection of such policies is frequently described as being based upon the criteria of efficiency and technical expertise (the idea that they will modernize and create growth whilst eradicating constraints upon the former) rather than upon ideological choice. Thus, Walter Little contends that 'there is virtual unanimity as to the kinds of macro-economic strategies to be pursued in contrast to the past when policy-making was bedevilled by ideological competition'.[9] The third essential element of the *Transitions* argument is that of 'uncertainty', which I will return to in the last section of this chapter.

Most authors of this school make a distinction between the processes of liberalization and democratization. Scott Mainwaring describes the former as the easing of repression within an authoritarian regime, while the latter would be the succeeding transition process to democratic rule. Liberalization begins with splits in the authoritarian coalition either because a sense of relative success causes some groups to want to relax control and others, of a more hardline persuasion, to resist this or, conversely, policy and legitimacy failures provoke regime disintegration. It then proceeds through interactions with opposition groups as ruling elites attempt to retain as much political power as possible. Liberalization ushers in changes to the political system to which other actors react; although it does not involve a commitment to democratization, it may well stimulate events which move out of authoritarian control.[10] This scenario could be equally applied to military to civilian transitions; to regimes based upon 'foundational pacts' which may now face periods of crisis (Mexico, Venezuela and Colombia) and to post-socialist and insurrectionary transitions.

There is no logical or inevitable reason why liberalization should lead to democratization. In the case of military to civilian transitions, for example, those elements of liberalization which took place before the military withdrew (the so-called *apertura/abertura* (the Spanish and Portuguese words for 'opening')), which differed country-by-country permitted the reappearance of a political space allowing limited debate, media coverage, the re-emergence of established political parties and the emergence of some new ones, and an increased respect for civil rights (although this has not become an absolute right). Once such a liberalized environment had been established, the political system could move on to democratization or redemocratization (depending upon previous political cultures), but it could also return to authoritarianism. Even if the first two options were to be followed, there would still be an enormous gap between the election of a civilian government and the creation of a democratic culture, with its attendant institutions and practices, which was embraced by the majority of citizens. Mainwaring argues that the first, minimal, stage would involve competitive elections, as near-universal suffrage as possible and the protection of basic civil liberties but that, at this stage, there could be no assumption that there was a consensus upon democratic values (this would also be dependent upon the type of political culture in existence before the advent of authoritarian rule).[11] It can be argued that what is vital in order to breach the gap between the tentative establishment of democratic government and its consolidation is the resurrection and reinvigoration of those groups within civil society who exist outside the boundaries of recognized and sanctioned political activity. This would need to be accompanied by substantive policy outcomes which citizens could identify as contributing to a widening and deepening of political, socio-economic and cultural opportunities within society, and the acceptance by Latin American states that they were both inefficient and corrupt and thus in need of major reform (which does not appear to be a close eventuality). With respect to policy outcomes, Mainwaring admits that social polarization renders the functioning of stable democratic institutions based upon the balancing of diverse sectoral interests very problematic.[12] Nevertheless, he assumes that it will continue.

An authoritarian regime must make an assessment of whether it can remain in government (some, the Argentinian *junta* in 1983, for example, will not enjoy this luxury) and whether staying will be as beneficial to it as departing. A military government will make this judgement on the basis of the degree of support it perceives it continues to receive from civilian elites, the latter's coherence and the intensity of popular mobilization. Authoritarian civilian regimes will make a similar calculation concerning their own unity, economic performance, degree of received legitimacy and how effectively they have managed to co-opt opposition politicians or manipulate popular movements. A regime such as the present Cuban one would also have to consider how well it had prepared for its succession and its relationship with opposition groups (in this particular case, this would mean Castro's attempts to negotiate with the Miami exile community, divisions within the latter and the foreign policy shifts of different US administrations).[13]

Each individual political system across the authoritarian military, civilian or state socialist spectrum will have its own complex set of power relationships between political actors which will exert a particular influence upon the processes of liberalization, democratization and democratic consolidation. The re-emergence of civil society – or its liberation from constricting ties – also reopens 'class, regional and group differences'. The role of transitional governments, from the pacted perspective, is 'to direct the social energies liberated by the disappearance of authoritarianism into a process of negotiation by means of the recreation of the party system'.[14] The role of parties is to mediate between diverse and potentially conflictual groups in order to prevent the growth of extremism. As previously noted, the liberal democratic pacted model has no patience with what it regards as the ideological politics of the Left (although it denies any ideological significance to that of the Right, particularly of the neo-liberal variety). A premium is thus placed upon the Latin American Left abandoning radical programmes in order 'to purchase the loyalty of the bourgeoisie'.[15] It is an accepted wisdom of this model that socio-economic transformations inspired by hopes of social justice would lead to the destabilization of regimes, as the privileged and propertied classes withdrew their support and began to yearn for the certainties of authoritarian rule. There is a need, however, to accept limited reform in order to pre-empt popular mobilization and possible destabilization. Whitehead acknowledges this while maintaining that 'in practice, it may take very little in material rewards to 'purchase the loyalty' of the lower classes'.[16] These statements say a great deal about the pacted model's assessment of the relative power of elites and popular sectors in Latin America and its belief that these arrangements will and should persist. Social justice is accepted as an ideally desirable ambition but, in the real world of practical politics, its accomplishment must be delayed in order to maintain the equilibrium of the system. The limited, institutional form of political democracy advocated by this model is to be regarded as the only route which might result in such a denouement.

The type of political culture which precedes such processes of transition and consolidation is of considerable importance. Authoritarian rule will have shaped policy, accepted and excluded political actors, determined which political issues are legitimate and created the climate of citizens' expectations. Military regimes, for example, attempted a 'substantial internal reorientation of existing civilian political forces'[17] through the suppression of political activity (Chile and Argentina); a reordering of the party system (Brazil) or the creation of government-controlled mass organizations (Peru). The PRI created a corporatist framework with the objective of legitimizing its rule, consolidating its monopolistic control over the Mexican state and preventing independent mass organization. This hegemony has weakened over time, beginning with the 1968 student riots, growing economic problems, internal party divisions and the emergence of an electorally combative opposition. In Cuba and Nicaragua, the governments sought to dismantle the power structures created by the Batista and Somoza dictatorships respectively and replace them with socialist institutions and political culture. However, they pursued this goal in distinct ways; Castro under the aegis of the Communist Party and the Sandinistas through the adoption of pluralism, elections and a commitment to gaining multi-class support.

A significant element in assessing the democratic effectiveness of post-authoritarian governments will be how successful they have been in breaking with the past and establishing their own distinctive political order. For example, critics would argue that post-military civilian governments in contemporary Latin America have singularly failed to address the heritage of military rule both in terms of continuing their socio-economic policies under the rubric of neo-liberalism, allowing the military tremendous influence over their own expenditure and, in the case of Peru, autonomy with respect to how the army has conducted its counter-insurgency war against Sendero Luminoso (SL, Shining Path). The military have also been in a position to veto judicial processes concerning their violation of human rights, despite popular demands that bringing the perpetrators to justice would be a valuable contribution to the building of democratic consciousness (when, in the case of Argentina, *junta* members were put on trial, the lack of severity of their sentences was farcical). It is interesting to note the resilience of civilian elites under military rule. Many of the political notables of the 1960s and 1970s returned to government office, often at the highest levels, in the 1980s. Thus Fernando Belaúnde Terry, ousted as President by the Revolution of the Armed Forces in Peru in 1968 returned – as President – in 1980, and Tancredo Neves, Goulart's Prime Minister before the 1964 coup, was elected to the Brazilian presidency in 1985 (although he died before his inauguration, being replaced by José Sarney). In countries which have experienced foundational elite pacts, politicians have had a long shelf-life (for example, the veteran Carlos Andrés Pérez, twice President of Venezuela),[18] as have parties

(AD and COPEI have dominated electoral politics in Venezuela since the 1958 Pact of Punto Fijo following the overthrow of the Pérez Jiménez dictatorship).[19] Even military governments' attempts to destroy party identification failed. Thus the Colorados and the Blancos would resume their domination of Uruguayan politics, and the Radicals and Peronists would together garner 90 per cent of the vote in the first Argentinian elections in 1983.[20] It is a paradox that military regimes which justified their intervention in politics by condemning the failure of civilian politicians to resolve major national problems, principally economic stagnation and the threat of subversion, were succeeded in office by such elites. The relationship between the two groups has unsurprisingly been a complex and often difficult one in the post-transition period, as will be indicated in the next chapter. Perhaps the most telling demonstration of the persistence of traditional elite politics was the defeat of the Sandinistas in October 1996 by Arnoldo Alemán, a politician with a strong *somocista* background – an ironic case of history coming full circle.

If we address – as the *Transitions* literature has done – military to civilian transfers of power, it is apparent that on entering governmental office, new governments could expect to enjoy a certain degree of public goodwill within the context of the end of dictatorship and repression and the restoration of citizenship. This honeymoon period would only, however, be translated into an enduring legitimacy if subsequently constitutional processes were respected, electoral promises kept and major social problems addressed. That is, such public support could not be regarded as unconditional. The pacted model, as outlined above, accepts that the political systems which emerged in the 1980s are based upon a narrow conception of democratic practice. Thus issues which are judged inimical to elite interests can be kept off the political agenda,[21] the Left's activities are circumscribed and mass non-participation in politics is regarded as healthy.[22] Writers have recognised this narrowness: 'In essence (they) seek to create a deliberate socioeconomic and political contract that demobilises emerging mass actors while delineating the extent to which all actors can participate or wield power in the future',[23] but many express the hope that once regimes are established and basic democratic structures and processes consolidated then such 'façade democracies', as Whitehead terms them, may acquire authenticity.[24]

The premise behind this line of argument is that democracy will become a habit once people grow accustomed to elections and other procedures, that is, once they internalize the rules of the new political game. However, the reverse might also happen, with democracy remaining superficial, expectations increasingly unsatisfied and unpopular governments resorting to acts of arbitrary authoritarianism which weak legislatures and parties are unable to prevent (such executive independence will be discussed in Chapter 2 with respect to presidents such as Carlos Menem of Argentina and Alberto Fujimori of Peru). Whitehead, in discussing how the contradiction between ensuring stability (as understood by ruling elites) and demands for participation and social justice aggravate the process towards democracy, calls for the pursuit of 'democratic political processes of persuasion, organisation, education and compensation' which, however, can only be developed over a very long time.[25] In the interim, his prognostication is gloomy: 'most Latin American democracies are likely to remain provisional, incomplete and unconsolidated'.[26] This is echoed by Schmitter, who has argued that without the creation of a strong civil society, a pluralist fragmentation of power-holding and a mature political consensus, Latin American states: 'may be compelled to choose from the restricted menu of a tame democracy based on . . . elite pacts, parliamentarism, coalition politics and proportional representation favouring centrist and right of centre parties'.[27] However, he does not appear to make a connection between the type of democracy proposed by the liberal pacted model and the outcomes that he predicts: that is, a political system based upon popular marginalization, a non-participatory ethos, a divorce between the political and the socio-economic, and an attempt to place urgently needed redistribution and reform on a back burner, is not destined to produce a democratic society. The 'democracy' it embraces is a negative one, while the radical model embraces an interactive definition, although critics of the latter suggest that its alternative may not necessarily be sustainable or, indeed, workable.

What I term the radical, participatory model of democracy is in fact a combination of a number of approaches which share, to varying degrees, the belief that democracy cannot be regarded as authentic unless it is participatory and rooted in popular experience. They take as their points of departure the new forms of activity and expression they identify with social movements and the role of a reconstructed Left within civilian regimes. All disagree with the model of pacted settlement with respect to the relationship between state and government; the role of political elites and their response to previous authoritarian rulers; the relationship between elites and people and, crucially, whether democracy should be procedural or substantive.

The *Transitions* model delineated the boundaries of the intellectual debate about the passage from authoritarian to democratic political systems. In his review of the book, Arthur MacEwan argues that O'Donnell and his colleagues, whilst maintaining that democracy was a non-ideological discourse, were deliberately setting an ideological agenda. They welcomed the demise of authoritarianism and the introduction of liberalizing and democratizing processes but they were also 'opponents of far-reaching social and economic change'.[28] This was because, he contends, they recognized a fundamental incompatibility between their understanding of political democracy and structural socio-economic transformations and, by implication, the participation of the mass of people in politics. Rejecting an exclusively and narrow political analysis of politics, MacEwan positions himself squarely in the radical camp by declaring the need for a holistic definition which encompasses both socio-economic indicators and popular participation. Petras and Morley concur: 'Throughout Latin America, powerful mass extraparliamentary socio-political movements have emerged as the central axis to any democratisation process and beyond, to be prominent actors in the redefinition of the relationship between state and society.'[29] Radical social movements' theorists have been castigated for taking an overly optimistic view of the democratic possibilities of their subjects and ignoring their shortcomings. Here the concept of *basismo* (literally, taking one's point of reference entirely from the base, that is, the practice and attitudes of popular sectors) is frequently introduced. This involves the notion that popular mobilization is intrinsically radical and is thus immune from criticism, despite obvious problems of organizational sustainability, levels of political awareness and impacts upon national decision-making (all of which are discussed in Chapter 4). There is a tendency to do this, although more sober assessments predominate. Thus MacEwan maintains that 'building popular movements that are themselves democratic would seem to be the only way to get where we want to go, even if success seems improbable'.[30] The inference being that, whatever the political and organizational obstacles, there is no real alternative to the slow, gradual and frequently tortuous build-up of popular democracy.[31]

The crucial distinction between the liberal pacted and radical participatory models hinges upon the relative weights they ascribe to procedural and substantive definitions of democracy. Thus the first model offers a limited perspective based upon 'the activities of actors who have or have not been given access to the formal levers of political change'.[32] It infers a 'bargaining about bargaining' approach between designated political groups. Radical theorists contend that it is both unrealistic and undesirable to differentiate the political from the socio-economic spheres. MacEwan argues that is it impossible to compartmentalize democracy in this manner: first, because the formal political process constantly interfaces with social life; second, that people's desires for improved living conditions and opportunities cannot be postponed indefinitely and finally, that the significance of formal procedures such as competitive elections and legislative rituals must be questioned if they operate within the context of extremes of wealth differentiation and deprivation (understood in its broadest sense of constricted access – based upon class, ethnic and gender classifications – to what may be regarded as democratic freedoms such as health, employment, educational and cultural opportunities). Whilst Adam Przeworski has contended that democracy does not and indeed perhaps cannot equal a just society,[33] Paul Cammack criticizes post-authoritarian governments as conservative regimes which are committed to the marginalization of popular concerns and of contentious issues. They are 'cautiously reformist, slow to eradicate inequality, elite-dominated and manipulative rather than genuinely participatory'.[34] The liberal pacted model, the radicals argue, believes in an abstract level playing field to which political actors have equal access and can thus engage in political activity with comparable skills and expertise. The radicals respond to this depiction with their own 'take' upon Latin American societies as highly stratified, dominated by elites and notorious for their exclusion from political and socio-economic power of the poor, who constitute the greater part of their populations.

Advocates of the pacted model do not ignore the narrowness of its definition of democracy. Thus Whitehead has described it as 'democracy by default'[35] and Rustow, as democracy 'on the instalment plan'.[36] Whitehead argues that this form of politics involves a lowering of popular expectations and greater inequity and that neo-liberal policy-making 'condones a considerable amount of interim illiberalism' (such as, for example, restrictions upon trade unionism) although protesting that it will eventually result in political and economic stability. Whitehead, himself, proposes a *'viable* programme of social democracy' based upon 'processes of persuasion, organisation, education and compensation' as an antidote to the need to 'reconcile political democratization with economic efficiency and social participation'[37] which, he feels, the pacted model does not adequately address. For Jorge Nef, the model has an 'overwhelming preoccupation with preserving a given socio-economic and institutional order – that is, liberal capitalism and US regional hegemony' which, he believes, could lead to a new era of instability (given the cleavages neo-liberalism creates).[38] Frightened by the threat of popular mobilization and the anxiety that broader-based governing coalitions would institute socio-economic programmes detrimental to their own privileged positions, political, economic and military elites have colluded to prevent these developments but, nevertheless, they still seek legitimacy. Castañeda points to the dilemma of 'giving the poor the vote and allowing their votes to be counted when they represent the majority of a society's inhabitants (which) leads to demands, policies and ruptures that . . . have historically tended to provoke military coups and the end of representative democracy.'[39]

Radicals maintain that the consequences of elite collusion have been far-reaching. Marxist parties have abandoned their long-term revolutionary programmes and concentrated upon becoming acceptable political actors in the hope of government office, and thus the socio-economic needs and political demands of the poor are underrepresented and therefore marginalized. Egalitarianism – understood by many as a fundamental tenet of democracy – is not regarded as a societal goal; indeed, liberals view it as dangerous to democratic consolidation. It has been replaced by the goals of economic efficiency and political stability encapsulated by the orthodoxies of neo-liberalism and pacted elite settlements. Advocates of the radical model would accept many of the criticisms made by the neo-liberals regarding the ineffectiveness of previous economic strategies, and particularly the need for the reform of inefficient, unrepresentative and corrupt state structures, but they disagree profoundly with the policy implications the latter have put forward.[40] They point, in particular, to what they recognize as a major contradiction between the export-oriented, foreign capital 'friendliness' which neo-liberalism desires and the economic precariousness and marginalization of the popular sectors which this produces and which, they contend, negates the idea of 'consensus' which the pacted model suggests exists. They also consider that the liberal approach, in its divorce of political from economic democracy, ignores the impact decisions about wages, prices, employment and investment priorities have upon an individual's ability to act politically to the greatest extent of his or her possibilities – that is, the notion of citizenship á la Rousseau, Mill or Marx. Additionally, it ignores the international financial context within which Latin American states make economic policy. This is particularly apposite with respect to the interconnected issues of debt servicing and neo-liberal restructuring. Arthur MacEwan maintains that 'economic life, in the context of imperialist domination, has continually regenerated the conditions of social conflict and political instability'.[41] He argues that the continuing dominating influence of external governments, institutions and agencies will prohibit the consolidation of a civil society imbued with a strong democratic identity and commitment which might be able to break the persistent historical cycle of political illegitimacy.

However, as already noted, the liberal pacted model is quite capable of criticizing itself. Writers who may accept its general tenets, nevertheless, have anxieties about this dichotomy between political and socio-economic democracy. Thus, in their book on the debt, Stallings and Kaufman conclude that this divide is 'arguably the most basic issue on the agenda for the future', although without specifying how the 'issue' would be addressed or when the 'future' would take place.[42] Samuel P. Huntington, in his influential attribution of a 'modest meaning' to democracy, argues that it can only flourish in the middle ground and that there is no room for 'gross inequalities' of income distribution.[43] Thomas Skidmore recalls that some fellow-participants at a conference organized by the Carter Center in 1986 disliked the narrow definition of democracy and declared the need for a major restructuring of the socio-economic order and mechanisms for popular involvement, as well as a recuperation of national sovereignty, particularly with respect to economic decision-making. He offers what he regards as significant internal and external factors which will be decisive in establishing resilient democracies. His domestic indicators include consensus on the rules of the game and strong democratic traditions (neither noticeably present in the histories of Latin American states); strong parties; a democratized military; and social reform (again, the last three are not evident characteristics of contemporary politics). Amongst the external conditions were resolution of the debt crisis and the need for more favourable trading arrangements between Latin America and other markets, as well as economic co-operation within the region.[44] One would want to add changes in relationship with both the USA and international financial institutions such as the World Bank and the International Monetary Fund (IMF).

The radical perspective is more multifaceted and less intellectually cohesive than the pacted model, with some writers concentrating upon the condition of Latin American Marxism in a post-Soviet world, others focusing upon the lessons to be drawn from socialist experiments such as Cuba, and a third current evaluating the political and transformative potential of new social movements While the liberal pact model is perceived as accepted wisdom, the radical model's role is to challenge this orthodoxy. A well-rounded radical critique has been offered by James Petras, both alone and with various collaborators. He argues that the paradigm of 'pacted democracy' makes a fundamental conceptual mistake in confusing the roles of 'state' and 'government'. The former is the *permanent* structure of power, which is underpinned by Latin American class relations, whilst the latter represents those executive and legislative institutions which can change without affecting the enduring nature of the state: 'the journey towards democracy thus represents both a rupture with past governments and a continuity with previous state structures'.[45] Democracy is not an absolute condition: the class nature of the state, its power-sharing arrangements, institutions and political economy determine the content and the substance of democracy. State elites share a common – if not always unanimous – perspective on their own best interests and concur on the need to restrain popular mobilization. This understanding is obscured by O'Donnell and others: 'who attempt to narrow the discussion of the political system to regime changes and the accompanying electoral procedures without examining the large historical/structural configurations within which those changes take place.'[46]

The pacted model's emphasis upon procedural political change accomplished during transitions and consolidations 'in liberal regimes neglects continued and pervasive authoritarian practices in politics and authoritarian values within political cultures. Petras and Vieux point to the continuities in personnel of military, bureaucracy and judiciary in individual states; the continuities of policy; the persistence of violations of human rights (what they term a 'culture of fear'[47]) and the application of anti-union and anti-popular legislation. They characterize as intrinsically undemocratic states which are not responsive to popular needs: 'today in Latin America electoral machines attempt to subordinate and disarticulate the social movements, to atomise the electorate and to discourage political vision'.[48]

The importance of participatory democracy, the status of social movements within the state and a holistic approach towards democracy incorporating socio-economic as well as political elements are amongst the main concerns of the radical model. Another consideration is the role the Latin American Left can play within contemporary politics. There are different approaches to this question, distinguished by their degrees of commitment to a self-reconstruction by the parties themselves.

The experience of living under sustained military or authoritarian regimes, taken with the shift in world politics following the fall of Soviet-style state socialism, have combined to produce significant changes in much left-wing thinking and practice. The former inculcated a respect for formal democratic freedoms previously denigrated by Marxist theorists, whilst the latter suggested that the Left could no longer deceive itself with claims to ideological supremacy. New strategies had to be developed, styles of political behaviour transformed and more reciprocal and egalitarian relationships developed with the popular sectors. For those radicals of a more orthodox persuasion, it was vital that change should be careful and should not undermine basic theoretical commitments. Thus Burbach and Nuñez – admittedly, writing in 1987 before the fall of the Soviet Union and the Eastern European bloc – criticized 'the new revisionists' who, accepting that Marxism was defunct, had 'an almost romantic belief that the masses and mass movements are the only hopes for the future'. Although other social groups such as the peasants and the urban poor were important elements in any socialist programme, 'the working class remains at the core of this process and the historic subject of all popular revolutions'. Additionally, despite calls for the democratization of internal party structures and decision-making and the elimination of the elite/mass approach, the need for a political vanguard persisted. Those arguing against such a vanguard 'ignore the reality that the popular classes in the early stages of most struggles are almost invariably influenced, if not dominated, . . . by the values of the established order'.[49]

Other left-wing writers and activists have recognized that their political and organizational criteria had to change to keep abreast of broader developments, but were not convinced that the intrinsic lines of battle had altered. Discussing the possibilities of democratization in El Salvador following the end of the civil war, Shafik Jorge Handal[50] distinguished between long-term and immediate considerations. He rejected 'the new thinking', which talked about political consensus and convergence, arguing that there was no similarity between developed and dependent capitalism whose relationship was still that of exploiters and exploited. Central America continued to be vulnerable to US intervention (the invasion of Panama in 1989 was a case in point), and the politics of Latin and Central America remained those of violence and repression in both governmental and economic spheres. Neo-liberal policies caused tremendous shocks to society, and particularly to the poor. Why should the latter be expected to tolerate poverty and deprivation and not react violently? For Handal, a socialist strategy was still the only one that could resolve the fundamental problems of the region, but it must be one which had discarded the dead wood of ingrained programmes and attitudes, and which acknowledged the importance of democracy. El Salvador and other countries had to pass through a democratic transition as a prelude to the passage towards socialism. This must not just involve lip-service to democracy, but rather a thoroughgoing commitment to the creation of structures and processes. The establishment of a pluralist political system, wide political debate, agrarian reform, the provision of basic infrastructure, the rebuilding of civil society after the ravages of war, the demilitarization of Salvadorean society (of both military and guerrillas) – all of these were indispensable elements without which a movement towards socialism would be doomed. He advocated decentralization of decision-making in the political arena and self-management in the economic, both of which would be facilitated by participatory mechanisms under popular rather than state control. All this notwithstanding, Handal maintained that democratic foundations would not produce socialist outcomes unless the entire process was guided by a revolutionary vanguard. Although he stressed the need for safeguards to prevent its entrenchment in power, these strictures appeared rather sanguine. Handal's position reflects an incapacity shared by many on the Left to move away from the idea that the revolution has to be made on behalf of those perceived as unable to make it themselves.[51]

In his and Barry Carr's review of contemporary left politics in Latin America,[52] Steve Ellner makes the point that although considerable inroads have been made into electoral politics (in Peru, Brazil, Mexico, Uruguay and Colombia, for example), parties have not shown evidence of staying power (in 1989, the PT of Brazil came close to winning the presidential election, but its 1994 and 1998 results were disappointing), and there is a marked tendency to embrace moderate, non-threatening policies. This latter may have its awards – thus in 1994 the MAS became a junior partner in Rafael Caldera's Social Christian Convergencia-dominated government in Venezuela – but also its drawbacks (the MAS found it was being eclipsed on the left by Causa R).[53] The consequences of its involvement in pacted systems for the Left have included increasing ideological vagueness, uncertainty about constituencies and attempts to maintain heterogeneous coalitions both within and outside party structures. Ellner contends that the only way the Left can have an effective presence within democratizing systems is if it assumes a more radical stance of an anti-neo-liberal character and predicated upon a militant rather than conciliatory political style.[54] This, of course, would raise the spectre of military intervention as well as speculation as to the probable response of the USA. Jorge Castañeda believes that the Left would have tremendous if not insurmountable problems in contesting state power. He argues it would be far more productive for left parties to harness themselves to the momentum created by popular mobilization and to concentrate their efforts at the local governmental level.[55] Whether the Latin American Left is capable of exerting more influence at either the national or local state levels will depend upon a variety of factors, including its own commitment to authentic democratization and the willingness of other political actors – both internal and external – to permit its participation.

How are the experiences of Latin American socialist transitions to be located within the two theoretical models discussed in this chapter? They have been few in number and only one – the Cuban Revolution – has achieved longevity (although not necessarily permanence). I would argue, however, that there are certain general criteria – the relationship between elites and masses, the existence of participatory mechanisms, methods of institutionalizing power and of providing service provision amongst them – which can be applied to all political systems. There has been a general reticence among Latin American radical theorists to offer objective criticism of either Cuba or the FSLN in power in Nicaragua (1979–90), inspired by an unwillingness to give succour to the enemies of socialism. Thus, Max Azicri rejects attempts to measure Cuba in liberal democratic terms, arguing that a 'conceptual framework based on Marxist–Leninist theory' should be applied and the Revolution 'judged by its own avowed political and societal goals and cultural and ideological premises'.[56] Certainly, this is an important critical consideration, but in an era when the vast majority of Latin American socialists have accepted the legitimacy of elements of formal democracy such as competitive elections, constitutional guarantees and engagement with government which they had previously castigated as shams, surely these issues should also contribute to the debate. It is also vital to recognize the differences between the Cuban and Nicaraguan Revolutions and to understand why they 'succeeded' – although this is obviously a relative evaluation – and why the Central American insurgencies of the 1980s or Sendero Luminoso in Peru have failed to take state power. I will concentrate here upon some general issues to be raised about the nature of the political model in Cuba and Nicaragua which will be examined, from different angles, in succeeding chapters.

Both socialist states came into being as the result of revolutionary transitions from personalized, corrupt dictatorships whose regimes were characterized by the 'absence of mechanisms for political participation – of a tradition of collective debate and decision-making – in the marginal classes'.[57] Once in power, they initiated programmes of institutionalization and socio-economic transformation, at the same time as being subjected to external pressure – the economic blockade orchestrated by the USA which pushed Cuba into the Soviet camp and the *contra* insurgency promoted by the USA – which had a significant (and in the Nicaraguan case, decisive) influence upon their political outcomes. The two countries followed distinct programmes of institutionalization. Cuba did not adopt a stereotypical 'Marxist–Leninist' path; the Partido Comunista de Cuba (PCC, Cuban Communist Party) was not established until 1965; there have certainly been serious infringements of human rights and the prohibition of political debate, but not systematic repression, and the post-1959 period has been characterized by Castro's highly personalist rule.[58] Azicri maintains that the governmental structures which were in place by the 1970s aimed to direct the informal mobilization which characterized the 1960s into 'clearly established avenues for . . . citizens' participation in the political process'.[59] What needs to be queried, however, is how hierarchical and stratified this process has been and whether the relationships between the PCC and the highest state organ, the National Assembly of Popular Power, and official mass organizations such as the Federación de Mujeres Cubanas (FMC, Federation of Cuban Women) are ones between equals or between dominant and subordinate institutions. If we obey Azicri's stricture and evaluate the Cuban political system purely on the basis of its realization of socialist democracy – amongst which he identifies the principals of both mass political participation and the decentralization of decision-making – how true to the model has its practice been? I will be looking at the different stages the Cuban Revolution has gone through – the foundational stage of the 1960s, institutionalization in the 1970s and the rectification initiatives of the 1980s and 1990s – in the next chapter in an effort to assess the nature of its socialism.

The Nicaraguan Revolution of 1979 – although influenced by and sharing a common intellectual heritage with the Cuban of twenty years earlier – followed a distinctive path characterized by its pursuit of multi-class support both during the insurrectionary and governmental periods. The Sandinistas also stressed the importance of high levels of popular participation and the close relationship between the FSLN and the masses.

Carlos Vilas has enunciated the difference between liberal democratic and Sandinista conceptions of citizenship. While, for the former, the citizen is an 'isolated individual' defined by his or her productive and property capacities and autonomy with regards to the state, 'For the Sandinista revolution, what converts the *individual* into a *citizen* is precisely the break with this reciprocal isolation and the voluntary integration into mass organisations, so that insofar as this integration takes place, the *practice* of their new political, social, economic and cultural rights has real life.'[60] There were various constraints upon the achievement of this vision. One, Vilas identifies as the tremendously low levels of national development inherited from the Somoza regime which had 'institutionalised the subordination of the economy and government to the domination of U.S. imperialism'. This meant that 'rather than a *transition to socialism*, the Sandinista revolution is entangled in a difficult *transition to development*'.[61] However, Nicaragua's attempts to pursue development were handicapped by the overriding constraint upon the ability of the Revolution to survive which was the *contra* war. Coraggio and Irvin suggest that the best way of assessing how democratic a revolutionary regime is to see 'how far it gives rise to autonomous mass organisations representing majority interests and how such organisations mediate between the new institutions of state and civil society'.[62] The problem – for Nicaragua – was how to prioritize popular mobilization and control within the context of civil war, US aggression and the economic destabilization which accompanied this. One would have to add the fact that despite its avowal of pluralist convictions, the FSLN was in many ways an authoritarian organization (it believed that it remained a vanguard party in the Marxist–Leninist understanding of that term, despite its democratic imagery) which became increasingly distant from its popular constituency and which, after its volte-face policy move towards economic restructuring from 1987, and the widespread distribution of economic favours to supporters which followed the 1990 election, appeared to have lost its reputation for moral integrity.

The contradiction at the heart of the FSLN's political programme was that between its courtship of the national bourgeoisie and the Nicaraguan middle classes (thus, private property was given legal protection and, although the state was to have a decisive role in the commanding heights of industry, the market was not to be replaced by state planning and the bourgeoisie were to be given a niche, albeit constricted, within the political system), and its endorsement of popular hegemony. There are strong parallels here with the situation in Chile under the Unidad Popular (UP, Popular Unity) government of Salvador Allende (1970–73).[63] Rather than representing the popular sectors, as a socialist state might be expected to do, the FSLN played a mediating role between classes and was eventually regarded by the mass organizations as having shown bias towards the bourgeoisie.

Despite a stated belief in electoral politics – demonstrated by the tolerance of opposition parties and the press – the institutional consolidation of the Nicaraguan Revolution was delayed until the 1984 elections (when the FSLN won a majority), because the Sandinistas argued that it was vital to allow for the building up of popular organizations so that they could carry 'effective weight within the formal political institutions of the state';[64] this, however, also gave the opposition an opportunity to organize. The state was committed to strengthening civil society but, over time, the dictates of war and its political strategy of class conciliation led it to contest the autonomy and attack the interests of its popular constituency. Luís Serra makes the point that the need to defeat the *contra* overrode all other considerations. Thus the FSLN lost peasant support because of its often authoritarian practices, such as the confiscation of produce brought to market in the interests of the war economy, forced migrations, the disastrous impact of the February 1988 adjustment package, the poor treatment of indigenous communities, and the general climate of militarization and violence. As the civil war continued, peasants found themselves caught between the opposing factions and the issue of peace became the dominant one. Also, given that the opposition, led by Violetta Chamorro and backed by the US, could promise this and the FSLN could not, the outcome of the 1990 elections should not have been surprising. In his assessment of the Sandinistas, Serra offers a general criticism of both liberal and radical models of politics in that both have an 'instrumental conception of political participation'; his argument is that both overvalue elite leadership and the professionalization of politics and patronize the ability of the popular sectors to determine their own destinies, thus encouraging apathy and indifference.

The FSLN, committed to a pluralist model of democracy, accepted (albeit charging fraud) its electoral defeats in 1990 and 1996, and although it retains control of the army, it has not attempted an extra-legal seizure of state power. Under first the Chamorro and now the Alemán governments, the socio-economic progress undeniably made and the participatory ethos created after 1979 have faced dismantlement. The consolidation of the transition from revolutionary to ever-more conservative rule which the 1996 election result represented has virtually erased the Sandinista experience from Nicaragua's political history. Will Cuba follow a similar course? The Cuban political system remains dominated by the Communist Party, but has clearly entered a transitional period which is likely to result in some form of pacted settlement between the incumbent government and those Miami exiles willing to negotiate with it in a post-Castro environment (and, undoubtedly, this process will be affected by the attitudes of intransigent exiles and the USA). If the structures and political culture created by the Cuban Revolution disappear, the only 'already existing' example of a Latin American socialist society will have disappeared, leaving the surviving Left with no available templates.

I conclude this chapter with a brief discussion of a preoccupation which is common to both the liberal and radical approaches. This is the question of democratic uncertainty and disillusionment (referred to as *desencanto* in Spanish) felt by citizens which may, over time, undermine the legitimacy of states and thus the development of mature and representative political systems. The two models find different causes for their anxieties.

The liberal perspective suggests that there are no certain outcomes in politics, and particularly not in processes of such complexity, involving so many variables, as those of transition and consolidation. The need for regime stability (in order to pre-empt a return to previous authoritarianism, which itself bestows a difficult and corrosive legacy upon succeeding governments) will mean freezing demands for greater social justice and attempting to restrain popular mobilization. Political elites will have to walk a tightrope between reaction and democratic progress. Implicit in this view is the notion that democracy is itself fragile and that political actors bear a heavy responsibility in protecting and preserving it. Groups representing social and political interests are obliged to be involved in a continuous process of transaction, mediation and compromise. Inevitably, all will be disappointed with outcomes at different junctures. For Adam Przeworski: 'The process of establishing a democracy is a process of institutionalising uncertainty. . . . In a democracy, no group is able to intervene when outcomes of conflicts violate their self-perceived interests.'[65] The maintenance of the political system is predicated upon losers accepting defeat gracefully, knowing that in the future they will be recompensed. A major shortfall of this theory – as noted earlier – is that some groups, who lack the necessary resources and influence within the system, will be penalized more than others. A radical critique is that the state is not a disinterested arena; groups with influence can accept short-term disappointments because they believe that their long-term interests will be safeguarded, but those lacking such influence can expect nothing. In defence of the liberal model, Przeworski has argued that constitutional guarantees and procedures can offer some defence to weaker social sectors (for example, minorities might be given veto rights over specific legislation in order to augment their sense of security). This might be helpful, but not for groups suffering from a wide range of political, social and economic disadvantages and, such as the poor, not constituting a minority.

Liberal writers have expressed misgivings concerning the pace and depth of democratic consolidation. O'Donnell has admitted that his pessimism has grown since the mid-1980s and he now believes that these political transformations will be lengthier, more difficult and 'even reversible'.[66] This could produce dissatisfaction and the risk that a democratic political culture cannot become entrenched. The reason for this was the twofold nature of the transitions. The first stage was that from authoritarian to democratizing regime and the second, from infant to maturing democracy. O'Donnell argues that the nature of the first stage may have important repercussions for the second. Comparing the implosion of authoritarianism (using the example of Argentina in 1983, which swiftly followed the 1982 defeat in the Malvinas/Falklands War) with a slow transition as experienced by Brazil (opened in 1974 by President Geisel, but not ending until 1985), he argues that the former might allow democratic government greater flexibility (and, thus, a greater chance of success) than the latter. The abrupt departure of a disgraced regime meant that, in the

Argentinian case, the military were able to exercise far less influence over subsequent civilian governments (although the history of attempted coups during the Alfonsín administration does not attest to this). The Brazilian case was more ambiguous in that the military regime had been less repressive and was more in control of the transition. Civilian elites had both positive and negative memories of military rule and might, therefore, be less concerned about a resumption of such rule. The military were able to exert significant influence even after they returned to barracks. O'Donnell suggests that if anti-authoritarian sentiment is weak then the commitment to democracy may also be less strong. This could result in what he terms a 'slow death' scenario: a gradual disintegration of democratic processes and a possible revival of authoritarianism. He further contends – going against the grain of the *Transitions* model – that the consolidation of a sustainable democracy could be in doubt if elitist political practices continue and elites remain in control of government.[67]

While proponents of the liberal model have expressed anxiety about the outcome of transitions from authoritarian to democratic government, they do not share the radical theorists' in-built distrust of the democratic credentials of the former. Thus for Petras, the process of democratization which began in the 1980s was merely a 'fragile interlude' between authoritarianisms,[68] with liberal democratic façades masking authoritarian structures and values. Munck has argued that the same period was characterized by 'capitalist restructuring', 'social disintegration' and a 'crisis of traditional political identities'. There was little indication of the emergence of 'new institutions' and a new 'way of doing politics' which had been thought possible at the start of the democratic decade.[69] By this, I assume he means the practice of social movements, their proactive definition of participatory democracy and their call for a deprofessionalization of politics. Elites acted to exclude the social movements by resuming traditional political arrangements. However, Munck detects a growing disillusionment with the latter under the weight of the 'savage privatisation' of neo-liberal restructuring and its social implications and increasing public condemnation of government corruption[70] and inefficiency, as well as charting the dwindling importance of political parties as conduits for popular opinion. The result has been a disengagement from democracy and possible openings for reinvigorated authoritarianism under the guise of anti-party, populist politicians. I have previously mentioned the case of Peru under Fujimori, but one could also cite the surreal example of President Abdalá Bucaram of Ecuador. After various highly publicized escapades, the self-styled 'El Loco' ('the madman') was forced to leave office in February 1997, barely six months after his inauguration, following concerted national opposition involving a general strike, Congressional rebellion and his repudiation by the military.[71] This might be viewed as a triumph for democracy but, equally, it may be seen as evidence of profound crisis within the political system and a major confrontation between people and state which will have tremendous implications for Ecuador's future.

As with all radical theorists, the core of Munck's critique is that authentic democracy cannot grow in societies marked by structural socio-economic and political inequalities and inequities. He argues that there is an intrinsic incompatibility between the 'rolling back of the state' thrust of neo-liberalism and social justice. Neo-liberal policies are promoted as being efficient and rational, but their consequences for citizens delegitimizes the latters' relationship with government. Political cultures which do not place a high value upon social justice must inevitably lose the ability to engage their populations' loyalties. With respect to the idea of *desencanto*, he maintains that 'the demobilised civil society it implies and the withdrawal from the public arena to the private is a poor basis on which to build a democratic citizenship and stable political institutions'.[72] This, he recognises, has an unfortunate knock-on effect on the potential radical democrats have for offering an alternative model to neo-liberalism, given 'the decentring of politics and the destructuring of social and political identities' which the latter creates.[73] Disillusionment with politics embraces both right, centre and left parties and also has a detrimental impact upon popular participation in social movements. Working within an unfriendly political and economic environment and dealing with the 'wear and tear' (*desgaste*) of everyday experience, the hopes that vast social sectors bear with respect to the prospects for 'real' democracy in Latin America appear empty. The following chapters hope to offer a prognosis of the possibility of 'real' democracy, beginning with an exploration of the nature of 'official' political actors and institutions.

Notes

1 J. C. Portantiero, 'Foundations of a New Politics', *NACLA. Report on the Americas*, XXV: 5 (May 1992), 19.

2 G. O'Donnell, P. Schmitter and L. Whitehead (eds), *Transitions from Authoritarian Rule: Prospects for Democracy* (Baltimore, MD, Johns Hopkins University Press, 1986).

3 T. L. Karl and P. Schmitter, 'Modes of Transition in Latin America, Southern and Eastern Europe', *International Social Science Journal*, 128 (May 1991), 281.

4 A. Knight, 'Mexico's Elite Settlement: Conjuncture and Consequences', in J. Higley and R. Gunther (eds), *Elites and Democratic Consolidation in Latin America and Southern Europe* (Cambridge, Cambridge University Press, 1992), p. 113.

5 O'Donnell *et al. Transitions*, vol. 4, p. 34.

6 *Ibid.*, p. 62.

7 P. Cammack, 'Democratisation: a Review of the Issues', *Bulletin of Latin American Research*, 4: 2 (1985), 44.

8 O'Donnell *et al. Transitions*, vol. 4, p. 12.

9 W. Little, 'Democracy in Latin America: Problems and Prospects', *Democratization*, 1: 2 (Summer 1994), 206. This position has its lineage in an earlier debate concerning the 'end of ideology'. See D. Bell, *The End of Ideology: On the Exhaustion of Political Ideas in the Fifties* (New York, Free Press, 1965) and S. P. Huntington, 'Postindustrial Politics: How Benign Will It Be?', *Comparative Politics*, 163 (January 1974).

10 In S. Mainwaring, G. O'Donnell and J. S. Valenzuela (eds), *Issues in Democratic Consolidation. The New South American Democracies in Comparative Perspective* (Notre Dame, IN, University of Notre Dame Press, 1992), pp. 298–302.

11 *Ibid.*, p. 300.

12 *Ibid.*, p. 311.

13 Although the first Clinton administration committed itself to a fresh perspective upon its Latin American policy, its approach towards Cuba retained the USA's traditionally aggressive stance; heavily influenced by the need to retain the political support (and campaign financing) of the Miami exiles, led by the late Jorge Mas Canosa, President Clinton acceded to the passing of the draconian Helms–Burton Cuban Liberty and Democratic Solidarity Act in 1996. See P. Brenner and P. Kornbluh, 'Clinton's Cuba Calculus', *NACLA. Report on the Americas*, XXIX: 2 (September–October 1995).

14 L. Meyer, 'Democracy From Three Latin American Perspectives', in R. A. Pastor (ed.), *Democracy in the Americas: Stopping the Pendulum* (New York, Holmes & Meier, 1989), p. 34.

15 L. Whitehead, 'The Consolidation of Fragile Democracies: A Discussion with Illustrations', in Pastor (ed.), *Democracy*, p. 80.

16 *Ibid.*

17 Cammack, 'Democratisation', 42.

18 In the periods 1974–78 and 1989–93, although his political resilience did not prevent Congress impeaching him for the misuse of funds (M. Coppedge, *Strong Parties and Lame Ducks. Presidential Partyarchy and Factionalism in Venezuela*, Stanford, CA, Stanford University Press, 1994), p. 1.

19 Acción Democrática (Democratic Action) and the Comité de Organización Política Electoral Independiente (Committee for Independent Political Electoral

Organization). The nature and limitations of Venezuela's 'partyarchy' are discussed in Chapter 2.

20 R. Munck, *Latin America. The Transition to Democracy* (London, Zed Books, 1989), p. 106; Munck makes the point that the victory of Raúl Alfonsín and the Unión Cívica Radical (UCR, Radical Civic Union) broke the mould of the previous Peronist/anti-Peronist discourse in Argentinian politics, although his subsequent actions as President were not conducive to establishing a new political course.

21 A classic exposition of what has been termed 'non-decision-making' is to be found in P. Bachrach and M. S. Baratz, 'Two Faces of Power' and 'Decisions and Non-Decisions: An Analytical Framework', *American Political Science Review*, LVI: 4 (December 1962) and LVII: 3 (September 1963), respectively.

22 In *Who Governs? Democracy and Power in an American City* (London, Yale University Press, 1961), R. A. Dahl's thesis is that a mature liberal democracy's health can be ascertained by the low incidence of mass involvement in politics (passivity meaning satisfaction with the workings of pluralism and the effectiveness of governing elites).

23 Karl and Schmitter, 'Modes', 281.

24 Whitehead, 'Consolidation', p. 148.

25 *Ibid.*, p. 156.

26 *Ibid.*, p. 158.

27 As paraphrased by J. Nef, 'The Trend Towards Democratisation and Redemocratisation in Latin America', *Latin American Research Review*, XXIII: 3 (1988), 141.

28 A. MacEwan, 'Transitions from Authoritarian Rule', *Latin American Perspectives*, 15: 58: 3 (Summer 1988), 116.

29 J. Petras and M. Morley, *Latin America in the Time of Cholera: Electoral Politics, Market Economics and Permanent Crisis* (New York, Routledge, 1992), p. 168.

30 MacEwan, 'Transitions', 130.

31 Writing in 1973, many years before he would become President of Brazil, the then left-winger and dependency theorist, Fernando Henrique Cardoso, stressed the need to 'create a climate of freedom . . . that will allow the reactivation of civil society . . . so that it can express itself in the political order and can counterbalance the state'. Quoted by M. Keck, *The Workers' Party and Democratisation in Brazil* (New Haven, CT, Yale University Press, 1992), p. 45.

32 MacEwan, 'Transitions', 117.

33 'We cannot avoid the possibility that a transition to democracy can be made only at the cost of leaving economic relations intact, not only the structure of production but even the distribution of income', in O'Donnell *et al.* (eds), *Transitions*, vol. 3, p. 63. In contrast, Margaret Keck identifies the contradiction between formal citizenship and vast socio-economic inequality as the central – and seemingly intractable – dilemma of the pacted model (Keck, *Workers'*, p. 23).

34 Cammack, 'Democratisation', 45.

35 Whitehead, 'Consolidation', p. 148.

36 D. Rustow, 'Transitions to Democracy: Towards A Dynamic Model', *Comparative Politics*, 2: 3 (April 1970), quoted in O'Donnell *et al.* (eds), *Transitions*, vol. 4, p. 38.

37 Whitehead, 'Consolidation', pp. 155–6. I shall return to the possibilities of this reconciliation in the Conclusion.

38 Nef, 'Trend', 151.

39 J. G. Castañeda, *Utopia Unarmed: The Latin American Left After The Cold War* (New York, Vintage Books, 1994), p. 338.

40 Castañeda argues that the Left must repudiate 'the free-market dogma being rammed down the throats of Latin American societies and economies' by advocating a new industrialization strategy based upon 'a long-term alliance between the business community and the state' and labour, that is, linking the private and public sectors rather than separating them. *Utopia*, p. 462.

41 MacEwan, 'Transitions', 124.

42 R. Kaufman and B. Stallings, 'Debt and Democracy in the 1980s: The Latin American Experience', in Kaufman and Stallings (eds), *Debt and Democracy in Latin America* (Boulder, CO, Westview Press, 1989), p. 221.

43 S. P. Huntington, 'The Modest Meaning of Democracy', in Pastor (ed.), *Democracy*, p. 134.

44 T. Skidmore, 'The Future of Democracy: An Analytical Summary', in Pastor (ed.), *Democracy*, pp. 135–8.

45 J. Petras, 'The Redemocratisation Process', in S. Jonas and N. Stein (eds), *Democracy in Latin America. Visions and Reality* (New York, Bergin & Garvey, 1990), p. 95.

46 Petras and Morley, *Latin America*, p. 166.

47 J. Petras and S. Vieux, 'The Transition to Authoritarian Electoral Regimes in Latin America', *Latin American Perspectives*, 83: 21: 4 (Autumn 1994), 7.

48 *Ibid.*

49 R. Burbach and O. Nuñéz, *Fire in the Andes. Forging a Revolutionary Agenda* (London, Verso, 1987), pp. 46–8. This approach perpetuates the traditional arrogance of many on the Left, as well as offering a misreading of the political and economic importance of the working class, which has been severely impaired by de-industrialization caused by the diversion of investment to the export sector under the aegis of neoliberal restructuring, accompanied by anti-trade-union policies.

50 Ex-guerrilla, General Secretary of the Communist Party and coordinator of the Frente Farabundo Martí de Liberación Nacional (FMLN, Farabundo Martí National Liberation Front) when it became a legal party in 1992.

51 S. J. Handal, 'A Proposal for El Salvador', in S. J. Handal and C. M. Vilas, *The Socialist Option in Central America* (New York, Monthly Review Press, 1993), pp. 35–78.

52 B. Carr and S. Ellner (eds), *The Latin American Left. From the Fall of Allende to Perestroika* (Boulder, CO, Westview Press, 1993).

53 A discussion of the relative politics of these two movements can be found in Chapter 3.

54 Carr and Ellner (eds), *Latin American Left*, p. 18.

55 Castañeda, *Utopia*, pp. 366–73.

56 M. Azicri, 'Twenty-Six Years of Cuban Revolutionary Politics: An Appraisal', in Jonas and Stein (eds), *Democracy*, p. 173.

57 L. Serra, 'Democracy in Times of War and Socialist Crisis. Reflections Stemming from the Sandinista Revolution', *Latin American Perspectives*, 77: 20: 2 (Spring 1993), 23.

58 The identification of Castro with the Revolution poses dilemmas. One is that it can be argued that such charismatic control is incompatible with the growth of popular democracy, particularly in the light of the patron–client relationships which have bedevilled all Latin American political systems of whatever ideological persuasion. Another is that it will create a succession crisis when Castro leaves the political scene.

59 Azicri, 'Twenty-Six Years', 146.

60 C. M. Vilas, *The Sandinista Revolution* (New York, Monthly Review Press, 1986), p. 251 (original emphasis).

61 *Ibid.*, pp. 265 and 268, respectively. The parallels – in terms of economic and cultural backwardness and foreign intervention – with the early years of the Soviet Union are interesting.

62 J. L. Coraggio and G. Irvin, 'Revolution and Democracy in Nicaragua', *Latin American Perspectives*, 45: 12: 2 (Spring 1985), 24.

63 The UP's attempts to attract the middle classes in order to consolidate its electoral mandate diluted its legislative programme and resulted in the disaffection of the popular classes. Its adoption of the middle ground dissatisfied all sectors and the *impasse* was eventually resolved by the 1973 coup.

64 Coraggio and Irvin, 'Revolution', 29.

65 A. Przeworski, 'Some Problems in the Study of the Transition to Democracy', in O'Donnell *et al.* (eds), *Transitions*, vol. 4, p. 58.

66 G. O'Donnell, 'Transitions, Continuities and Paradoxes', in Mainwaring *et al.* (eds), *Issues*, p. 17.

67 He discusses these obstacles with reference to Brazilian political culture in *ibid.*, particularly pp. 41–8.

68 Quoted by R. Munck, 'After the Transition: Democratic Disenchantment in Latin America', *European Review of Latin American and Caribbean Studies*, 55 (December 1993), 8.

69 *Ibid.*, 9.

70 The credibility of governments has been challenged in the wake of seemingly endless corruption scandals, including the various bribery and 'narcodollars' allegations directed against Carlos Menem's ruling coterie; claims that Ernesto Samper's presidential campaign of 1995 in Colombia was financed by the Calí drug cartel; the disgrace and self-enforced exile of ex-President Salinas of Mexico following drug and political assassination accusations, and the 1993 impeachment of Brazil's President Collor de Mello for massive misappropriation of public funds (a case of taking privatization to its logical conclusion!).

71 *Guardian* (6/2/97), 13 and *Independent on Sunday* (9/2/97), 14.

72 Munck, 'After', 15.

73 *Ibid.*, 17.

2
Official politics

The prospects for the consolidation of democracy . . . depends on
how the relationships among key groups – the military, the bourgeoisie, state bureaucrats and labour – coalesce during specific
conjunctures.[1]

To this list, one would wish to add other players, including
the churches, the media, political parties and business interests. Catherine Conaghan, in her study of the relationship
between state and domestic capital in the Andean countries,
argues that democracy is the 'product of class alliances and
pragmatic choices'.[2] This chapter examines the relations between significant political actors and the nature of the political
systems they preside over. Their interrelationship with other
elites is touched upon in both this and later chapters, and the
obstacles they may pose to democracy are considered in Chapter 6. Given the limitations of space and the inadequacy of a
single, general volume to address all aspects of 'official' politics, I will be concentrating upon themes, similarities and contrasts between such actors and systems rather than undertaking
an in-depth survey of any one in particular. It must be borne in
mind that political systems are not static entities, but experience persistent change. Certainly during the 1990s, the authoritarian and exclusionary styles of governing parties – such as
the Mexican PRI – and neo-populist presidents – such as Menem
of Argentina – have been challenged by mainstream political
actors demanding more representative and inclusionary democracy. Thus the 'new politics' which I speculate about in the
title of this book is not confined to popular mobilization, but
has also been taken up by established parties. Whether this
project can be successful is discussed in varying ways throughout the text.

Much of the literature on contemporary Latin and Central American politics stresses that elite interaction is the only method of establishing democracy. Thus Samuel Huntington felt able to insist that 'democratic regimes that last have seldom, if ever, been instituted by mass popular action. Almost always, democracy has come as much from the top down as from the bottom up.'[3] It may, however, be regarded as a more complicated process. Recognizing that interaction between governing elites – be they political, financial, military or cultural – is an important ingredient, it is necessary to accept that mass mobilization gives elites the leverage they require in order to become influential players, at least at the transition stage (later on, they may deny this). Mainwaring argues that popular action 'redefines the political scene' and thus facilitates elite activity.[4] Elites need masses to win elections, but the important question is how their subsequent relationship develops, and what 'the people' obtain from such 'democracy'. Here the democratic credentials of governing elites will need to be assessed. Given their historic monopoly of political, economic and social power and their narrow perspective upon the application of and participation in that power, are such elites now willing to embrace what Ronaldo Munck has termed 'political renewal'? By this is meant authentic democratic practice which requires that political actors identify themselves with democratic values and work to sustain them.[5] From this viewpoint, it is clear that traditional elites may not be described as democratic but may be seen as *potentially* democratic. This may appear to be a problematic assessment in terms of democracy but it is one that many commentators seem to tolerate. With respect to consolidating political systems, Mainwaring contends that elites do not need to be committed to democracy initially; rather, it should be accepted that they will act in an instrumentalist fashion (that is, in their own interests).[6] However the hope is that, in order to secure democratic consolidation, they will acquire such commitment over time.

The experience of established 'liberal, pacted ' systems such as those of Mexico and Venezuela does not support this prognosis as their democratic discourse and practice has been of a narrow nature. Similarly, the very distinct experiments in socialist government undertaken in Cuba and Nicaragua have also been debilitated by a constricted democracy, reflected in both the relationship between governing elites and popular

masses and by the lack of authentic representation and accountability in political institutions. To understand the continuing
dominance of elites in widely varying political systems, one
must address the nature of their foundational pacts, that is,
the arrangements made between elites to create and perpetu-
ate such systems, and the historical circumstances in which
these came about. The limitations of these pacts, particularly
with respect to popular expectations and their satisfaction,
are demonstrated most forcefully during periods of crisis (of
a political or economic nature, provoked by war or external
circumstances, popular mobilization or insurgency), when the
stability and legitimacy of regimes are threatened. Those contemporary systems which have experienced military to civilian transitions since 1980 have had to engage with problems
set in motion during the periods of military rule. Socialist
governments have had to contend with an inheritance of
poverty and deprivation as well as external pressures (thus
the impact upon Cuba of the US blockade and of its membership of the Soviet bloc, and the effect of the US-supported
contra war upon Nicaragua). Even those countries with what
have been regarded as the most entrenched systems have
found themselves in difficulties since the late 1960s. I will
begin by considering the nature of the foundational pacts in
Mexico, Venezuela and Colombia and the difficulties they have
encountered.

The so-called consolidated political systems of Venezuela
and Colombia can be described as both polyarchies and con-
sociational democracies, that is, regimes which are based upon
recognition of the need for competing elites to compromise
by accepting limitations to their power.[7] They do so in order
to ensure system maintenance, which is itself predicated upon
minimal mass participation and resistance to structural change,
despite profound socio-economic cleavages and the persistence
of inequality. Moderation in policy-making, and political conflict which is restricted to intra- and inter-party competition,
are key features of such political cultures. John Peeler argues
that the aims of the party systems of Venezuela, Colombia and
Costa Rica are to 'define, structure and limit voter choice to a
narrow range of options which are mutually acceptable to competing elites'.[8] The political evolution of these countries must,
therefore, be significant when evaluating the long-term prospects for post-military consolidating regimes as they, too, are

based upon the idea of elite pacts and exclusionary practices. This, in essence, is the gist of the *Transitions* model enunciated by O'Donnell and his colleagues, and summarized in Chapter 1. Mexico differs from these polyarchies in that this is a political order which has been orchestrated by a dominant party since the late 1920s. The PRI has monopolized power through a combination of co-optation, corruption and selective repression.

The Mexican, Venezuelan and Colombian political systems have all encountered political crisis in the contemporary period, albeit crises which possess their own distinctive characteristics. Colombia has had to deal with both insurgency and the growth of the drugs trade; the latter has permeated the state apparatus, the legitimacy of which is now totally compromised by the depth and intensity of corruption of a society which endures a culture of seemingly uncontrollable violence. Ungovernability appears to be a possibility. The beginning of the Mexican crisis dates back to the student demonstrations of 1968 and the repressive response of the Díaz Ordaz government.[9] The PRI's political monopoly has been challenged by increasing intra-elite tension, as represented by the tension between modernizing *técnicos* and reactionary *políticos*.[10] The political crisis which has dominated Mexico since the late 1980s has been exacerbated by deepening economic problems; this has also been an important element in the Venezuelan case. In both countries, oil wealth had 'lubricated the political process'.[11] It did this by allowing governments to spend themselves out of political trouble through state expenditure and investment. With the collapse in oil prices of the 1970s, the consolidation of the debt crisis and the pressure upon governments to implement austerity programmes (including the retraction of state spending), this option disappeared. The repercussions with respect to regime cohesion, increasing popular radicalism (protesting against the new political economy) and the possibilities for political opposition were immense.

Until its political crisis of 1989–93, Venezuela had long been portrayed as one of the most stable political systems in Latin America, having engaged in competitive elections every five years since 1958 (although left-wing parties were periodically excluded). After the 1958 overthrow of the Pérez Jiménez dictatorship, the two major parties – the social democratic AD and COPEI (which was of a Christian Democratic persuasion)

– signed the Pact of Punto Fijo, which created an institutional arrangement whereby they would alternate in government (although AD proved to be the dominant political presence). The parties committed themselves to a strong role for the state in economic management, a mixed economy, and a political policy based upon class conciliation.

Subsequent electoral politics were monopolized by AD and COPEI, whose influence invaded interest groups, the judiciary, the media and all other state institutions. Interestingly – for Latin America – the military were kept at a distance from political life; their consent could be secured so long as high government expenditure benefited the armed forces, but the economic crisis provoked dissatisfaction and resulted in two abortive coups.[12] Factionalism was rife in both parties, but their continuing internal power struggles did not challenge the consensus between them upon which the system rested. However, it did present an image to the Venezuelan public of competition between highly personalized elites who appeared to have little interest in policy, regarded themselves as immune from criticism and were consumed with political ambition. Coppedge has described the Venezuelan political system as a 'partyarchy' within the context of a presidential system.[13] The party system was fuelled by patronage with AD and COPEI controlling and distributing public offices. There was an unequal division of power between the executive and legislative branches of government. Congress attempted to block budgetary measures and dissect legislative processes, resulting in policy stalemate. Successive presidents resorted to rule by decree in order to avoid such intervention; this produced a system characterized by crisis management. The absence of democratic control and public accountability, the high incidence of corruption, and fraudulent electoral practices contributed to public disillusionment with professional politicians. It was not an authoritarian political culture, but neither was it a democratic one. It appeared able to ensure stability, but only insofar as it was able to satisfy the economic expectations of the population.[14]

The Venezuelan state used its oil revenues to buy political support; thus, it offered huge subsidies to the private sector and wooed the working class with the legislative protection of trade-union rights and substantial welfare provision. However, oil wealth was not distributed equally, economic management was both wasteful and corrupt and the oil revenue was not used to generate authentic economic expansion.[15] The policy of economic patronage and clientelism carried within it the seeds of destabilization in that it was dependent upon oil money.[16] The end of the oil boom resulted in massive indebtedness and the need for retrenchment which compelled President Carlos Andrés Pérez to introduce a severe austerity programme in February 1989. This provoked massive riots and the imposition of a state of siege; hundreds of people were killed by the authorities. Coppedge argues that the economic crisis stimulated the riots but that people also 'turned to extraconstitutional solutions ... out of frustration with the functioning of formal channels of representation'.[17] It appeared that both the economic and political underpinnings of Venezuela's foundational pact were disintegrating. In 1992, two coup attempts received considerable public support,[18] while Andréz Pérez was impeached in the same year for the misuse of public funds.

However, although the political system was severely dented by the events of 1989–92, it has demonstrated its resilience although subject to considerable change. Politics have opened up in the 1990s with the growth in influence of left-wing parties (Causa R's presidential candidate obtained 22 per cent of the 1993 vote) and popular groups who have challenged the dominance of the AD/COPEI axis. Rafael Caldera became President in 1993 in an election characterized by a lack of popular endorsement, with approximately 40 per cent of the electorate abstaining and allegations of widespread fraud.[19] Lacking a congressional majority, Caldera sought alliance with AD, COPEI, Causa R, the MAS and even supporters of the old dictator Pérez Jiménez. This lack of political identity was a good reflection of the instrumentalism which is endemic in Venezuelan public life. Caldera's commitment to relax austerity measures and pursue social justice was obstructed by falling oil prices and a large budget deficit and debt. The Venezuelan state has also failed to reassert civilian control over the military.

Other political systems exhibit the features of the Venezuelan model to a greater or lesser extent. I will briefly consider Costa Rica and Colombia before turning to Mexico. Both are based upon competition between elites with narrow policy agendas and have strong traditions of popular non-participation in the face of a corrupt party spoils system. Despite having proportional representation in Congressional elections, the limited political strength of left-wing parties has meant that they are unable to contest government power.[20] In the face of wide income differentials, the elites have resolutely opposed what Peeler has termed 'political democratization and economic equalization'.[21] In Costa Rica, following a brief civil war, the 1948 Figueres–Ulate pact established a political system over which the dominant party, the Partido Liberación Nacional (PLN, National Liberation Party), has presided (although many factional splits have enabled opposition parties to win elections). Executive powers are more diluted than elsewhere, as the legislature has sufficient powers to force a president to negotiate and civil liberties are respected. However, Costa Rican politics is characterized by low participation, and since the economic crisis, social welfare provision has been reduced, although until the late 1990s, stability has been preserved.[22]

Peeler contends that, of the consolidated systems, Colombia is the furthest away from the democratic ideal; over recent decades, the legitimacy of its political system has been undermined by the challenge of counter-elites (drug cartels and guerrillas) and permeated by drugs-linked corruption and violence. We may be able to talk about the ongoing deconsolidation of Colombian politics. Following *la violencia*,[23] formal power-sharing occurred during the National Front period (1958–74), but subsequently the Conservative/Liberal hegemony has created an exclusionary political system. Ricardo Vargas Meza argues that until the introduction of the new Constitution in 1991, 'these two parties ruled under a permanent state of siege in order to control rebellion, social protest and political opposition'.[24] In the 1980s and 1990s, the increasing precariousness of the state, the growth of military and paramilitary influence, and the exposure of enormous governmental corruption (symbolized by claims that President Samper's 1994 campaign was financed by the Calí drug cartel) have strengthened discussion of crisis. The victory in the first round of the presidential elections of June 1998 of an independent candidate, Noemi Sanin – an ex-Conservative who had campaigned for open government – shocked the two major parties. Although defeated in the final round, her performance may be seen in the future as marking the end of the Liberal–Conservative control over politics. It was certainly regarded as demonstrating public disillusionment with already existing politics. The second round gave victory to Andrés Pastrana (candidate of the Conservative Party), who has pledged himself to change, both in terms of reforming government and radical social investment, but his government is likely to be obstructed by Liberal control of Congress and the seemingly insurmountable dilemmas of drugs and guerrillas.[25]

Mexican politics cannot be identified with democracy (although it may be evolving towards it); rather, one would have to talk of a process of corporatism and of a symbiotic party–state relationship which, until 1988, achieved the most complete domination of a political system of any country in Latin and Central America in the twentieth century. Judith Adler Hellman has contended that Mexico is exceptional in that it has never been as authoritarian as those states which have endured military rule or personal despotisms, but that it has been democratizing far slower than other countries and a democratic outcome still remains uncertain.[26] Following the 1968 political crisis, successive governments introduced various reforms, including the 1977 law which gave opposition parties the right to take part in elections (although the PRI's democratic commitment was somewhat comprised by its continued fraudulent efforts to steal electoral victories), and the 1990 Electoral Reform law, which established that a first-place party with 35 per cent of the vote in federal elections was assured a majority in Congress.[27]

The Mexican system is Presidential, with incumbents exercising virtually autocratic powers for six-year, non-renewable terms and enjoying the right, in conjunction with the party machine, to nominate their successors. The Presidency has been described as a 'six-year dictatorship' around which all other elements and institutions circulate.[28] The power of the office is such that democratic reform will be contingent upon its commitment to it. The inability of the other state institutions – the legislature, the judiciary, the bureaucracy – to exercise control over successive presidents has resulted in a highly skewed balance of power. Thus as the President is granted constitutional control over Congress as the 'supreme head' of the PRI, the former's powers of impeachment are impeded. Presidents have the authority to initiate legislation and constitutional amendments and have employed these powers to increase their authority. In addition to selecting his successor, a President also appoints Cabinet ministers, federal and state governors, mayors, officials and judges. Thus a huge and highly corrupt spoils system pervades public life.[29] The consequences of the hegemony of *presidencialismo* have been the absence of both constitutional restraints upon arbitrary executive power and political accountability to the electorate.

The PRI's domination of Mexican politics – termed the process of *continualismo* (literally, the state of continuing) – was subject to serious economic and political pressures in the 1980s and 1990s. The exhaustion of the import substitution industrialization strategy [30] and the deepening of the debt crisis led the government of Miguel de la Madrid (1982–86) to implement neo-liberal policies (which included lowering protective tariffs and welcoming unregulated foreign investment, as well as selling off parastatals). This provoked protests from domestic manufacturers (whose economic activity was not directed at the export market, and who were not linked to transnational capital[31]), trade unions and the popular sectors. The relationship between government, large and medium domestic business and finance capital and the export elites has not always been harmonious. Thus, the domestic private sector reacted angrily to President López Portillo's nationalization of the banking system in 1982. Business elites generally have been ambivalent in their response towards a democratization process which would involve a relaxation of the PRI's hegemony, arguing that a limited reform process would be incapable of preventing the floodgates of popular mobilization and political instability from opening. However, the events of 1988–98 suggest that such a process may be forced upon both political and economic elites.

The political challenge to the PRI came first from the Right, with the PAN gradually moving away from its allotted role of tame opposition,[32] and then from the centre-left PRD, which received a certain degree of support from the popular movements. The PRD emerged in 1986 as the Corriente Democrática (Democratic Current), a group of reform-minded PRI grandees which most notably included Cuauhtémoc Cárdenas, son of President Lazaro Cárdenas. They called for democratization of the party system and the state, constitutional reform (and pre-eminently a curb on presidential power), the restoration of the state's central role in economic management and the pursuit of economic nationalism. They also demanded a return to the roots of the Revolution through a reaffirmation of its commitment to promote the interests of the poor. Initially intended as a lobby within the PRI, the party leadership, supported by the dinosaurs, forced their expulsion. Contesting the 1988 elections as the Frente Democrático Nacional (FDN, National Democratic Front), the dissidents put forward Cárdenas as their presidential candidate. Huge popular mobilizations, political violence and assassinations accompanied the electoral process. Many observers believe that Cárdenas won with 31.29 per cent of the vote, whilst others accept that the PRI's Salinas was the victor, but that, with very high abstention figures and evident fraudulent practices by the government, the legitimacy of the PRI's rule had received its most serious dent up to the late 1990s. Mexico had passed from 'a hegemonic party system ... to a dominant party system'.[33] PRI candidates could no longer depend upon safe seats, and a degree of genuine competition had emerged at national, state and local levels. The rise of opposition politics has clearly strengthened the hand of reformists and modernizers within the governing party itself, although their efforts continue to be hampered by old-style *políticos* who have no desire to see the PRI's control relaxed.

The demise of the PRI state cannot be regarded as inevitable. One factor pointing to its survival – although, maybe, as a reconstructed model of government – may be the lack of consensus amongst both the political and popular opposition as well as the latter's particular vulnerability to co-optation by the state. It has been argued that the establishment of a direct relationship between petitioning groups and the presidency bypasses other forms of mediation such as that between popular groups, political parties and state institutions at local, state and federal levels. Despite this obvious constraint, Harvey has maintained that 'the decreasing capacity of the regime to meet popular demands and institutionalise their political expression' must have an important impact upon the PRI's fortunes.[34] Harvey is also critical of the PRD, contending that it has failed to 'develop a competing hegemonic project of its own' and has not yet discovered how to represent the broad opposition to PRI rule.[35] Its focus upon electoral politics – and indeed its own provenance (coming from within the governing elite, its political ambitions could be regarded as suspect) – have had a negative impact upon its relations with the popular movement.

It can be seen that the Latin American states which experienced military to civilian transitions in the 1980s share many of the characteristics and problems attributed to the so-called consolidated political systems. I do not intend to examine the actual transitions,[36] nor do I have the space to examine any country in detail. Instead, I highlight specific aspects of political history and practice in order to compare them with the more mature political systems outlined above, and to consider how they fit into the 'official' model of democracy discussed in Chapter 1. From a radical model perspective, James Petras contends that the political compromises made in order to secure military to civilian transitions have exercised a strongly limiting influence upon subsequent political activity and decision-making. Those elites restored to government have passed the screening process imposed by the military and other interested bodies such as large domestic and international capital; their acceptance of the strictures of the latter groups 'prevents them from initiating new policies, redefining international obligations and pursuing profound institutional innovations in the state. The result is a new cycle of democracy, instability, popular dissatisfaction, increasing reliance on the military, and a return to authoritarian rule.'[37] The defining characteristics of these regimes include continuity with the past in both the polity and the economy; very slow, incremental change; attempts to divide the opposition by seeking understandings with dissident political elites and attempting to incorporate popular organizations; resistance to any resolution of human rights issues stemming from military rule; and acceptance of neo-liberalism as the dominant discourse.

Ronaldo Munck has taken a more flexible approach than Petras in stating that, despite the elitist nature of the transitional settlements, the 'new' democracies which emerged were 'more open and fluid processes' rather than being simply 'repetitions of past patterns'.[38] He points to left-wing electoral victories, the fragmentation of traditional political loyalties and their replacement with support for populist non-party politicians who 'succeed in creating a fragile and false sense of cohesion and identity on the basis of an emotive appeal'.[39] He further cites the mass criticism directed at rising levels of corruption and the impeachment of presidents Collor de Mello and André Pérez as proof that democratic values have become embedded in these societies; the inference being that traditional elites can no longer get away with everything and that the political trajectories of Latin American states are moving in new and possibly unpredictable directions.

Frances Hagopian has addressed the manner in which the political system was reconstituted following the departure of the Brazilian military from government in 1986. The Brazilian was a top-down transition, although the military's management of the process was thrown off balance by the growth in electoral strength of the oppositional Partido do Movimento Democrático Brasileiro (PMDB, the Brazilian Democratic Movement Party), which challenged the regime's tame official party, the Partido Social Democrático (PDS, the Social Democratic Party). Pivotal in upsetting the *junta*'s strategy was the Minas Gerais political elite (the most influential in the country, headed by Tancredo Neves, the future President-elect), which, having supported the 1964 coup, began to turn against the regime in the early 1980s. The tide of opinion moving against the military government was apparent during the opposition's 1984 campaign against the former's intention to hold indirect presidential elections. Although the campaign failed, its momentum convinced Neves that he could play the game on the military's terms and still have a good chance of winning. Thus despite the fact that the political elite eventually chose the democratic option, its democratic credentials must be regarded as highly suspect. Although Neves won the election, the military retained sufficient influence to compel him to make concessions, which included no legal action being taken against military personnel in the light of human rights abuses, no discrimination being practised against the PDS and other regime supporters, and allowing them access to public-sector and state appointments. Hagopian argues that this deal 'smuggled into the new democracy . . . antidemocratic political practices inherited from both the military regime and its civilian predecessors'.[40] The newly fused elite embraced exclusionary politics, its objective being to ignore non-elite interests and to block political reform and economic redistribution. It existence also perpetuated the weakness of the Brazilian party system. Hagopian concludes that in the new Brazilian democracy, mass political participation, decision-making and partisan debate have been 'sacrificed systematically to the particularistic calculations of a closed elite', and the consequence has been that anti-democratic practices have become ingrained in public life.[41]

The first civilian government of José Sarney did introduce a programme of reforms, including the restoration of political and citizenship rights, the end of censorship, the enfranchisement of illiterates and the right to strike, and the 1988 Constitution granted equal rights to women, banned torture and introduced the eight-hour day.[42] However, this progress was hampered by the fact that many of these rights often appeared more true on paper than in practice. Concentration of power within the executive branch of the state reduced Congress's ability to bring the government to account, the bureaucracy continued to be staffed by traditional elites, and the military retained its constitutional prerogative to ensure that law and order was maintained. The presidency of Collor de Mello witnessed the unleashing of a massive spoils system with a free-market economic model, facilitating structural corruption. The first administration of Fernando Henrique Cardoso (1994–98) appeared to inaugurate a new era in Brazilian politics. A highly influential dependency theorist in the 1960s and 1970s, his political journey to the centre-right was symbolized by the Real Plan (introduced when he was economy minister under his predecessor Itamar Franco). The Plan, named after the new currency, aimed to attack hyperinflation and ensure economic stabilization. Cardoso proposed to do this by welcoming massive amounts of foreign investment and the privatization of hitherto state-owned enterprises. His success in curbing inflation enabled him to defeat the political challenge of Luís Inácio (Lula) Da Silva and the PT in the 1998 presidential elections.[43]

Competitive elections and competing parties have been embedded in the consciousness of Uruguayan politics since the 1870s. The trend between 1865 and 1958 was for the rule of the Colorados, although this was interspersed with periods of military rule and the challenge of the Blancos, who represented regional, ranching interests in contrast to the urban and commercial groups whom the dominant party, situated in the capital city of Montevideo, spoke for. The two parties colonized the state bureaucracy. The pacted settlement began to break down following the Blancos' success in winning both legislative and Presidential elections for the first time in 1958. The Colorados returned to power in 1967, but the competition between them and the Blancos intensified at the same time as the state had to contend with severe economic problems, labour unrest and the challenge of the Tupamaros guerrillas.[44] Both parties courted the military, culminating in the military coup of 1973, which created a collegiate leadership with the erstwhile Colorado president, Juan María Bordaberry, as its civilian figurehead. The Uruguayan political system had been considered by many commentators as the most reminiscent of European practice and the one mostly likely to survive authoritarian threats. The period of military rule, which lasted until 1985, contradicted this complacency.

The generals constantly argued that they had no intention of remaining in power and that their sole purpose was to make the country safe for democracy. In line with this position, generally disbelieved, they held a referendum in November 1980 which was intended to endorse their new, highly restrictive Constitution. To their surprise, the referendum registered a 'No' vote and the military, to the even greater surprise of the Uruguayan people, prepared to leave office. Over the next five years, the military negotiated a transitional arrangement with the Blancos and Colorados, whilst excluding the Left and popular movements.[45] The result was the1985 election of President Julio María Sanguinetti. The political system which has operated in Uruguay since then has been described as a *reforma pactada* (pacted reform), based upon the belief that 'it was the capacity of party elites rather than social groups to act together that would determine the success of the attempted transition to democracy'.[46] The two traditional parties have lost their hold over the political system as the Left has grown stronger. However, its inclusion is predicated upon its acceptance of the rules of the game. Political activity has moved towards the centre, with the right wings of both Blancos and Colorados losing influence.[47]

The consolidation of elite settlements in Chile, Argentina and Peru has followed distinctive trajectories, which have been shaped by their particular historical backgrounds and the nature of the relationships between principal political, military and economic players. Thus, Chilean politics was historically based upon a triangular ideological division (left/centre/right) which Marvelo Cavarozzi has termed the 'irreconcilability between the major political camps'.[48] This partisanship was a major cause of the 1973 coup against Salvador Allende. Party activity was violently interrupted during the years of the Pinochet regime, but partisan alignments re-emerged in the lead-up to the 1989 transition and still remain in the 1990s. The difference is that, whereas before 1973 political parties pursued exclusive strategies, they are now prepared to compromise with each other (in line with one of the defining tenets of the model of liberal pacted democracy). Thus, the Concertación government (literally 'based upon agreement') which succeeded Pinochet in 1989 was made up of the centre-right Partido Demócrata Cristiano (PDC, Christian Democratic Party), the left-wing Partido Socialista Chilena (PSC, Chilean Socialist Party) and the Partido Pro Democracia (PPD, Pro-Democracy Party). The re-emergence of civilian politics into the 1990s has, however, been dominated by the Pinochet Constitution of 1980, which granted the military the role of 'guardianship', that is, the right of intervention should they fear political instability. The Constitution also gave the Chilean Right (which together accounted for one-third or more of the electorate) a veto over all key policy decisions (this was done through the designation of a number of safe seats in the Senate). The Right has consistently endorsed the continuity of the political economy of neo-liberalism pursued by the military regime. These arrangements preclude either any sharp policy shift or attempts at constitutional amendment by incumbent centre-left governments. The military – headed by General Pinochet until his retirement in 1998, upon which he became senator-for-life under the same 1980 Constitution – has remained entrenched at the heart of power in the Chilean political system, with military officials defining the parameters of policy initiatives and prohibiting investigation and resolution of human rights issues. The Concertación's acceptance of this situation amounts to appeasement of the military's political project and legitimization of its legacy.[49]

The Argentinian political system had also been been shaped by confrontation between major political actors and this cleavage – represented by the Unión Cívica Radical (UCR, Radical Civic Union, usually known just as the Radicals) and Peronist parties – persisted after the collapse of the military regime in 1983, confirming that no elite settlement existed. Cavarozzi and Landi described this as the lack of 'a common antiauthoritarian programme'.[50] However, both parties experienced serious divisions as the 1980s progressed which facilitated the rise of Carlos Menem as an increasingly independent politician. Between 1989 and 1991, he governed with little or no input from his Peronist party; subsequently, an organizational overhaul transformed it into a loyal state party on the lines of the PRI (although far less firmly institutionalized). Menem's aggressive economic neo-liberalism[51] was accompanied by a political style based upon a non-ideological, populist appeal to Argentinians which effectively bypassed the party system and a huge concentration of executive power. He governed in close alignment with the military, business and the right-wing Unión del Centro Democrático (UCD, Union of the Democratic Centre). However, Menem's political pre-eminence was threatened from the mid-1990s in the run-up to the 1999 presidential elections. The challenge came first from the Frente Para Solidaridad (FREPASO, National Solidarity Front) which formed in 1994 and in 1997, entered into alliance with the UCR as the Alianza Para Empleo, Justicia y Educación (Alliance for Jobs, Justice and Education). They campaigned on an anti-corruption platform, calling for greater accountability in public office, a reduction in executive power and a commitment by the state to address social issues. The Alianza's Presidential candidate, Graciela Fernández Meijida, looked set to pose a serious threat to Menem in the next national elections if the 1997 Congressional elections in which it obtained 45.6 per cent of the national vote was to be treated as a yardstick.[52]

Peruvian politics in the 1990s gave most cause for concern about the nature of democratic consolidation and the possibility of a regression to authoritarianism. As such, it merits some detailed consideration in order to judge whether it might be a model that other systems could follow. After the departure of the generals in 1980, it appeared that the political system had settled into a pattern of procedural democracy, the Left apparently accepted as a legitimate political actor and the military seemingly confined to the sidelines. However, this optimistic picture had a downside in that the continuing insurgency of Sendero Luminoso brought the military back into the political equation and led to the imposition of a state of siege over large areas of the country. Also, an economic crisis provoked popular mobilization which, in its turn, frightened the political, military and financial elites and also contributed to a disenchantment with party politics which facilitated the election of Alberto Fujimori in 1990. Henry Dietz states that 'By 1990, Peru's gross national product had shrunk by 25 per cent in two years, inflation had reached an annual rate of 7,600 per cent, poverty had engulfed more than half of the population, the political party system was in shambles and Sendero Luminoso had become an intimidating omnipresence.'[53] It has been argued that authoritarianism is endemic in Peruvian political culture.

Political parties of all persuasions have been weak structures, revolving around charismatic leaders and lacking well-defined programmes. Parties were seen as the mechanisms by which leaders could manage electorates and were used as transmission belts for the distribution of patronage and corruption. Pasara's phrase 'la personalización del poder' ('the personalization of power') sums up a situation where political leaders represented their parties, and the political fortunes of the latter in government depended upon the reputation and public perception of the former.[54]

The 1980 election, which heralded the military to civilian transition, appeared to inaugurate an era of democratic politics. The APRA presided over the 1978–79 Constituent Assembly and was involved in discussions with Morales Bermúdez's military regime. Defeated in the elections by Fernando Belaúnde's Acción Popular (AP, Popular Action), it agreed to play the role of loyal opposition and was rewarded by three of its members entering the new Cabinet. Both Belaúnde and his successor, García, used their large Congressional majorities to rule through presidential decree (thus, for example, the imposition of states of emergency, which severely curtailed civil liberties and challenged the legitimacy of the justice system), which increased public disdain for the legislative system. Both governments were also characterized by extensive patronage machines and major corruption scandals (the magnitude of allegations against García forced him to flee to Colombia after Fujimori's *autogolpe*). A positive note with respect to the creation of a political consensus was the electoral involvement of the majority of left-wing parties and their repudiation of armed struggle. Although the Left's political progress was substantial during the first part of the 1980s, after the 'high' of the Izquierda Unida (IU, United Left)'s capture of the Lima municipality in 1983 and its candidate's impressive showing in the 1985 Presidential elections, it rapidly lost cohesion and influence. The party system was so enfeebled by the end of the 1980s that President Fujimori was able to govern in the 1990s with virtually no organized party-political opposition.

No politicians of the 1980s proved capable of dealing with the twin problems of the economy and Sendero's insurrection. The AP government (1980–85) continued the military's structural adjustment programme and made no attempt to address the social polarization this caused nor to reform a corrupt and inefficient state. The personal political style of President Belaúnde was constructed by his reliance on a close, personal circle and technocratic advisers which bypassed both Congress, his own party and the domestic industrial and business community. Thus, industrialists' demands for state support went unheeded and workers' pleas for social equity were ignored.[55] Belaúnde depended upon his relationship with large transnational business which constituted the core of his governmental strategy; this did not create a positive context for the creation of a political culture based upon consensus.

When Alan García was elected *aprista* President in 1985, he was motivated by a desire to resolve the economic and political problems represented by the Peruvian international debt and its repercussions for the domestic economy, and the difficulties involved in a military solution of Sendero Luminoso's political challenge. García's economic nationalism, interventionist view of government and populist style led him to argue for social justice, enter a public dialogue with Peruvians over the heads of party and state bureaucracies and defy the IMF in contesting its decisive role in economic management. His declaration that normal debt repayment was inconsistent with growth and that Peru would only pay interest equivalent to 10 per cent of its annual export revenue (the money saved being redirected to boost domestic economic growth) was politically popular, but amounted to nothing when he was ostracized by the IMF and other creditors.[56] The nadir of García's presidency came in July 1987 when he nationalized the private banks; this aroused huge opposition in financial circles which culminated in his being forced to withdraw the measure by Congress and the law courts. As recession and inflation spiralled and the trade deficit increased, García – now a lame-duck president – was forced to resort to a series of IMF-sponsored austerity packages which sealed his political coffin. Similarly, his desire to control the military in terms of its management of the insurgency and its response to human rights collapsed when he endorsed the Lurigancho prison massacres of *senderistas* (members of SL) in 1986. Afterwards, the operational independence and impunity of the military in areas under counterinsurgency control increased.[57]

The Peruvian Right was revived by its campaign against García's bank-nationalization project and several parties, including AP and the Partido Popular Cristiano (PPC, Popular

Christian Party), came together with the Frente Democrático (FREDEMO, Democratic Front), whose presidential candidate in 1990 was the author, Mario Vargas Llosa. His victory seemed certain, but his patrician attitude and the indifference to suffering which his full-blown neo-liberal economic policies suggested facilitated the election of the virtually politically unknown Alberto Fujimori (who was supported in the second round of the contest by both the APRA and IU). Fujimori's political strategy was to say one thing and do another; his policy acrobatics wrong-footed his potential political opponents (thus, the restructuring policies he implemented were far more savage than those posited by Vargas Llosa). His Cambio 90 (Change 90) was not a political party but rather a personal electoral vehicle; nevertheless, Fujimori appealed to a broad spectrum of groups who felt excluded from elite politics in Lima and wanted a resolution to the crises in the economy and the war against Sendero.[58] In office, Fujimori increasingly governed in conjunction with a closed political circle and with full military endorsement.[59] After initial suspicion, both military and business elites rallied to his side; the former when it recognized his commitment to defeating SL (which compared favourably with what they regarded as the ambivalent policies of both Belaúnde and García), and the latter when his complete embrace of free-market economics became evident. In the early 1990s, Fujimori's administration was credited with curbing hyperinflation and with evident successes in the war against Sendero (culminating in the capture of its leader, Abimael Guzmán, in 1992).

The deepening concentration of power in the executive branch was predicated upon the collapse of national party politics (demonstrated by Fujimori's landslide victory in 1995), although parties did retain considerable support at the municipal level. Fujimori's political style consisted of using the media and personal appearances to create a direct link between himself and voters which bypassed traditional allegiances. He talked of direct democracy through the use of referenda as a means of taking the task of national reconstruction away from ineffectual and corrupt politicians. Following the 1992 *autogolpe* with its draconian measures against Congress, an independent judiciary, parties and the press, he only submitted to hold elections again under pressure from the USA and European nations, who threatened to withhold humanitarian aid. The new Constitution of 1993 allowed for his re-election in 1995; it was expected that he would try for a third term as President in 2000. Fujimori's popularity declined significantly in the late 1990s. Following the controversial end to the MRTA occupation of the Japanese Embassy in April 1997 and a marked reduction in Sendero's activities, Fujimori found it difficult to base his popular appeal upon the anti-terrorist card, and opposition mounted against both his authoritarian leanings and the debilitating consequences of his wholehearted commitment to neo-liberalism. The regime was increasingly dependent upon the support of the military, which was seen to be the dominant partner in government. The negation of partisan political competition, the muzzling of independent and representative institutions and an intolerance for democratic checks and balances have been the major features of contemporary Peruvian politics. It has been suggested that Fujimori implemented a 'radical modification of the structure of government' grounded in his belief that already existing practices were inappropriate to resolve the country's problems. However, his negation of citizenship, the rule of law and the conventions of democracy do not augur well for the future.[60]

The final political system I consider in this chapter is the only one which identifies itself with socialist government, and that is the Cuban; that it is on the brink of a transition is clear, although of what kind is debatable. When Fidel Castro and his brother Raul decide to leave office (or are compelled through death or illness), the options are varied. There might be an internal succession from amongst a younger generation of Politburo members who would be amenable to enter negotiations with the more conciliatory and, increasingly, pre-eminent, Miami exiles who reject the intransigence of their fathers' generation. This would not be the scenario which past and present US administrations would prefer. In 1996, the US blockade of the island was further intensified by the introduction of the Cuban Liberty and Democratic Solidarity (Libertad) Act (better known as the Helms–Burton Act after the two right-wing Republicans who promoted it). This attempted to make American law international by penalizing companies doing business with Cuba (the arrogance of this stance infuriated many nations involved in building up their trade with Cuba, including Canada and members of the European Union). It also imposed a transition strategy which would involve no members of the present regime and which, in its offer to help 'a free democratic Cuba', implied the dismantling of the socio-economic transformations since 1960.[61] The danger here was that hardliners within the Cuban hierarchy would use Helms–Burton to justify a continuance of the siege mentality and resist further expansion of what has undoubtedly been a growing acceptance of diverse opinion and expressions of cultural and gender difference. The impact of the blockade and the general policy of harassment directed at it over the decades upon the political evolution of the Cuban Revolution is evident, but the possible demise of its socialist nature cannot be attributed solely to external factors. There are many paradoxes and ambiguities inherent in the development of the political system since 1959 which have inhibited the construction of an authentic socialist democracy. Here I want to concentrate upon formal structures; I will be returning to a consideration of the Cuban state's relationship with popular organizations and women in Chapters 4 and 5 and discussing the political consequences of its economic policies in Chapter 6. As with other countries previously mentioned in this chapter, I will only be offering some general comments.

The history of the Cuban Revolution since 1959 can be divided into three broad periods. During the first foundational stage of the 1960s, the new government had to lay the foundations for the socio-economic and political transformation of a country which had been both neglected and plundered by the Batista regime. The 1960s witnessed wide-ranging debates about development strategies and the role of Cuba in the world, as well as a high politicization of social relations which was enhanced by the use of the media 'as a means of political orientation and ideological education'.[62] This process was underpinned by external threat and the promotion of egalitarianism as the ethos of the Revolution. The latter was expressed in terms of the government's commitment to ideas of fixed income and full employment, social security, health and education, and its encouragement of volunteer work (whether it be sugar-cutting, construction, literacy campaigns or militia duty) as a collective response to survival. The notion of *poder popular* (popular power) was regarded as both instrumental (creating the building blocks of the new socialist society) and normative (consolidating the Revolution's value system, which, at this time, was infused by Guevara's concepts of the 'new

man' and the superiority of moral over material incentives).
However, this emphasis upon revolutionary participation and
empowerment was debilitated by weak institutionalization of
the political system and a governing and management style
which was centralized, bureaucratic, personalist (in its icono-
graphy of Castro as the symbol of the Revolution) and, as the
Soviet connection grew, increasingly conformist.

Institutionalization began with the formation of the PCC in
1965 (from the fusion of Castro's 26th July Movement and the
Moscow-oriented Partido Socialista Popular or PSP, Popular
Socialist Party) although it did not hold its first Conference
until 1975. The Party oversaw a complete overhaul of the incipi-
ent governmental and party apparatus which produced a system based upon three pyramids. The PCC was the only political
party, the Council of Ministers provided the administrative
and bureaucratic elements of government and the Organs of
Popular Power were accorded a legislative and legitimizing
role. This was presented as 'the institutionalized participation
of the masses in state administration in general rather than
just in the election of their representatives'.[63] These three
institutions were allotted equal status within the state, but in
practice, the PCC has been the dominant partner. Responding
to criticisms that a one-party state cannot provide socialist
democracy, the Cuban leaders argued that the special circumstances of history and the nature of the revolutionary struggle
in the 1950s and 1960s bestowed an exceptional role upon the
PCC. However, it can be argued that in the absence of real
debate and power-sharing both within the party and within
political culture in general, until recently, fundamental questions would have to be asked about what kind of socialism the
Cubans aspired to.[64]

In 1986, Fidel Castro launched the Rectification Campaign,
which was intended to both address political and economic
anomalies and to revive the revolutionary ethos of the 1960s.
The collapse of the Soviet system between 1989 and 1992
created what was termed the 'Special Period for Crisis' in Cuba,
which encouraged a debate about what strategies should be
adopted to face an increasingly hostile world environment.
With the disappearance of safe markets for its goods, food and
manufactured imports from the Soviet Union and Eastern
Europe, and a persistent decline of world sugar prices, Cuba
embarked upon an austerity programme which aimed to ensure

its economic survival. Greater productivity and more efficient management, as well as an appeal to its citizens' sense of collective solidarity, were intended to safeguard the Revolution's social achievements. Accompanying economic liberalization was the realization that the PCC's political legitimacy needed to be revitalized and a new consensus between state and citizens created. For many Cubans, the notion of *poder popular* and empowerment had turned into apathy and alienation, as people struggled to find individual solutions to the ongoing crisis.[65] While issues of national identity and independence remained fundamental in Cuban political culture, commitment to a socialism which remained highly centralized and reluctant to accept and act upon criticism was in decline. Although the economic situation had improved by the late 1990s, it was apparent that the government could not rely upon the continuation of the enormous sacrifices made by the Cuban people in recent years unless it took the initiative and transformed the institutions of state into truly responsible and representative, participatory and democratic entities.

In this chapter, I have explored the establishment and consolidation of political systems and the interactions between political elites in contemporary Latin America. Three questions underpin this text: is elite government (whether in a liberal democratic or socialist context) the only possible form, trading greater political participation and more inclusionary socio-economic projects for stability; is elite government the most efficient and effective (Chapter 6 will suggest the contrary, arguing that present neo-liberal policies are destructive and may bring societies to the point of ungovernability) and, finally, is elite government responsible to and acting in the best interests of its citizens? Having given an idea of the nature of such government in this and Chapter 1, I will be addressing these issues in the succeeding chapters of this book. In examining the liberal pacted model of democracy, I stressed the importance of elite consensus with respect to the rules of the political game, the objectives of policy-making and the relationship of the state to civil society. However, I would wish to point out that this consensus is not a given condition and, even if it is achieved, may be neither permanent nor conflict-free. As always in the study of politics, one observes the reality to be more complicated than the theoretical model. Thus, elites may share a broad agreement with respect to the desired outcome

but differ on how to achieve it; there will always be disgruntle-
ment with policy priorities, shifting alignments and occasional
power struggles (sometimes, for example in the relationship
between governing and military elites, with recourse to confrontation in the form of threatened or attempted coups). If
these interactions become too conflictual then the elite settlement will enter a situation of crisis and regime breakdown
may ensue. Certainly, elements of tension and contradiction
are built into foundational settlements; an obvious example is
the threatening presence of military elites in post-transition
systems. Similarly, relations between governments and business elites, and within the latter between large firms linked to
transnational finance capital and those in domestic manufacturing, experience a process of ebb and flow, depending upon
economic performance and the perceptions distinct sectors of
business have as to the degree of their influence over government and decision-making. Business elites may have participated in promoting transitions from military to civilian rule,
but their commitment to democratization (whether it be in
consolidating or consolidated systems) will depend upon their
assessment of their own financial prospects and their views
on the desired parameters of public policy, particularly with
respect to social and redistributional matters and any attacks
upon domestic and foreign capital's highly privileged position.
Ronaldo Munck has contended that the contemporary state
has been colonized by business (one would wish to exclude
Cuba from this statement, although if the dollarization of the
economy continues at its present rate, this may not be possible for much longer), and that 'reform in the contemporary
context no longer has connotations of social justice and redistribution but of the destruction of public service provision
and disregard for the living conditions of the vast percentage
of populations'.[66] Business elites have organized increasingly
sophisticated lobbying strategies but may, nevertheless, still
feel excluded from decision-making because of the dominance
of executive power and the prominent role of state technocrats.
Their weight within the state is also affected by the fact they
are fragmented between export- and domestic-oriented concerns. In her discussion of Argentinian capitalism, Monica
Peralta Ramos paints a scene of fluid and flexible alliances
with the continuous emergence of factions and crossovers, as
different business groups vie to gain 'control of the state's

regulatory activity so as to make their specific interests predominate'.[67] The importance of elites other than elected political ones in determining the evolution of individual states brings to the fore issues of who the state and government serve, and how they can be made more accountable. The next chapters consider pressures upon the state to become less exclusionary and more democratically responsible.

Notes

1 C. M. Conaghan, 'Capitalists, Technocrats and Politicians: Economic Policy Making and Democracy in the Central Andes', in S. Mainwaring, G. O'Donnell and J. S. Valenzuela (eds), *Issues in Democratic Consolidation: The New South American Democracies in Comparative Perspective* (Bloomington, IN, University of Notre Dame Press, 1992), p. 234.

2 *Ibid.*

3 S. P. Huntington, 'Will More Countries Become Democratic?', *Political Science Quarterly*, 99 (1984), 212.

4 S. Mainwaring, 'Transitions to Democracy and Democratic Consolidation: Theoretical and Comparative Issues', in Mainwaring *et al.* (eds), *Issues*, p. 303.

5 R. Munck, 'After the Transition: Democratic Disenchantment in Latin America', *European Review of Latin American and Caribbean Studies*, 55 (December 1993), 9.

6 Mainwaring, 'Transitions', p. 309.

7 The classic exposition of the latter is to be found in A. Lijphart, *Democracy in Plural Societies. A Comparative Exploration* (New Haven, CT, Yale University Press, 1977).

8 J. A. Peeler, *Latin American Democracies. Colombia, Costa Rica and Venezuela* (Chapel Hill, University of North Carolina Press, 1985), p. 98.

9 This repression culminated in the massacre in the Plaza Tlatelolco in Mexico City and is described by W. A. Cornelius, J. Gentleman and P. H. Smith, 'Overview: The Dynamics of Political Change in Mexico', in W. A. Cornelius, J. Gentleman and P. H. Smith (eds), *Mexico's Alternative Political Futures* (San Diego, University of California Center for US–Mexican Studies, 1990).

10 The *tecnícos* – literally 'the technical ones' – are administrators, bureaucrats and reformist-minded politicians, while the *políticos* are those traditional/reactionary politicians, members of the PRI hierarchy and office-holders at municipal, state and national levels, who are often referred to as 'the dinosaurs'. The former have argued that state and party needed to reform themselves in order to stay in power, while the latter have been implacable in their desire to protect the status quo, particularly in the face of the electoral challenge of the PRD and the PAN.

11 J. A. Peeler, 'Elite Settlement and Democratic Consolidation: Colombia, Costa Rica and Venezuela', in J. Higley and R. Gunther (eds), *Elites and Democratic Consolidation in Latin America and Southern Europe* (Cambridge, Cambridge University Press, 1992), p. 82.

12 D. L. Norden, 'Democracy and Military Control in Venezuela: From Subordination to Insurrection', *Latin American Research Review*, 33: 2 (1998) provides a sound analysis of the role of the military in Venezuelan politics.

13 M. Coppedge, *Strong Parties and Lame Ducks. Presidential Partyarchy and Factionalism in Venezuela* (Stanford, CA, Stanford University Press, 1994), p. 5.

14 It has been suggested that if one ignores the view of Venezuelan politics as one of perceived stability, the resistance of incumbent elites to the democratization of the system and the economic crisis which has threatened its long-established practice of clientelism may stimulate the notion that younger transitional regimes may be better positioned to deepen democratic consolidation. This approach is discussed by M. Naim, *Venezuela in the Wake of Radical Reform*, quoted by S. Ellner, 'Recent Venezuelan Political Studies: A Return to Third World Realities', *Latin American Research Review*, 32: 2 (1997), 202.

15 D. C. Hellinger, *Venezuela. Tarnished Democracy* (Boulder, CO, Westview Press, 1991), pp. 131-7. There was a high concentration of economic ownership within the business elite whilst the internal market failed to grow.

16 This is the point argued by T. L. Karl, 'Petroleum and Political Pacts: The Transition to Democracy in Venezuela', *Latin American Research Review*, 22: 1 (1987).

17 Coppedge, *Strong Parties*, p. 5.

18 The army officers, known as '*los bolivarianos*', aimed to eliminate the existing government and to replace it with a civilian–military *junta*. They 'intended to maintain control long enough to carry out substantial changes in the political system that would prepare Venezuela for a "better democracy" ' (Norden, 'Democracy', 153).

19 Coppedge, *Strong Parties*, p. 17.

20 The Communist Party of Costa Rica was banned from 1948 until the 1960s and was only allowed to participate in elections in 1975.

21 Peeler, 'Elite Settlement', p. 130.

22 *Ibid.*, p. 103.

23 The 1948 assassination of the populist leader Jorge E. Gaitán provoked the civil war; the nature of peasant resistance would prove to be an important influence upon the guerrillas of the 1970s.

24 R. Vargas Meza, 'The FARC, the War and the Crisis of the State', *NACLA. Report on the Americas*, XXX1: 5 (March–April 1998), p. 24.

25 *Guardian*, 2/6/98, p. 14 and 23/6/98, p. 12.

26 J. Adler Hellman, 'Mexican Popular Movements, Clientelism and the Process of Democratisation', *Latin American Perspectives*, 20: 81: 2 (1994), 125–6.

27 Although Harvey contends that this innovation was nothing more than a subterfuge intended to institutionalize PRI control and to destroy the opposition's chances ('The Difficult Transition: Neoliberalism and Neocorporatism in Mexico', in N. Harvey (ed.), *Mexico. Dilemmas of Transition*, London, Institute of Latin American Studies and British Academic Press, 1993, p. 10).

28 J. L. Klesner, 'Political Change in Mexico: Institutions and Identity', *Latin American Research Review*, 32: 2 (1997), 187.

29 Attempts by reform-minded presidents will thus face immense resistance from entrenched political and bureaucratic elites. The PRI–State has also cajoled opposition politicians into acquiescence by offering them federal and state offices and direct material incentives.

30 Import substitution industrialization (ISI) was predicated upon the state's encouragement of domestic manufacturing (through investment, financial incentives and the imposition of protective tariffs designed to offset foreign competitors). This appeared successful between 1940 and 1960 when Gross Domestic Product more than tripled. By the late 1970s, manufacturing represented about 40 per

cent of national output and pundits talked about 'the Mexican miracle'. It was artificial growth, however, in that the shortage of capital (with which to purchase imported capital goods) forced the government to begin borrowing heavily. The external debt, which had been $3.2 billion in 1970, rose to $100 billion by the late 1980s. Its upward spiral was further aggravated by the oil crisis (Cornelius *et al.*, 'Overview', p. 4). The collapse of ISI produced a retraction in the manufacturing sector which led to high unemployment, food scarcities (agriculture had long been neglected in preference to industry), and increasing income disparities. The PRI's political economy, which had been based upon buying the support of potentially discontented social sectors, was breaking down.

31 Since the mid-1970s, the export-oriented private sector – represented by the Consejo Coordinador Empresarial (the Businessmen's Co-ordinating Council) – has consolidated its monopoly over financial activity (for example, the exclusion from the Mexican Stock Exchange of all but the top 200 firms, Harvey (ed.), *Mexico*, p. 13). This has been facilitated by the state's move away from a central role in economic management which, in its turn, has had a negative impact upon the economic health of small and medium-sized businesses and the number of bankruptcies has risen.

32 Formed in 1939, the PAN has its roots in the conservative middle class, the Catholic Church and the prosperous northern states. Accepting the political system designed by the PRI, it acted as a 'safety valve for political pressure' as well as lending credence to the government's democratic claims. Its political role changed in the 1980s as it adopted a more dissenting stance and achieved some significant electoral victories. However, its inherent weakness is that it remains a regional party and is unlikely to attract national support (S. Loaeza, 'The Role of the Right in Political Change in Mexico, 1982–1988', in D. A. Chalmers, M. do Carmo Campello de Souza and A. A. Borón (eds), *The Right and Democracy in Latin America*, New York, Praeger, 1992, p. 130).

33 Cornelius *et al.*, 'Overview', p. 19.

34 Harvey (ed.), *Mexico*, p. 11.

35 *Ibid.*, p. 10.

36 There is a huge literature. Amongst the general texts are P. O'Brien and P. Cammack (eds), *Generals in Retreat* (Manchester, Manchester University Press, 1985) and R. Munck, *Latin America. The Transition to Democracy* (London, Zed Books, 1989). Single-country texts include M. A. Garretón, *The Chilean Political Process* (Boston, Unwin Hyman, 1989) and C. G. Gillespie, *Negotiating Democracy: Politicians and Generals in Uruguay* (Cambridge, Cambridge University Press, 1991).

37 J. Petras, 'The Redemocratisation Process', in S. Jonas and N. Stein (eds), *Democracy in Latin America. Visions and Reality* (New York, Bergin & Garvey, 1990), p. 99.

38 Munck, 'After the Transition', 8.

39 *Ibid.*, 9.

40 F. Hagopian, 'The Compromised Consolidation: The Political Class in the Brazilian Transition', in Mainwaring *et al.* (eds), *Issues*, p. 261. The PMDB 'opened its ranks to those who had . . . profited from the military regime. In so doing, it actually diminished its potential to represent a broader segment of interests' (*Ibid.*, p. 271).

41 *Ibid.*, p. 281.

42 *Ibid.*, p. 272.

43 Cardoso's first term in office is analysed by S. Kaufman Purcell and R. Roett (eds), *Brazil Under Cardoso* (Boulder, CO, Lynne Rienner, 1997). In this volume, Roett

concludes that Cardoso's popular mandate was buttressed by his economic successes (although the Brazilian government's commitment to a severe austerity programme in autumn 1998 suggested that world economic problems had caught up with the President). However, his progress was blocked by Congressional power-brokers at local, regional and national levels who blocked much enabling constitutional legislation ('Politics at Century's End').

44 C. G. Gillespie, 'The role of civilian–military pacts in elite settlements and elite convergence: democratic consolidation in Uruguay', in Higley and Gunther (eds), *Elites*, provides the historical background to Colorado–Blanco hegemony.

45 Munck, *Latin America* gives a succinct summary of the tortuous process of negotiation.

46 Gillespie, 'The role', p. 187.

47 J. Peeler, *Building Democracy in Latin America* (Boulder, Westview Press, CO, 1998), p. 169.

48 M. Cavarozzi, 'Patterns of Elite Negotiations and Confrontations in Argentina and Chile', in Higley and Gunther (eds), *Elites*, p. 222.

49 J. Petras and M. Morley, 'Aylwin's Chile: The Nature of Latin American "Democratic" Transition' in Petras and Morley, *Latin American in the Time of Cholera. Electoral Politics, Market Economics and Permanent Crisis* (New York, Routledge, 1992) discuss the military's penetration of the Chilean state.

50 M. Cavarozzi and O. Landis, 'Political Parties Under Alfonsín and Menem: the Effects of State Shrinking and the Devaluation of Democratic Politics', in E. C. Epstein (ed.), *The New Argentinian Democracy. The Search for a Successful Formula* (Westport, CT, Praeger, 1992), p. 208. Thus in the 1983 elections, the Radicals won but the Peronists obtained 40 per cent of the vote and control of the Senate and were thus able to sabotage government legislation. The Radical Alfonsín government floundered over its inability to cope with mounting economic crisis and its inability to create a policy consensus amongst diverse groups such as the military, business and popular organizations. For the last two years, Alfonsín's was a lame-duck Presidency and Menem took office as Peronist President six months before the official handover date.

51 Known as the Convertibility Plan, his policies produced economic growth (the benefits of which were distributed in a tremendously unequal manner), the dismantling of the public sector, the privatization of the social welfare system and the deregulation of the labour market.

52 M. Novaro, 'Shifting Alliances, Party Politics in Argentina', *NACLA. Report on the Americas*, XXXI: 6 (May–June 1998), 15.

53 H. A. Dietz, 'Peru Since 1990', *Latin American Research Review*, 33: 2 (1998), 198.

54 L. Pásara, 'La "Libanización" en democracia', in L. Pásara and J. Parodi (eds), *Democracia, Sociedad y Gobierno en el Perú* (Lima, Centro de Estudios de Democracia y Sociedad, 1988), p. 33.

55 J. Cotler, 'Los partidos políticos y la democracia en el Perú', in Pásara and Parodi (eds), *Democracia*, p. 176.

56 The debt *impasse* is discussed in J. Crabtree, *Peru Under García: An Opportunity Lost* (Basingstoke, Macmillan, 1992). García's statist economic programme was undermined by his failure to reform the highly inefficient bureaucracy and unequal tax system. His efforts at income redistribution were confined to temporary employment programmes which left the poor as marginalized as ever from the official economy. His 1985–87 project of micro-regions, which would have entailed economic decentralization to the regions and provinces, was hampered

by the resistance of local politicians and the overriding need to keep the wheels of the political spoils system well oiled.

57 Pásara argued that violence now dominated the functioning of the state and was causing the implosion of its institutions ('"Libanización"', p. 18).

58 Fujimori emphasized his ethnic (he is a Peruvian of Japanese extraction) and non-Establishment roots. He attracted the support of the small business sector, the provinces, many popular groups; in all, as Dietz has argued, the 1990 election was one grounded in class and the perception of marginality (H. A. Dietz, 'Elites in an Unconsolidated Democracy: Peru During the 1980s', in Higley and Gunther (eds), *Elites*, p. 251). Fujimori's ability to present himself as in touch with dissatisfaction with the dominant political system has allowed him to establish control over it.

59 As the 1990s proceeded, the ascendancy of the military High Command and of the state security agency, the Servicio Nacional de Inteligencia (SIN, National Intelligence Service), caused many commentators to wonder if Fujimori was at best a junior partner in government and at worst, a puppet (the possibility of a coup is, as always, a permanent fixture in Peruvian political discourse). The point is made both in P. Mauceri, 'State Reform, Coalitions and the Neoliberal Autogolpe in Peru', *Latin American Research Review*, 20: 1 (1995) and F. Rospigliosi, 'Democracy's Bleak Prospects', in J. S. Tulchin and G. Bland (eds), *Peru in Crisis. Dictatorship or Democracy?* (Boulder, CO, Lynne Rienner, 1994).

60 G. Rochabrun, 'Deciphering the Enigmas of Alberto Fujimori', *NACLA. Report on the Americas*, XXIX: 1 (July–August 1996), 18. Rochabrun contends that the only obstacle to an ever-deepening authoritarianism will be the strength of popular resistance to it.

61 It is clear that the entrenched US position on Cuba was out of tune with world opinion. Thus in October 1998, the UN General Assembly voted by 157 for and two against (USA and Israel), with 11 abstentions, to press for the lifting of the blockade. The US's response was that it would do nothing until Cuba stopped its denial of human rights (*Guardian*, 16/10/98, p. 17). That the Cuban government has been responsible for diverse violations of civil liberties cannot be gainsaid, but it has not been responsible for systematic repression in the same manner as many states that the US has no problems in dealing with.

62 R. Hernández and H. Dilla, 'Political Culture and Popular Participation', in Centro de Estudios Sobre América (ed.), *The Cuban Revolution Into the 1990s. Cuban Perspectives* (Boulder, CO, Westview Press, 1992), p. 33. This politicization centred upon the legendary figures and incidents of the revolutionary war, principally Castro and, until his final departure from Cuba in 1966, Ernesto Guevara. Hernández and Dilla make the significant point that the experiences of the foundational stage are only now personal to middle-aged and older Cubans. For the young, these are only received myths which for many, particularly since the onset of the struggle for economic and political survival since the mid-1980s, may no longer have resonance. This notwithstanding, the personal appeal of Castro is still apparent to the visitor, as is that of Guevara, as demonstrated by the massive celebration of survival and resistance which accompanied his funeral in Santa Clara in October 1997. The political and personal rivalries and the debates concerning political and economic strategy and the relationship between Cuba and the Soviet Union, as well as with the rest of Latin America, are given fresh insights by J. G. Castañeda, *Compañero. The Life and Death of Che Guevara* (London, Bloomsbury, 1997).

63 G. Suárez Hernández, 'Political Leadership in Cuba', in Centro de Estudios Sobre América (ed.), *The Cuban Revolution*, p. 52.

64 While accepting that the Cuban political model was not perfect and that further democratization of the power structures and the substance of participation and *poder popular* was essential, Juan Antonio Blanco then went on the offensive when he wrote: 'We consider our party democracy to be supported by a structure of power that is equally democratic as and much more desirable and satisfactory than a "market democracy" in which the political-legal system is based on a polarized structure of economic and financial power' ('Cuba: Utopia and Reality Thirty Years Later', in Centro de Estudios Sobre América (ed.), *The Cuban Revolution*, p. 27). The account of contemporary regimes given in this book may cause the reader to react positively to this opinion, although this would not obviate the need to make far-ranging criticism of the depth and extent of Cuban democracy.

65 Economic policies since 1986 are discussed in Chapter 6.

66 Munck, 'After the Transition', 15.

67 M. Peralta Ramos, 'Economic Policy and Distributional Conflict among Business Groups in Argentina: From Alfonsín to Menem (1983–90)', in Epstein (ed.), *New Argentinian Democracy*, p. 99.

3

The Left and democracy

The Latin American Left has experienced tremendous changes in recent years which have compelled it to reconsider its place within political systems, its own strategies and its relationships with popular movements. There has been much discussion of a crisis on the Left, of parties hitherto certain of their political identity now cut adrift from their moorings and unsure of their purpose. The disintegration of the Eastern European regimes in 1989, followed by that of the Soviet Union, has had important repercussions. Many on the Latin American Left had welcomed perestroika, seeing in it the possibility of renovating socialism on more tolerant and participatory lines. Roberto Freire, a leading Brazilian Communist, has been quoted as saying that 'the fall of the Eastern bloc is one of the best things to happen to socialism in many years'.[1] However, the reality of the 1990s has been that of a decline, if not eclipse, of the international credibility of Marxist and socialist ideas and movements, underpinned by a right-wing offensive, represented by Fukuyama's triumphalism and by the pervasiveness of neo-liberal strategies which have displaced previous models of state-led economic development to which the Left has always subscribed. The 1990 and 1996 electoral defeats of the FSLN in Nicaragua and the precarious viability of the Cuban Revolution in the post-Cold War world have called into question any future socialist experiments. Some parties, such as the Chilean PSC and the MAS of Venezuela, have dropped all reference to socialism. In Mexico, the left-leaning PRD has sought to offer a serious challenge to the unravelling PRI hegemony, whilst left-wing parties are increasingly detached from contemporary politics. In the Southern Cone and Brazil, left-wing parties emerging from the ravages of military dictatorship (their experience of torture, imprisonment and exile convincing many of the value of defending human rights) have had to find their place within transitional and consolidating electoral systems. Moving from their traditional disparagement of liberal democracy as nothing more than a façade for elite manipulation and the defence of unequal class relations, they have re-evaluated democracy and the prerogatives of citizenship. The majority have abandoned any thought of armed struggle and now compete in national and local elections. Steve Ellner argues that 'the Left has broken out of its traditional ghetto and become a major protagonist in politics'.[2]

I would qualify this positive assessment by arguing that there have been both successes and failures, but that the political significance of the Left has not acquired critical mass. There have been notable achievements. In 1983, Alfonso Barrantes of the IU was elected mayor of Lima, and two years later came second in the Peruvian Presidential elections (although, subsequently, the Peruvian Left has gone into what seems terminal decline). The Uruguayan Frente Amplio (FA, Broad Front) and the Venezuelan MAS have achieved considerable success, as has the PRD, culminating in Cuauhtémoc Cárdenas's capture of the mayoralty of Mexico City in 1997. In the 1989 presidential elections, Lula of the Brazilian PT lost by only six percentage points (but his 1994 and 1998 campaigns produced disappointing results). In the 1990s, following the official peace settlement ending the civil war, ex-guerrillas, including the Movimiento-19's (M-19, Movement-19) erstwhile leader, Antonio Navarro Wolff, have been elected to the Salvadorean Constituent Assembly. Such advances have been offset by problems in relations between left-wing parties and popular movements, which have resulted in division and estrangement, and a reduction in voter alignment with political parties generally which have weakened the Left's opportunities. Whilst one could, therefore, talk of dramatic breakthroughs in the 1980s, the 1990s found 'the Left ... more disoriented and lacking in credible options than ever before'.[3] Thus whilst the Central American insurgencies in El Salvador and Guatemala finally ended in peace settlements in 1990 and 1996, respectively (although major problems remain unresolved and civil peace continues to be problematic), other left-wing movements resist the repudiation of violent political action with Sendero Luminoso in Peru and the Colombian Fuerzas Armadas Revolucionarias

Colombianas (FARC, Revolutionary Armed Forces of Colombia) still adhering to the notion of the armed overthrow of the state. Democratic participation has directed the Left's attention to its realistic chances of gaining power (what, for example, would be the international response to the election of a left-wing candidate as President in Brazil or Mexico?), and whether it is operating on a level playing field.[4] It has also been obliged to consider how democratic and participatory its internal organizational structures are and how its relationships with popular movements are conducted. One can identify both positive and negative assessments of the Left's attempts to wrestle with democracy.[5]

Historically, neither the Old nor New Lefts[6] attached great significance to questions of political representation, constitutional rule and citizenship. However, many writers have recognized how the theoretical discourse (or what Norbert Lechner has called 'the articulating axis of the Latin American debate'[7]) of the Left has shifted from a focus upon revolution in the 1960s and 1970s to a preoccupation with democracy in the 1980s and 1990s. Ronaldo Munck affirms that 'the antagonism between authoritarianism ... and democracy has largely superseded that posited between capitalism and socialism'.[8] Neither Munck nor Tomás Vasconi believe, however, that the issue of a socialist transformation of society is dead and buried. Vasconi has argued that much of the criticism of Marxism as reductionist (that is, that it explains everything in the political sphere by recourse to its economic origins, and that its obsession with class as the main determinant of political activity makes it incapable of understanding the significance of new social movements) is, in fact, a vulgarization of Marxism and a negation of its continued value as a methodological tool. He castigates those Marxists who have embraced liberal democracy so completely that they ignore the vast chasm between formal political democracy and socio-economic democracy (attainment of both, he argues, has always been the goal of Marxism, whereas liberal democracy is founded upon the acceptance of socio-economic inequality).[9] Richard L. Harris states that if revisionist Marxists embrace the existing social order as a necessary condition of the pacted political system, accepting it as legitimate, then 'they give a decisive advantage to their bourgeois opponents who are able to use their control over the economic and social structures of the prevailing capitalist system to preserve the status quo and manipulate the existing political processes to their benefit'.[10] Munck concludes that the Left cannot afford to distance itself from criticism of already existing systems of government and that 'only the fully egalitarian socialist extension of democracy can move towards the resolution of the grievous social and economic problems of the continent'.[11] For Munck, this could only be a possibility if left-wing parties transformed themselves with respect to their commitment to real popular control, the decentralization of power and the strengthening of civil society. Vasconi, on the other hand, whilst accepting some engagement with other popular sectors, continues to believe that the working class must remain central to any transformative strategy. Highly critical of the radical model of democracy – which he describes as 'left populism' – he maintains that it lacks the organizational thrust and political leadership that a revolutionary vanguard offers.

To talk of 'the Left' is to make a huge political generalization, ignoring historical and contemporary differences, but it is possible to identify three main ideological currents which have emerged from the socialism/democracy debate. Roberto Barros delineates them in the following manner. The first group – which might be called 'the intransigents' – has adhered to the view that existing pacted democracy in Latin America is formal and deceitful, and the Left should approach it as an obstacle which has to be overcome on the road to socialism. This perspective acknowledges the very definite limitations of existing democracy and the 'parameters for further democratization' which are constrained by economic neo-liberalism and creeping political authoritarianism, and infers that 'the possibilities for integrating popular demands through representative institutions are . . . extremely circumscribed'.[12] Whilst Barros concurs with the intransigents' analysis of the fundamental inadequacies of the pacted model, he is scathing in his critique of their continued loyalty to 'an authoritarian Marxism whose real concepts are objective interests, vanguard party, political revolution and the dictatorship of the proletariat'.[13] This ultra-orthodox approach continues to downgrade the role of 'the masses' to dependent subjects who require an education in political consciousness which only a vanguard can provide, and thus ignores the impressive, albeit slow, progress of popular movements in structuring their own strategies and consolidating their presence within political cultures. A good example of this perspective is found in Roger Burbach and Orlando Nuñez's book *Fire in the Andes. Forging a Revolutionary Agenda* (written in 1987). Claiming to accept the need for internal debate and greater egalitarianism in decision-making within left-wing parties, they continue to affirm the necessity of a revolutionary bloc led by the working class. In their view, popular mobilization which lacks this discipline is incoherent, open to manipulation by the dominant political order and inherently utopian.[14] These 'old school' marxists are clearly in a minority within the broad Left, and their numbers are declining.

The second group identified by Barros represents those who have turned away from Marxism and have concentrated their activities upon democratic consolidation. Discussion of 'revolution', 'class struggle' and the 'transition to socialism' has disappeared from their political agendas.[15] Barros considers that this perspective fails to recognize the unequal power relationships which permeate existing pacted democracies and which create impediments to a 'shared valuation of (the) legitimacy . . . (of) . . . democratic institutions'.[16] It also ignores the compromises left-wing politicians make in order to be recognized as legitimate political actors, and their implicit acceptance of the fact that the political agenda is inimical to popular interests. This Left must evaluate its position within contemporary political systems (a position which Barros regards as extremely weak), particularly as it falls between two stools: to support popular democracy will reduce its legitimacy in the eyes of the political establishment, whilst to try to demobilize it will alienate existing or potential voters and thus diminish its weight within the state. James Petras has contended that the revisionist Left has contributed to the pervasive influence of neo-liberalism because it has accepted the boundaries the latter has imposed upon political debate.[17]

The third tendency within the Left (and the one which most closely resembles the radical model described in Chapter 1) attempts to marry Marxist socialism and democracy, thus recognizing the momentum of popular radicalism and the new role left-wing parties should assume with respect to this. Adopting a critical position on past left theory and practice, it calls for 'The development of alternative forms of culture, organisation and struggle that challenge institutionalised norms and hierarchies and thereby contribute to the formation of popular subjects endowed with autonomy and will to actively engage in public life.'[18] This view moves away from the orthodox insistence on the prime political role assigned to the industrial working class and joins the post-Marxist retreat from class analysis. Chilcote discusses a radical force made up of diverse social groups based upon the fact that 'the struggle for socialism comprises a plurality of resistances to inequality and oppression'.[19] With the decline in the size and industrial muscle of the organized labour movement and the tremendous growth of the informal economy and of people living below the poverty line (it has been estimated that by 1990, 183 million Latin Americans or 44 per cent of the total population lived below the poverty line and that half of these lived in 'extreme poverty'[20]), writers have urged the democratic Left to confront the ever-increasing problems of the poor. The intensification of income differentials and the impact this has had upon access for the poor to employment, education, health, culture and other life opportunities (considered the right of citizens) is a profoundly serious trend and raises issues of discontent and the delegitimization of democracy (whether of a pacted or radical nature). Brazil's PT is often cited as a movement engaged in addressing this dilemma through its combination of municipal and national electoral activity, its close links to grassroots organizations and its efforts to maintain egalitarian party structures. Such a multifaceted approach does pose problems. One is that it may be impossible for a political movement to represent diverse social groups with possibly conflicting demands, another that focusing upon electoral involvement may inhibit the decentralization of decision-making called for by a participatory project. A third is that established political elites will be suspicious of such a dynamic programme, regarding it as threatening the stability of their pacted governing arrangements.

Although renovated and new left-wing parties have moved – with greater or lesser degrees of commitment and effectiveness – into the terrain of radical democratic politics, they have not as yet been capable of formulating a coherent political vision which could act as an alternative to neo-liberalism. The state has traditionally been seen by the Left as the central agent of change, but this view is no longer viable given the demise of state socialism in the Soviet bloc, experience of military rule (showing what the concentration of state power can do), the rolling back of the state under the aegis of economic restructuring, and a virtually universal recognition that Latin American state structures are in urgent need of modernization to eradic-ate bureaucracy, corruption and general inefficiency. It can be argued that the Left needs to develop new political and eco-nomic strategies and place the cultural and ethical values of radical participatory democracy at their heart. According to Jorge Castañeda, it also needs to separate the disillusionment caused by the end of 'already existing socialism' from what he sees as a 'generalised perception of defeat' on the Left. He believes that 'the conditions in Latin America that gave birth and recognition to the left in the past are as pervasive as ever, and in fact have become more severe with recent trends'.[21]

Municipal, state and regional politics – rather than nationally-based competitions – have provided the arena where the Left has been most successful in electoral politics, and where it has been offered the opportunity to experiment with progressive reforms with the aim of both greater social justice and the introduction of participatory mechanisms.[22] Local politics may be the crucible in which the Left can forge both its alignment with the radical model of democracy grounded in grassroots organization and a rearticulation of the relationship between state structures and civil society. Castañeda maintains that 'Municipal democracy should be the centre–piece of the left's democratic agenda, not so much because the region's problems can be solved at this level but because it typifies the kind of change that is viable, significant and constitutes a stepping stone for the future.'[23] As left-wing candidates and coalitions have established significant footholds in municipal government in Latin America's largest cities, as well as in rural areas and in individual states and departments, their advance has coin-cided with most national governments devolving major re-sponsibilities to local government, particularly in terms of service provision, as part of their commitment to the rolling back of the central state. This decentralization process is com-patible with the neo-liberal agenda, but it might also be used to facilitate more popular involvement in and control over decision-making, as well as ensuring that municipal govern-ment satisfies local needs in a more diligent fashion.

Some general observations can be made in terms of the con-straints that left-wing parties working in municipal government have to contend with. They must deliver services efficiently if they are to retain the public's support, but they undertake this task in difficult circumstances. National neo-liberal economic policies have resulted in the intensification of poverty and its attendant ills (malnourishment resulting in health problems, inadequate infrastructure and services), but the handing down of powers to local government means that it is the latter which has to address these issues and manage the crisis. Left-wing municipalities are elected on the basis of programmes which promise to alleviate social deprivation, but the enormity of the problems makes the job very daunting, particularly for politicians with little previous experience of the day-to-day administration of local authorities.

Left-wing municipal governments are also elected because of their commitment to changing the political culture by offering more open and accessible management and creating opportunities for widespread popular representation. There are many examples of good practice in this respect, but the overhauling of institutional life will be a protracted and difficult process which must cope with both the resistance of local elites and the inevitable disenchantment that slow and often problematic progress will provoke in popular groups. There is an additional contradiction between the pragmatic policies that elected mayors and councils have to pursue in order to govern (and satisfy their constituents), and the ideological stances of their party stalwarts. All parties which have been involved in municipal politics have had to contend with internal divisions over questions of tactics and policies which have impaired their efficient functioning. William R. Nylen, in his discussion of the PT's record in rural local government in Brazil, argues that political activists facing the uphill task of solving seemingly insurmountable problems may have to contend with poor community response, which can lead to a widening gap between PT administrators and the groups they are trying to work with. It could also encourage the return of traditional elitist and patronizing attitudes towards 'the people' and, thus, a move away from the participatory impetus. Since the late 1980s, the PT has engaged in a debate about its role in local government and the implications for popular democracy. Nylen identifies two positions which he terms the 'orthodox' and the 'heterodox'. The former endorses the view that municipal involvement is important only insofar as it furthers the revolutionary cause (that is, as a means of getting the party message across to broad sectors of the community), whereas the latter is committed to democratizing the contemporary state through the creation of an alternative politics. In his 1992 book, *The PT's Way of Governing*, Jorge Bittar argued that the heterodox perspective offered the party an opportunity to create new bases of support and to establish a new style in public service, shaped by an ethos of social justice and realized through popular participation.[24]

The remainder of this chapter will consider the varieties of ways that national Lefts have attempted to come to terms with a democratic model and how they have succeeded in re-creating their own identities. The latter challenge can be viewed from two angles: one is the relationship between left-wing parties and dominant systems, and the other is their need to transform their links with popular movements. Social movements remain suspicious, believing that the Left will attempt to subvert the independence of community, peasant, indigenous, environmental and women's groups. The Left's credibility has to be established. In their efforts to reconstitute themselves in a new political climate, left-wing parties must engage in a critical dialogue with their own histories – in order to expose dogmatism and sectarianism – as well as reassessing previous experiments in socialism, pre-eminently the Cuban Revolution.[25] Since 1959, the Latin American Left has floundered over its inability to offer an objective criticism of Cuba with respect to the latter's violation of human rights, its suppression of political discussion and its narrow cultural perspectives.[26] The Left has always endorsed Cuba's considerable achievements, but its overriding consideration was to avoid giving sustenance to the enemy – that is, the USA – within the context of the Cold War. Similarly, solidarity with the FSLN in Nicaragua produced an unwillingness to criticize such policies as economic austerity measures and *la piñata*.[27] The challenge facing the Latin American Left is aptly summed up by Margaret E. Keck. Arguing that the Left must convince public opinion that 'social equality . . . is in the interest of society as a whole', she accepts that 'reclaiming this fundamental dimension, while shedding the accumulated baggage of failed experiments with models that produced new forms of inequality in the name of socialism, is extraordinarily difficult'. For Keck, 'the effort to rethink socialism is inextricably linked to the effort to broaden and deepen democracy'.[28]

Traditional left-wing parties – communist, socialist, Trotsky-ist, Maoist and those advocating armed struggle – have responded to changing political circumstances in contemporary Latin America in a variety of ways. Most have experienced intense, internal debates often ending in division and further fragmentation of movements long known for their endemic instability. Few exert significant political influence and many appear to have been banished to the sidelines of national political activity. Newer parties such as the PT, MAS, Causa R and FA, propose the adoption of organizational forms and political programmes which are closely aligned to the interests of popular movements. They have had their share of political success, but Brazil's PT is perhaps the only one to have harnessed a vision of a grassroots, radical democracy to an effective strategy for electoral growth. In Central America, ex-guerrillas reconstituted as politicians have, despite their lack of electoral experience and resources, made advances, although it must be questioned as to whether they can ever contemplate winning state power. The obstacles in their path include their own ideological splits, the resistance of entrenched elites, the fragmented nature of the political systems they operate within[29] and the attitude of the USA. All left-wing parties who are committed to electoral activity are working within political environments where many citizens feel alienated from politics *per se* and distrust most politicians, whatever their place on the ideological spectrum. With increasing socio-economic differentiation and a trend towards political authoritarianism, it is going to be very difficult for left-wing parties to democratize themselves and offer attractive and possible government alternatives. I wish now, through a consideration of specific left-wing parties – both 'old' and 'new' – to evaluate the problems they face and the strategies they have adopted.

Many writers have commented upon the tremendous shock administered to the Chilean Left by the military coup against Salvador Allende and the Unidad Popular (UP, Popular Unity) government on 11 September 1973.[30] Exceptionally for Latin America, left-wing parties – principally socialist and communist, but also radical Catholic – had enjoyed legality, electoral success, legislative weight and even occasional governmental presence, as well as creating strong bases within the working-class and popular movements. Although left-wing parties did endure periods of repression, they generally regarded themselves as legitimate actors within the Chilean political system, taking their democratic rights for granted. This illusion was brutally exposed by the coup and the elimination of 'subversion' which followed it, and the Chilean Left was compelled to come to terms with exile and a sense of failure which led it into a lengthy debate about culpability, identity and future prospects. It embarked upon simultaneous processes of organizational fragmentation and then regrouping and moves towards alliance (*convergencia socialista*, socialist convergence). The ideological and strategic trajectories taken by individual parties departed from their previous incarnations with the PSC, historically the more radical, undergoing division, with a majority moving towards a social democratic position and the Partido Comunista Chilena (PCC, Chilean Communist Party, which traditionally had been the more conservative) pledging itself to armed struggle in 1980, and even allying with its erstwhile strongest critic, the guevarista Movimiento de Izquierda Revolucionaria (MIR, Movement of the Revolutionary Left) in a series of actions in the period 1983–86. The political landscape was complicated by the existence of smaller groups on the Christian Left as well as independent intellectuals, some of whom gravitated to the socialist and others to the communist camps.[31]

The PCC's strategy after the coup and throughout the 1970s was to adhere to an orthodox insistence upon the creation of a broad, anti-fascist front which would involve not only left-wing and popular forces but also progressive elements within the military and the Church, although excluding what it regarded as the *ultra* Left. It hoped to exploit continuing divisions within the PDC, which initially supported the Pinochet regime but subsequently moved to an oppositional stance. However, the authoritarian 1980 Constitution, which signified the institutionalization of military rule, convinced the party (and particularly young militants impressed by the 1979 triumph of the Sandinistas) that gradualist tactics were not working, and its discourse was remodelled around 'the right to rebellion'. Collaboration with the MIR in a series of bank raids, kidnappings and shoot-outs distanced the PCC from other left-wing parties who were moving in the opposite direction and concentrating upon alliance-building with the PDC in the search for a negotiated transition. The PCC and other members of its front organization, the Movimiento Democrático Popular (MDP,

Popular Democratic Movement), were unable to offer a serious military challenge to the regime and were subject to fluctuating repression. As opposition forces joined together in the Coalition of Parties for a 'No' vote in the 1988 plebiscite (a rejection of Pinochet's attempt to retain the Presidency) and participated in the general election of the following year, it became clear that the PCC had made a grave misjudgement and it belatedly joined the 'No' lobby.

Factionalism within the PSC (which had been divided throughout the UP government) intensified in the post-coup period, culminating in formal division in 1979. Rifts were based upon political disagreements (particularly over whether the PSC should seek alliance with the PDC), as well as contradictions between militants living in exile and those constituting the resistance at home, generational experiences and personality clashes. The Almeyda socialists initially adopted an orthodox Marxist–Leninist strategy, arguing for the vanguard role of the working class and aligning themselves with the PCC, but later sought wider allies, campaigned for the 'No' vote and in 1989 constituted themselves as a legal party, the Partido Amplio de Izquierda Socialista (PAIS, Party of the Broad Socialist Left). The Altamirano PS called for a popular front and the continuation of Allende's *via chileno socialismo* (Chilean road to socialism) within the perspective of a peaceful and democratic transition. This view led it into the AD, with the PDC and participation in the campaign for electoral registration which preceded the 1988 plebiscite.[32] The Socialists' ability to affect political events was undermined by organizational and political reconfigurations during the 1980s, but after 1986 they achieved a broad consensus which was characterized by a rejection of revolutionary violence and acceptance of the need for alliance with other political forces in order to force the military out of office. Their commitment to pluralist democracy went hand in hand with a repudiation of a Marxist vocabulary, pre-eminently the phrases 'the dictatorship of the proletariat' and 'class struggle'.

Following their victory in the 1988 plebiscite, most left-wing parties continued in alliance with the PDC and endorsed its candidate, Patricio Aylwin, in the 1989 Presidential elections (although the PDC rejected a formal alliance with the PCC). Socialists were repaid by ministerial positions within the first and subsequent coalition governments, but the Communists, the MIR and other resolutely 'orthodox' groups were excluded. The PCC experienced severe divisions during the 1990s and its political profile remains low. Brian Loveman has argued that the 'renovated' Chilean Left, having internalized the lessons of 1973, has become a pragmatic and social democratic force which – in exchange for governmental office – has been prepared to support economic adjustment programmes and accept the political constraints embedded in the 1980 Constitution. In line with the role of such a Left within a pacted transition, it has been 'hesitant to mobilize popular forces to demand redistribution of income or support calls for institutional reforms'.[33]

The context in which the Peruvian Left must be placed is its historic weakness in national political terms as well as its ideological fragmentation, its experience of military rule between 1968 and 1980,[34] the subsequent transition to civilian government[35] and a dramatic decline in its fortunes from 1983, when one of its leaders, the Maoist Alfonso Barrantes, was elected Mayor of Lima, and 1985, when he contested the Presidency with Alan García, to the 1990s, when its political presence has been all but extinguished. Many writers have commented upon how the nationalist, modernizing, reformist programme of the Revolution of the Armed Forces under General Juan Alvarado Velasco stole the Left's thunder.[36] Neither the Moscow-oriented PCP (later known as the PCP–Unidad, or Unity) nor Trotskyist, Maoist or pro-Cuban groups knew how to react to the military's endorsement of a 'social democracy of full participation' and its support for – albeit controlled and corporatist – mass mobilization.[37] The PCP, believing that the military could act as a progressive force by carrying through a revolution from above that it would never be given an opportunity to do itself, tried to act as a loyal opposition (involving it in attempting to rein in labour activism and defending the gains of 'the Revolution'), but found itself second-guessed by the regime at every stage.[38] The 'ultras' (as the PCP termed its critics on the Left) talked of fascism and the existence of a pre-revolutionary situation without putting forward any substantial programme or strategy of their own. Relations between reformists and radicals were acrimonious, particularly as the latter's involvement with labour and popular activism increased and the PCP's previous hegemony was challenged. Both sides were surprised by the eruption of an increasingly militant union and popular movement during the 'Second Phase' regime of General Morales Bermúdez (1975–80), in response to its dismantling of earlier reforms, and its political economy, which was dominated by the IMF's restructuring 'austerity packages'.[39]

A series of general strikes and continuous labour and popular mobilization, as well as its own internal divisions over policy, forced the military government into inaugurating a two-stage electoral transition process in 1977. The Left entered an intense period of debate about its future political role and a series of unity discussions and realignments. The majority of left-wing parties accepted the need to jettison their traditional disparagement of formal democracy and engage in electoral politics whilst a minority, of which the PC del P – SL was the most significant, chose boycott. SL would launch its armed insurrection to coincide with the 1980 general election which ushered in Fernando Belaúnde's civilian government. However, there was no consensus as to how the Left should deal with democracy. In the run-up to the Constituent Assembly elections in 1978 and during its year-long existence, radicals and reformists continued to quarrel both between and amongst themselves. Whilst the PCP–Unidad and the Partido Socialista Revolucionaria (PSR, Revolutionary Socialist Party, which brought together ex-military radicals and supporters of the 'First Phase' reforms) sought to preserve the Velasco legacy and aspired to be accepted as legitimate actors, Vanguardia Revolucionaria (VR, Revolutionary Vanguard), the MIR, the three Trotskyist parties and other smaller groups regarded the elections as a demobilizing manoeuvre on the part of the regime and, in the main, chose to regard the Assembly as little more than a platform for propaganda and thus failed to have much impact upon the actual business of constitution-writing.[40] The surprisingly large vote obtained by left-wing parties in the 1978 Constituent Assembly elections gave warning that their supporters wanted them to be actively involved, whatever their own inclinations, in democratic politics.[41] As the transition process evolved, the parties of the reformist and radical Left made increasingly desperate attempts at unification. However the collapse of the Alianza Revolucionaria Izquierda (ARI, Revolutionary Left Alliance) in February 1980 meant that five left-wing alliances contested the Presidential and Congressional elections in May of that year, thus dissipating their electoral strength and throwing away the opportunity heralded by 1978.[42]

Despite the disappointment of the 1980 election results, the creation of the IU in the autumn of 1980 appeared to signify a pragmatic departure from previous ideological rigidity on the Left and the party subsequently enjoyed considerable electoral success at both municipal and national levels, culminating in Barrantes's election as Mayor of Lima. Rochabrún has contended that the Left 'was pushed . . . into the framework of the established order' in the wake of popular mobilization, but once there it 'adapted to the functioning of the powers of the state'.[43] This was influenced by its entrance into the realm of the day-to-day administration of municipal affairs and by its urgent need to disassociate itself from Sendero Luminoso, and thus escape the attention of the counter-insurgency policies which the government was directing at the latter. This proved to be unsuccessful; many left-wing activists were caught up in the repression which accompanied the escalation of the insurgency. Political office-holding and IU's desire to be seen as legitimate led it to stress moderation, which resulted in it distancing itself from popular mobilization and failing to lead opposition to Belaúnde's supply-side economic policies. This is not to say that the IU's experience of municipal government in Lima and elsewhere was negative, but it had to deal with many difficulties.[44] Nevertheless, prospects for the Left in the mid-1980s appeared reasonably sound: 'In our country today there co-exist in a single space the strongest guerrilla movement in South America, the legal left with the greatest political presence (IU) and the historically most important reformist political party of the continent in power: APRA.'[45] Barrantes's 1985 presidential campaign against the APRA's García represented the highest point of the Peruvian Left's fortunes, but his defeat signified the beginning of its decline. The 'unity' of the IU was always precarious, but Barrantes's adoption of a co-operative strategy towards the García government brought accusations of corruption and betrayal, with radicals claiming that the alliance had been tainted by its proximity to the state and the weakening of its links to its popular base. The eventual result was that the IU split, with Barrantes leaving in 1987 to form the more openly reformist Izquierda Socialista (IS, Socialist Left). Both organizations fielded candidates in the 1990 elections but their performance was unimpressive. This was part of a general climate of disaffection as voters abandoned traditional party loyalties and flocked to Fujimori and Cambio 90.

It is clear that the persistence of SL's insurrection has seriously hampered the Peruvian Left's prospects, but Gorriti's contention that 'if Sendero had not existed, the process of (IU's) incorporation into the system would have been much more marked and complete and, today, the marxist left would be one of the fundamental pillars of democratic stability' seems remarkably sanguine, given the Left's endemic and apparently unavoidable tendency towards self-destruction.[46]

Throughout the 1980s and during the 1990s, the Mexican Left was on the defensive as it was overtaken by the PRD and, most recently, by the Zapatistas in their ability to mount serious opposition to the PRI regime and to demand modernization and democracy.[47] The Left has failed to develop a critique of state economic policies, although it has been involved to a certain extent with *paros cívicos* (civic strikes) and radical unions as the latter have mobilized in an attempt to survive the consequences of the economic crisis. Left-wing groups of different ideological persuasions have tried to create co-ordinating bodies, but the crisis has 'exacerbated the difficulties inherent in any attempt at unification'.[48] A considerable degree of debate within left-wing circles has concentrated on whether support should be given to the PRD and whether the latter can be regarded as 'of the Left'. Barry Carr believes that it must be (which definition would give the Mexican Left a far larger presence within the political system). He identifies three groups which he describes as the independent Left, the loyal or 'satellite' Left and the *neocardenistas*. The first, which has included the Partido Comunista Mexicano (PCM, Mexican Communist Party), the Partido Mexicano Socialista (PMS, Mexican Socialist Party) and the Trotskyist Partido Revolucionario de los Trabajadores (PRT, Revolutionary Workers' Party), as well as various local *frentes* (fronts), defence committees and social movements, has consistently opposed the PRI government, whereas the second – including the Partido Popular Socialista (PPS, Popular Socialist Party) and the Partido Socialista de los Trabajadores (PST, Socialist Workers' Party) – has traded critical support for the PRI for financial reward. When the Corriente Democrática emerged within the PRI, it was described by one of its leaders, Porfirio Muñoz Ledo, as 'a populist–nationalist current of the Mexican Revolution – but we do not stand for socialism'.[49] Following its expulsion from the PRI, the renamed FDN received the support of many on the Left in the 1988 elections. These included 'a number of leading Trotskyists who considered the mass mobilisations around the Cárdenas campaign a springboard for socialist politics and a sign of the disintegration of the corporatist structures in place since the late 1930s'.[50] The 1988 election results transformed the FRD (which would become the PRD in the following year) into the second largest political force in Mexico. Its independent socialist allies found their share of the vote diminished, whilst 'loyalists' acquired greater electoral weight.[51]

Despite the PRI's continued ability to 'massage' election results, the 1988 elections were considered to be a major political breakthrough on the part of the Left which identified with the PRD. The hope was that exposure of the bankruptcy of PRI rule would stimulate popular mobilization and provide a springboard for a socialist transition. There have been reservations related to the exact nature of the PRD's radicalism, and whether its 1988 results constituted a defining moment in Mexican politics or should be considered merely as a protest vote against the PRI. The independent and loyalist Left – hoping to travel towards state power in the PRD's slipstream – have also been slow to introduce democratic procedures into their internal party mechanisms and to repudiate hierarchical and personality-centred practices. The Left has failed to build strong links with urban and rural movements and to incorporate their demands into its strategic objectives. No left-wing party has managed to build a mass base and, individually, these parties have to be seen as being marginal to the political process. Collectively, the 'Left's' prospects are obviously dependent upon the fortunes of the PRD, but its post-1988 electoral performances have not, as yet, constituted a breakthrough. This can be partly explained by the PRI's determination to hang on to power and its resolve to use any means necessary to achieve this. The experience of the PRD in municipal and state politics has also had an impact, as the party's efforts to honour election promises concerning service provision have been seriously hampered by the national government's economic problems and its reluctance to divert funds to local authorities. Carr argues that an additional factor is 'widespread public cynicism and the long-standing tendency to see all political action (including that of the Left) as tainted by corruption, demagoguery and struggles among rival *camarillas* (clans)'.[52] In recent years, the PRD has sought to bolster its position by embarking upon a series of negotiations and agreements with other parties, social movements and the EZLN. However, the contradiction which is inherent in this process is that these groups represent different political agendas, some of which may be intrinsically antagonistic. Given the PRD's ambivalent political identity and the Mexican Left's political impotence, the possibility of a future socialist debate appears extremely unlikely.

The contemporary character of Venezuelan left-wing politics has been shaped by its response to the post-1958 power-sharing arrangement between AD and COPEI. The Partido Comunista de Venezuela (PCV, Venezuelan Communist Party) had resisted the coup which installed AD in government in 1945, but eventually the two parties came together (in a relationship of mutual suspicion and one which alienated many communist supporters) to oppose the Pérez Jiménez dictatorship (1948–58). Subsequently, the PCV adopted a policy of collaboration with what it termed the 'national bourgeoisie', which antagonized parties to its left and many of its own militants. A second, major, factor was the political aftermath of the PCV's decision to launch an armed insurrection directed at the increasingly authoritarian and repressive Betancourt government in 1962. The result was a disastrous defeat and many dissidents left the party in protest. Some, such as Douglas Bravo and his colleagues in the Fuerzas Armadas de Liberación Nacional (FALN, Armed Forces of National Liberation), remained committed to the armed struggle whilst others, including Teodoro Petkoff and Pomeyo Márquez, eventually formed the Movimiento al Socialismo in 1971.[53] Initially, the MAS criticized the PCV leaders for their reformism and called for a more radical and dynamic socialist agenda. Claiming to be influenced by Eurocommunism, it described itself as a 'New Force' which would work within the legal, electoral system, attract support from sectors apart from the traditional working class and embrace political pluralism. Over time, the MAS came to stress its democratic rather than socialist principles and sought to convince AD and COPEI of its legitimacy as a political actor. Thus, it offered critical support to the first AD presidency of Carlos Andés Pérez (1974–79) and made overtures to progressive elements within both the Church and the military to work with it to contribute to the modernization of the country (all of which was strangely reminiscent of the very tactics it had earlier criticized the PCV for). It argued that it was creating a niche within the system rather than confronting it. In reality, the MAS did not make inroads into either the working class or popular sectors and its constituency was mainly middle-class and student-based.[54] Given that both AD and COPEI were catch-all parties (with AD, in particular, traditionally enjoying substantial support amongst workers and peasants), the prospects for the MAS achieving electoral take-off were slim and its electoral performances disappointing. Thus it obtained 5.7 per cent of the vote in the 1983 elections, with the PCV receiving 1.8 per cent, but AD and COPEI garnering 49.9 per cent and 28.7 per cent, respectively. The MAS might have become the largest single force on the Left, but its national presence was negligible.[55] The Left's seeming inability to effect an electoral breakthrough was not helped by a public perception that the various left-wing parties were engaged in permanent battle with each other and that they were internally fragmented. The MAS provided a perfect example of this perception. It was extremely reluctant to enter into united fronts with the PCV and others and thus the total left vote was always split (thus, it insisted on running Petkov as presidential candidate in 1983 and 1988, despite the fact that the independent, veteran left-winger, José Vincente Rangel, appeared to have a much better chance at success) and its own factionalism was legendary. Party policy endorsed the concept of 'the legalisation of tendencies' which might, on paper, seem to be a democratic recognition of diversity, but in practice kept the MAS locked in interminable political squabbles and highly competitive personality-based struggles.[56]

Whilst the Venezuelan economy was riding the wave of the oil boom, successive governments were able to offer improved living standards and prosperity; political stability appeared secure and mass activism highly unlikely. However, with the onset of recession in the early 1980s (as discussed in Chapter 2) and the application of neo-liberal austerity programmes by both COPEI (under President Campíns, 1979–84) and AD (the Lusinchi government, 1984–89), and the second Pérez administration, 1989–94, the Left was forced to re-evaluate its own political strategies. The MAS divided between a more moderate social democratic wing (most of whom had left by 1985), and those arguing for greater criticism of governments and their privatization programmes and greater identification with popular struggles, which had a more overtly socialist stance. The late 1980s witnessed intensifying mobilization, particularly the mass demonstrations of February 1989 which resulted in hundreds and possibly thousands of deaths.[57] Labour opposition to economic shock-treatment policies and to privatization of state-run basic industries such as steel involved left militants, particularly those from Causa R (which had emerged in the 1970s and whose veteran leader, Andrés Velásquez, won the governorship of the state of Bolívar in 1989). The MAS also fared better in the 1989 elections, with strong contenders in gubernatorial contests in four states, a victory in one state and a respectable 20 per cent share of the municipal vote. It would go on to win four states in 1992, although Petkoff lost the race for the mayoralty of Caracas to the Causa R candidate. The AD stranglehold upon Venezuelan politics appeared to be ending; in the 1989 elections, parties of the Left, including the PCV and even COPEI, entered electoral pacts in order to mount a serious opposition to incumbent AD politicians. In 1993, the veteran COPEI politician, Rafael Caldera, was elected at the head of a new party called Convergencia (Convergence) which represented a breakaway anti-neo-liberal faction. His electoral success was facilitated by the 1993 impeachment of AD's Carlos Andrés Pérez for massive misappropriation of public funds. Caldera's candidacy had been supported by the MAS; the party's reward was a number of government appointments, including Petkoff as Planning Minister. In 1996, the Caldera government performed a political volte-face by embracing privatization; in accordance with IMF strategy, Petkoff has supervised cuts in federal spending and the creation of a friendly environment for foreign investment. This development has caused splits in both the MAS and Causa R between what have been termed 'pragmatists' and 'programmatic anti-neo-liberals' (the latter's 1997 split has been seen by some commentators as the beginnings of the end of its political influence).[58]

I turn now to the Brazilian PT, which is rightly regarded as the most important party to form on the Latin American Left in recent decades. Created in 1980, it originated from a militant 'new unionism' which emerged in the ABCD industrial region around São Paulo and was particularly strong in the automobile industry.[59] Margaret Keck comments that 'many working-class leaders were no longer willing to leave the act of interpretation to others – they wanted to create an organisational opposition for workers to speak for themselves'.[60] From the onset, the PT rejected professional politics and strongly identified with social movements. It proposed a double strategy of institutional progress via electoral competition and endorsement of a revitalized civil society with respect to its promotion of popular mobilization. It can be suggested that this was bound to produce intractable tensions as the PT was sucked into electoral activity and, following its successes, local and national office-holding. Having committed itself to a non-hierarchical and participatory ethos[61] and to the creation of a clear issues-based politics as opposed to the personality-led, populist and thoroughly fragmented nature of the rest of Brazilian political activity, nevertheless the PT has been criticized for authoritarianism and ineptitude in municipal government and for distancing itself from its roots within popular politics.

The PT was largely marginalized during the 1980s as a consequence of the internal problems caused by the double strategy and the continuation of elite control of the political system. Its breakthrough year appeared to be 1989, as Collor de Mello only managed to defeat Lula by six points (53 to 47 per cent) in the presidential elections. The closeness of the race suggested that the PT had the potential to become a governing party, although it may be that the result was as much a comment upon the huge domestic opposition to government corruption and a deteriorating economic situation as approbation of the PT. Keck suggests that the PT was the 'vehicle for the expression of widespread dissatisfaction with the status quo', but queries whether this was sufficient to transform it into a durable political movement, capable of government.[62] This synopsis appeared to be borne out by the disappointing results of the 1994 Presidential election. Lula had expected to win (capitalizing on the corruption scandal which had led to the resignation of Collor de Mello in December 1992), but the PT's complacency was shattered by an alliance between the right wing, the PSDB and the caretaker government of Itamar Franco to support Fernando Henrique Cardoso's candidacy.[63] Despite this setback, the PT's electoral presence continued to grow within Congress and, most visibly, in municipal government. In 1988, it achieved the election of 36 mayors in 13 states, including three state capitals, with Luiza Erundina (a woman from the deprived north-east of the country) taking São Paulo (she lost it in 1992 but the party retained control in Porto Alegre, won

Belo Horizonte and came close in Rio itself); this upward trend continued throughout the 1990s.[64] In 1996, the PT was the most voted-for party in Brazil's hundred largest cities.[65]

The PT's increasingly high municipal profile has enabled it to test its views on grassroots democracy (and for us to evaluate Jorge Castañeda's contention that municipal democracy is the Latin American Left's future[66]). The experience has been one fraught with problems, as PT officials have struggled to reconcile party principles with administrative procedures, and there have been incidents of corruption and, indeed, the need to expel mayors and others from the party. Attempting to provide basic services under the difficult circumstances of national privatization programmes and economic austerity has, inevitably, resulted in a popular perception of inefficiency.[67] This has been compounded by criticism from the *núcleos* (the PT's base units) and the popular councils (which comprise representatives of the social movements) that the party was becoming institutionalized and was neglecting its mobilizational role. A high incidence of popular input into policy-making and government has been obstructed by disagreements over priorities and the creation of patron–client relationships between PT officials and community groups.[68]

The PT's attempt to create a 'new politics' may be problematic, but it has introduced concepts (such as participation and the notion of a transparent, accountable state) which have, hitherto, been noticeably absent from the Brazilian political scene. The PT has also gone further than other left-wing parties in coming to terms with democracy and its relationship to socialism. Breaking the mould of conventional politics and embracing the idea of popular empowerment is bound to be a difficult business and the PT's problems attest to this. It has, however, succeeded in appealing to a broad swathe of the population, including white-collar workers as well as industrial unions, both *favela* (shanty-town) inhabitants and landless peasants (thus breaking the traditional urban/rural dichotomy), women and liberation theologists. Such an alliance should be regarded as an experiment in the promotion of active mass citizenship. The challenges it now faces is how to survive in electoral politics and maintain its principles and how to govern and maintain a mass relationship. Castañeda has written about the 'inconveniences of too much democracy' (including slow decision-making, internal debates and a public image of indecisiveness) but argues that these impediments are preferable to the absence of democracy.[69] The danger is that the PT's delivery of improved service provision and of accountable government will be too slow and its commitment to electoral politics too strong to sustain popular support. The future remains unknown, but the fact that the PT has promoted the idea of mass democracy for millions of Brazilians may be an enduring and important achievement.

Other left-wing parties have adopted similar strategies to that of the PT, albeit with varying degrees of success. One of the oldest, the FA, was formed in 1971 by ex-Communists, socialists, Christian Democrats, progressive military officers and ex-guerrillas and won 18 per cent of the national vote in the Uruguayan elections of the same year (including 30 per cent of the vote in Montevideo, the capital, where almost half of the population live). Its progress was frozen by the period of military rule (1973–83) but it was still able to obtain 21 per cent of the national vote in 1984 (again, with a similar concentration in the capital). Subsequently, the FA split between those advocating broad, democratic aims (known as the Nuevo Espacio, New Space) and those remaining loyal to a socialist position (although one more social democratic than Marxist). Their combined vote in the 1989 elections (with the Frente gaining 21 per cent, and control of Montevideo, and Nuevo Espacio 9 per cent) equalled the turnout enjoyed by the Colorado Party (which, with the Blancos, has long dominated Uruguayan politics, but whose hegemony was now being challenged by the FA as a third force). In the 1994 national elections, the FA achieved 31 per cent of the vote with its candidate, Tabaré Vázquez, coming within 35,000 votes of becoming President.[70] In common with the PT, the FA's most impressive performance has been at the level of municipal government, where it has attempted to propagate the concepts of welfare provision, decentralized management and popular participation and to offer resistance to the prevailing orthodoxies of neo-liberal economics. It has also benefited from a general disillusionment with the two traditional governing parties following the restoration of civilian rule, as they have been found wanting in terms of both effective policy-making and democratic representation. The FA may be able to escape the public repudiation of conventional party politics which is evident throughout the continent, but to do this it must present a distinct and authentic political identity. The problem with broad left fronts is that they are, by nature, indistinct and constantly fluctuating entities. Concentrating upon their 'electability' factor and adopting a fluid progressive image, they hope to attract wider social sectors and identify themselves with democratic institutions. Their major problem (apart from the burden of their ideological past in terms of commitment to and enhancement of popular participation) is that they are operating in national circumstances, and their global sources, which are beyond their control. Here one would cite such factors as the impact of economic austerity, the legacy of authoritarian malpractice and human rights violation, the pervasive corruption which is endemic in Latin and Central American states and the vulnerability of these states to external intrusion (whether it be in terms of continuing debt renegotiations, anti-drugs programmes or the Realpolitik practised by dominant world powers).

As I reach the end of this chapter, I have not discussed the guerrillas who reject incorporation into existing political systems. I have concentrated upon what one might call, without any prejudicial intentions, left-wing parties who have entered these systems (intransigents would probably describe them as having been tamed by the latter). I talk about guerrilla movements in contemporary Latin America (and specifically in Mexico, Peru and Colombia – although I draw strong distinctions between the Zapatistas and the others with respect to their political agendas) in my discussion of the challenges to the hegemony and legitimacy of the state in Chapter 6.

I wish to finish this chapter with some thoughts upon the future of the Left in Latin and Central America. Its history has been one of division, both within and across national borders and, also, under the impact of international ideological divisions. An advance of recent years has been the setting up of the São Paulo Forum which, since 1990, has attempted to group diverse organizations (including the PT, the PRD, the FSLN and the FA, as well as unions, social movements and non-governmental organizations (NGOs) and socialist parties from the rest of the world) in a broad, catholic and continuing debate concerning the Left's role in contemporary Latin and Central America. The third Forum, held in Nicaragua in 1992, issued the Managua Declaration, which condemned neo-liberal economic policies for 'an inevitable worsening of people's living standards, limiting their rights, denationalisation and the opening up of our countries to unrestrained foreign capital and investment'. It called for the development within Latin America of an alternative economic strategy which would revolve around autonomous decision-making, social justice and democracy and which would expect a reformed and responsible state to play a central regulatory role as the promoter of social equity. The resolution of the debt problem, the ending of unequal terms of trade, the imposition of controls to prevent the environment from the ravages of multinational devastation and the protection of indigenous peoples were amongst the priorities it identified.[71] Later Forums have attempted to build bridges between warring factions within political parties and trade unions in individual countries as well as cementing links across borders (within Latin and Central America but also with US and other external organizations). It is important that such dialogues continue to develop, although one may wonder how much is rhetoric and how much substance, and one may query how significant a political player the Latin American Left can be in the next century. The odds – in terms of the pervasiveness of free-market economic commitments on the part of governments, the corruption and inefficiency of the state, the brooding presence of the military, voter passivity and decreasing political partisanship – appear to be stacked against it. In addition, the transformation of left-wing parties from hierarchical and doctrinaire to participatory and tolerant has been extremely problematic. Ronaldo Munck encapsulated this dilemma when he asserted 'there is still an old left which appears to have learned nothing from the experiences of the last 20 years and a new democratic left which has not yet found its bearings'.[72]

Notes

1 J. G. Castañeda, *Utopia Unarmed: The Latin American Left After The Cold War* (New York, Vintage Books, 1994), p. 244.

2 S. Ellner, 'The Changing Status of the Latin American Left in the Recent Past', in B. Carr and S. Ellner (eds), *The Latin American Left. From the Fall of Allende to Perestroika* (Boulder, CO, Westview Press, 1993), p. 2.

3 *Ibid.*, p. 4.

4 Chapter 1's discussion of the constraints imposed by the pacted model of democratic transition and consolidation included the inhibition of radical reform in order to forestall military intervention, and the attempted suppression of popular mobilization.

5 Although some writers question the seriousness of the engagement. Thus Carlos Vilas has declared that 'the abdication of . . . critical thought [on the Left] is astounding' ('What Future for Socialism?', *NACLA. Report on the Americas*, XXV: 5 (May 1992), 16).

6 The defining moment for 'Old' and 'New' being the response of pro-Moscow parties as well as Trotskyist and Maoist parties to the Cuban Revolution; following 1959, most left-wing parties experienced processes of schism and fragmentation. Divisions were along strategic and ideological lines (debates focusing upon the viability of armed struggle as compared to pursuing a peaceful road to socialism) and were also frequently generational, with many younger militants adopting Ernesto Guevara's precepts. José Rodríguez Elizondo gives a comprehensive account of the impact of the Cuban Revolution upon Old and New Lefts and their views upon insurgency in *Las Crisis de las Izquierdas en América Latina* (Caracas, Editorial Nueva Sociedad, 1990).

7 Quoted by R. Munck, 'Farewell to Socialism? A Comment on Recent Debates', *Latin American Perspectives*, 65: 17: 2 (Spring 1990), 113.

8 *Ibid.*

9 T. A. Vasconi, 'Democracy and Socialism in South America', *Latin American Perspectives*, 65: 17: 2 (Spring 1990).

10 R. L. Harris, *Marxism, Socialism and Democracy in Latin America* (Boulder, CO, Westview Press, 1992), p. 208.

11 Munck, 'Farewell', p. 116.

12 R. Barros, 'The Left and Democracy', *Telos*, 68 (1986), 55, 57.

13 *Ibid.*, 57.

14 R. Burbach and O. Nuñez, *Fire in the Andes. Forging a Revolutionary Agenda* (London, Verso, 1987).

15 Harris, *Marxism*, p. 197 discusses the Venezuelan MAS whilst Brian Loveman ('The Political Left in Chile, 1970–90', in Carr and Ellner (eds), *Latin American Left*, pp. 23–39) considers the evolution of large sections of the Chilean Left in this context.

16 Barros, 'Left', 65.

17 J. Petras, 'State, Regime and the Democratization Muddle', *Latin American Studies Association Forum*, 18: 4 (1988), 10.

18 Barros, 'Left', 65.

19 R. H. Chilcote, 'Post-Marxism. The Retreat from Class in Latin America', *Latin American Perspectives*, 65: 17: 2 (Spring 1990), 5. E. Laclau and C. Mouffe, in *Hegemony and Socialist Strategy. Towards a Radical Democratic Politics* (London, Verso, 1985), argue for a new hegemonic project which recognizes diversity in social experience and attempts to create linkages between groups oppressed, by virtue not only of their class position, but also because of their gender and ethnic profiles as well as those concerned with 'issue politics', such as environmental problems.

20 Vilas, 'What Future', 14.

21 Castañeda, *Utopia*, p. 240.

22 Despite greater visibility in national elections, left-wing parties have so far only managed to become either junior partners in centrist governments (Chile and Venezuela) or oppositions exercising varying degrees of political leverage (Brazil, Mexico, Uruguay, Nicaragua).

23 Castañeda, *Utopia*, p. 366.

24 Cited by W. R. Nylen, 'The Workers' Party in Rural Brazil', *NACLA. Report on the Americas*, XXIX: 1 (July–August 1995), 32.

25 Thus, the UP government in Chile, the Nicaraguan Revolution and insurgencies in Peru and Colombia, as well as in Central America, need to be addressed in terms of their respective failures to transform the state, consolidate relationships with popular sectors, agree upon strategic policy choices and repudiate authoritarian practices.

26 Amongst issues which need to be considered are the Cuban state's treatment of homosexuals and its exercise of censorship with respect to literature and the cinema.

27 As mentioned earlier (p. 30), in 1990 the outgoing FSLN government made generous distributions of land, property and funds to its own members and party loyalists. *La piñata* (literally, the opening of a net) was regarded by many observers as a violation of the FSLN's reputation for financial probity.

28 M. E. Keck, 'Brazil's PT: Socialism as Radical Democracy', *NACLA. Report on the Americas*, XXV: 5 (May 1992), 29.

29 Thus, in the November 1995 elections, the newly created Frente Democrática Nueva de Guatemala (FDNG, New Guatemalan Democratic Front) received 7.7 per cent of the presidential vote and became the third largest party in Guatemala, but given the tribal nature of Guatemalan politics it is unlikely to make much further progress (in that its electoral appeal is limited to a certain constituency and it does not have crossover appeal); S. Jonas, 'Left establishes its presence in Guatemalan elections', *NACLA. Report on the Americas*, XXIX: 4 (January–February 1996), 1. This is a problem common to all left-wing parties, particularly those emerging from insurrectionary periods.

30 Texts include J. Faúndez, *Marxism and Democracy in Chile. From 1932 to the Fall of Allende* (New Haven, CT, Yale University Press, 1988), C. Furci, *The Chilean Communist Party and the Road to Socialism* (London, Zed Books, 1984) and B. Pollack and H. Rosenkranz, *Revolutionary Social Democracy – The Chilean Socialist Party* (London, Pinter, 1986).

31 Carlos Bascuñan Edwards discusses the impact of liberation theology upon the Movimiento de Acción Popular Unitaria (MAPU, Movement of United Popular Action), the Movimiento Obrero Campesino (MOC, Workers' and Peasants' Movement) and Izquierda Cristiana (IC, Christian Left) and their ambivalent politics in *La Izquierda sin Allende* (Santiago, Editorial Planeta Espejo de Chile, 1990), pp. 117–22.

32 Clodomiro Almeyda had been Allende's vice-president whilst Carlos Altamirano was party Secretary-General until 1979. Jorge Arrate and Paulo Hidalgo chronicle the political and personal divisions on the left in *Pasión y Razón del Socialismo Chileno* (Santiago, Las Ediciones del Ornitorrinco, 1989).

33 B. Loveman, 'The Political Left in Chile, 1970–1990', in Carr and Ellner (eds), *Latin American Left*, p. 37.

34 This is discussed by, amongst others, J. Nieto, *Izquierda y Democracia en el Perú, 1975–80* (Lima, Centro de Estudios y Promoción del Desarrollo, 1983) and N. Haworth, 'Radicalisation and the Left in Peru, 1976–90', in Carr and Ellner (eds), *Latin American Left*.

35 The post-1980 political situation is discussed by J. Crabtree, *Peru under García. An Opportunity Lost* (Basingstoke, Macmillan, 1992), H. Pease García, *Democracia y Precariedad Bajo el Populismo Aprista* (Lima, Centro de Estudios y Promoción del Desarrollo, 1988), L. Pásara and J. Parodi (eds), *Democracia, Sociedad y Gobierno en el Perú* (Lima, Centro de Estudios de Democracia y Sociedad, 1988) and P. Mauceri, *Militares, Insurgencia y Democratización en el Perú, 1980–88* (Lima, Instituto de Estudios Peruanos, 1989).

36 The military's political programme and philosophy is analysed by D. Booth and B. Sorj (eds), *Military Reformism and Social Classes: The Peruvian Experience, 1968–80* (London, Macmillan, 1982) and C. McClintock and A. Lowenthal (eds), *The Peruvian Experiment Reconsidered* (Princeton, NT, Princeton University Press, 1983). Guillermo Rochabrún has written that the military reforms 'resulted in unprecedented conditions for democratic functioning in terms of the incorporation into political life of new broad, organised and autonomous contingents' ('Crisis, Democracy and the Left in Peru', *Latin American Perspectives*, 15: 3, Summer 1988).

37 A revealing insight into the different parties' views is to be found in M. Lauer, *El Reformismo Burgués* (Lima, Mosca Azul Editores, 1978).

38 The communist Confederación General de Trabajadores del Perú (CGTP, General Confederation of Peruvian Workers) found its hegemonic position within the organized labour movement challenged by *clasista* (class-conscious) radical unions, particularly those of the teachers and miners, who repudiated the hierarchy's reluctance to support strikers and to criticize the government's labour policies. Militancy increased following the July 1977 General Strike (the first in Peru since 1919); there was growing confrontation between workers and employers, backed up by the police and gangs of strike-breakers. Both the CGTP and the PCP–Unidad experienced schism in the 1977–78 period as calls for internal democracy and an identification with popular struggles grew.

39 The Peruvian economy experienced a severe balance of payments deficit and spiralling inflation. Its borrowing from international banks and the IMF increased. The latter insisted upon economic restructuring in return for granting standby credits. The packages included wage freezes, price hikes on food and gasoline, cuts in social services, the end of collective wage agreements and the suspension of cost-of-living allowances. Unemployment and deprivation intensified.

40 VR was, by the Left's standards, a relatively catholic church of ex-Communists, ex-Trotskyists, ex-Maoists and pro-Cuban advocates, with some strong links to the popular and union movement. It played a central role in the abortive unification process. The MIR originated as a splinter group within the APRA; it was a leading participant in the guerrilla war of 1965. Following its defeat, it underwent constant splits until reuniting in 1979. The three Trotskyist parties formed the 'socialist bloc' which contested the 1980 elections; Hugo Blanco of the Partido Revolucionario de Trabajadores (PRT, Workers' Revolutionary Party) would have been the unity candidate for President if the ARI had survived. Nieto argues that the radical Left's contemptuous response to the Assembly was a misreading of popular desires for a legal endorsement of citizenship rights; *Izquierda*, p. 84.

41 The two radical electoral fronts obtained 16.91 per cent of the national vote and the two reformist fronts, 12.5 per cent (E. Bernales, *Crisis Política: Solución Electoral?* Lima, Centro de Estudios y Promoción del Desarrollo, 1980, p. 70). This confirmed that the PCP–Unidad had lost its hegemonic position on the Left.

42 The five Left-wing alliances collectively obtained 13.7 per cent of the Presidential vote and 17.2 per cent of the Congressional returns (S. Woy-Hazleton, 'The Return of Partisan Politics in Peru', in S. Gorman (ed.), *Post-Revolutionary Peru. The Politics of Transformation* Boulder, CO, Westview Press, 1982, p. 55).

43 Rochabrun, 'Crisis', p. 91.

44 The IU adopted a practical programme, including the improvement of housing stock and health facilities and various projects which led it to collaborate with community organizations. Henry Pease (who would head the IU after Barrantes's departure) described the municipal experience as 'a school for democracy' (quoted by Haworth, 'Radicalisation', in Carr and Ellner (eds), *Latin American Left*, p. 52.

45 Nelson Manrique, quoted by Rochabrún, 'Crisis', p. 90.

46 G. Gorriti Ellenbogen, *Sendero. Historía de la Guerra Milenaria en el Perú* (Lima, Editorial Apoyo, 1990), p. 32.

47 Indeed, even the right-wing PAN has made electoral advances through presenting itself as committed to democratization, while the Left has remained conspicuously quiet about its democratic credentials.

48 B. Carr, 'The Mexican Left, the Popular Movements and the Politics of Austerity, 1982–85', in B. Carr and R. Anzaldúa Montoya, *The Mexican Left, the Popular Movements and the Politics of Austerity* (San Diego, University of California Center for US–Mexican Studies, 1986), p. 9. Discussions concerning unification led to the dissolution of the PCM in 1981 and the emergence of broader organizations such as the Partido Socialista Unificado de México (PSUM, Unified Socialist Party of Mexico) in the same year.

49 B. Carr, 'The Left and Its Potential Role in Political Change', in W. A. Cornelius, J. Gentleman and P. H. Smith (eds), *Mexico's Alternative Political Futures* (San Diego, University of California Center for US–Mexican Studies, 1990), p. 369.

50 B. Carr, 'Mexico: The Perils of Unity and the Challenge of Modernization', in Carr and Ellner (eds), *Latin American Left*, p. 91.

51 *Ibid.*, pp. 91–2.

52 *Ibid.*, p. 95.

53 The insurrection is discussed by R. Debray, *The Revolution on Trial* (Harmondsworth, Penguin, 1978), vol. 1 and R. Gott, *Rural Guerrillas in Latin America* (Harmondsworth, Penguin, 1970), part 2.

54 Castañeda, *Utopia*, p. 170.

55 S. Ellner, *Venezuela's Movimiento al Socialismo. From Guerrilla Defeat to Innovative Politics* (Durham, NC and London, Duke University Press, 1988), p. 134.

56 S. Ellner, 'The Venezuelan Left: From Years of Prosperity to Economic Crisis', in Carr and Ellner (eds), *Latin American Left*, pp. 146–7 describes how attempts were made to curb factionalism from the mid-1980s onwards. Other reforms included the decentralization of the MAS's organizational structure with primaries being held for the first time in 1990 and a woman, Argelia Laya, elected party President. Other parties, including the PCV, followed suit with respect to internal democratization. However, factionalism continues to be a debilitating tendency and left-wing leaders still build their power bases through personal followings.

57 *Ibid.*, p. 140.

58 S. Ellner, 'The Politics of Privatization', *NACLA. Report on the Americas*, XXXI: 3 (November–December 1997), 6–9.

59 ABCD is an acronym of the cities of Santo Andre, São Bernardo do Campo, São Caetano and Diadema. Since the introduction of the 1944 Labour Code, Brazilian trade unions had been organized in a corporatist manner with collaborationist leaders with close ties to management and the Ministry of Labour. After 1964, the military regime imposed strict anti-strike legislation and abolished job security regulations: 'the . . . purpose . . . was both to decrease salaries and to attract foreign investment by ensuring a "safe climate" vis-á-vis labour' (M. H. Moreira Alves, 'Cultures of Fear, Cultures of Resistance', in J. E. Corradi, P. Weiss Fagan and M. A. Garretón (eds), *Fear at the Edge. State Terror and Resistance in Latin America*, Berkeley, University of California Press, 1992, p. 187). In 1975, the Metalworkers Union of São Paueo do Campo and Diadema elected a new radical slate of union leaders headed by Luis Ignácio da Silva ('Lula'), who would become the PT's most charismatic leader, and orchestrated a campaign of civil disobedience and wildcat strikes which gradually spread to other industries. The 'new

unionism' stressed militant independence from both government and party influence, including the manipulative activities of the pro-Soviet Partido Comunista Brasileiro (PCB, Brazilian Communist Party).

60 M. E. Keck, *The Workers' Party and Democratisation in Brazil* (New Haven, CT, Yale University Press, 1992), p. 60.

61 Thus, it called for mass consultations on policy issues at all levels, demanded the accountability of elected representatives, permitted the existence of factions as well as double militancies (allowing members to belong to other social organizations) and pursued gender and ethnic equality through its adoption of fixed quotas for women and black militants (although both have complained that discriminatory practices remain). Toleration of factions might be regarded as a democratic necessity, but it has meant that the PT operates as a frequently unstable and shifting coalition with a consequent absence of strategic unanimity and a public image of disunity. Keck, *Workers' Party*, pp. 114–22 discusses the political divisions within the PT.

62 Keck, *Workers' Party*, p. 17. The PT's electoral success was helped by the fact that Lula was supported by both the Partido Social Demócrata Brasileiro (PSDB, Brazilian Social Democratic Party) and Leonel Brizola's Partido Democrático Trabalhista (PDT, Democratic Workers' Party) during the second round. The latter – which drew upon the populist legacy of Getulio Vargas's Partido Trabalhista Brasileiro (PTB, Brazilian Workers' Party) – had strong working-class support in the states of Rio de Janeiro and Rio Grande do Sul. These relationships posed the danger of clouding the PT's radical credentials, as well as linking it to parties which were hierarchical and highly traditional in their approach towards leaders and followers (M. H. Moreira Alves, 'Something Old, Something New: Brazil's Partido de Trabalhadores', in Carr and Ellner (eds), *Latin American Left*, p. 228.

63 Cardoso's background as an academic dependency theorist enabled him to be promoted as someone who could make a difference to the economy, while Lula was portrayed as incapable of grappling with hyperinflation. He was also subject to strong press villification with respect to his views on abortion and homosexuality and allegations of corruption. Lula's campaign tactics (his lengthy tours of the country, or *caravanas*), his obviously proletarian origins and his denunciation of the social apartheid which permeated Brazilian society frightened the middle class. Cardoso received 54 per cent of the vote as compared to Lula's 27 per cent (S. Branford and B. Kucinski, *Brazil: Carnival of the Oppressed. Lula and the Brazilian Workers' Party*, London, Latin America Bureau, 1995, p. 4.

64 *Ibid.*, p. 60.

65 P. de Mesquita Neto, 'Interview with Lula', *NACLA. Report on the Americas*, XXXI: 1 (July–August 1997), 16. However, he also acknowledged that substantial change had taken place: 'if you compare the PT ten years ago and today. Ten years ago, the PT was more present, more active in the social struggle. In 1997, the party is more present in the political struggle' *(ibid.)*. Lula regarded this as a negative evolution. In 1996, he withdrew from the Presidency of the PT in order to concentrate on supporting social mobilization via his Citizenship Institute.

66 As discussed on p. 76.

67 The problems of the PT's municipal governance are discussed by Branford and Kucinski, *Carnival*, pp. 196–215.

68 M. E. Keck, 'Brazil's PT: Socialism as Radical Democracy', *NACLA. Report on the Americas*, XXV: 5 (May 1992), 27.

69 J. Castañeda, *Utopia*, p. 361.

70 L. Stolovich, 'Uruguay: The Paradoxes and Perplexities of an Uncommon Left', in S. Jonas and E. J. McCaughan (eds), *Latin America Faces the Twenty First*

Century. Reconstructing a Social Justice Agenda (Boulder, CO, Westview Press, 1994), pp. 173–4, 184. The FA's history has been bedevilled by factionalism, diverse ideological currents and the intervention of external agents such as the Partido Comunista de Uruguay (PCU, Uruguayan Communist Party) and the ex-guerrillas of the Movimiento de Liberación Nacional-Tupamaros (MLN-T, National Movement of Liberation-Tupamaros). The former's continued adherence to the principle of democratic centralism did not help to enhance the FA's democratic ethos. The PCU had provided the FA with 40 per cent of its votes in 1989 but following the collapse of the Soviet Union, its control dissolved enabling the more radical MLN-T to exert more influence within the FA.

71 'The Managua Declaration', quoted in *Barricada Internacional* (Nicaragua, August 1992), p. 16.

72 R. Munck, 'After the Transition: Democratic Disenchantment in Latin America', *European Review of Latin American and Caribbean Studies*, 55 (December 1993), 17.

4

The politics of the poor

Counterpoised to the practices and values of the official political sphere and the semi-official world of left-wing politics is the growing momentum over recent decades of popular or informal democratic activity, known collectively as the new social movements. I wish in this chapter and the next – where I focus upon women's mobilization – to define and evaluate the nature of these movements, as well as to determine how they are to be regarded from the perspective of the liberal pacted and radical participatory models of democratic consolidation and empowerment.

Popular organization, and the emergence of an overwhelming diversity of forms of expression and activity, have been constant features of consolidated, if increasingly beleaguered, regimes such as the Mexican, military to civilian transitions such as the Chilean, and socialist experiments, as in Nicaragua in the period 1979–90. The new social movements constitute a very broad spectrum of experience and innovatory response, although all are shaped by one particular characteristic, which is that they represent the needs and demands of sectors traditionally marginalized by narrow political regimes and exclusive socio-economic structures. In essence, the politics of popular democracy is the politics of the poor. The incapacity of the state to engage with the daily experience of the majority of Latin Americans is not a new phenomenon. Numerous writers have described the failure of governments to address rural and urban deprivation and, in particular, the consequences of massive migration to cities and spiralling demands upon inadequate infrastructure and service provision.[1] The state's inability to meet these demands and its refusal to commit to structural socio-economic reform have typically resulted in it resorting to clientelist and corporatist solutions.[2] These policies have been posited upon the notion of the poor as malleable, passive, deferential, resigned to their role within society and, therefore, grateful for any material favours bestowed upon them. This 'culture of poverty' thesis, first proposed by Oscar Lewis in his work on Mexico City in the 1950s,[3] has been contested, with authors such as Susan Stokes arguing that the political attitudes of the urban poor are both more differentiated and complex.[4] This is not to suggest that patron–client relations and government attempts at corporatist manipulation are not endemic. Indeed, they are present in all systems, regardless of their ideological complexion (and, are not restricted to the state, but also essayed by political parties and churches). Thus, the PRI in Mexico courts community leaders persuading them to sign *convenios de concertación* (pacts of agreement) with federal and municipal governments in order to integrate them into the state apparatus.[5] It has been argued that while the FSLN was formally committed to endorsing popular mobilization and locating mass organizations within the heart of the Nicaraguan state, in practice it undervalued their priorities and attempted to impose a top-down management style upon them. Critics concede that the demands of war may necessarily ease out democratic participation, but argue that the growing distance between state and popular organizations undercut the former's legitimacy. The increasingly fraught relationship has become more public since the FSLN's defeat in the 1990 elections. The organizational secretary of the Confederación Sandinista de Trabajadores (CST, Sandinista Workers Confederation) stated:

'We used to believe that change came from the top down, that the State was the mechanism. Now we don't have the State or the Party. . . . Now change must come from the group most affected by the current economic crisis. The popular movements, not the Party, are the vanguard.'[6] This response would be endorsed by the radical participatory model of democracy, but it does not explain how the popular movements can defend their interests in the conservative environment introduced by the Chamorro government and now consolidated by the right-wing Alemán regime.

The liberal and radical schools of thought hold very different conceptions of the power and perceived role of popular mobilization within contemporary political systems. While the former would wish it to be minimal, invisible at best and co-opted at worst, the idea of mass democracy is central to the latter although, as discussed in Chapter 1, definition of this 'democracy' is a contested one within the literature. The 'transitions' view is that popular mobilization was a non-essential element of military to civilian processes, which occurred only *after* the liberalization phase facilitated the opening of political spaces within regimes. Once the transition happened, conventional wisdom was that human rights activists and self-help groups organizing within shanty towns should withdraw from such assertive political activity and allow professional politicians to resume doing what they did best. Thus popular groups were regarded as amateurs, incapable of decision-making and strategic management. Georgina Waylen, amongst others, has argued that this attitude towards new social movements has meant, paradoxically, that there may be more opportunity for popular activism during military rule and in processes of transition (including revolutionary ones) than in post-transition situations. She maintains that this was because 'the nature of the state was potentially more fluid at this moment of transformation than at other times'.[7] The outcome of the transition in Chile – and, by implication, elsewhere – was narrow, conservative and resolutely anti-popular. Ignoring the kick-start that popular opposition gave to the move to oust Pinochet, the post-1989 experience of these groups has been the efforts of government and political parties to intervene in their affairs and to marginalize their needs.

Radical faith in the political potency of the new social movements rests in the belief that they initiate transformative social strategies through the occupation of different kinds of political space and the application of more diverse languages and forms of activity than those present within 'official' politics. Maruja Barrig contends that 'social movements develop broad agendas and seek to modify norms as well as institutions. Many argue that there is a more radical exercise of democracy within social movements than can be found in conventional political institutions.'[8] Popular mobilization thus challenges prevailing political practice as well as the policy priorities which it endorses (and here the liberal/radical dialogue comes to the fore: the former argues that the socio-economic and political demands of the poor have to be discounted in order not to antagonize the military, while the latter sees their satisfaction as the sine qua non of a democratic society). However, can social movements 'play a role in reshaping the political and institutional system rather than remaining "marginal" to it without losing their identity?'[9] In pursuing their demands, popular groups have no choice but to engage with the institutionalized political terrain, but once they do they are faced with multiple choices of action, as they decide how to negotiate with inefficient and uncoordinated bureaucracies and shifting party alliances. They will have to defend their organizational integrity because 'negotiation with the state has to be conducted in a context that may and does include clientelism, patrimonialism, corruption and electoral fraud'.[10] They may also have to change their methods and priorities in order to make them more acceptable to officialdom, with the likelihood that this will moderate their demands and dilute the distinctive and innovatory character of their activism. All this would be consistent with their acquiring legitimacy within pacted and consolidated systems, but at the cost of being tamed by them. The corollary, however, is that states which wish to be regarded as liberal democratic need at least to be seen to be responding to popular demands for services, and the protection of citizenship rights and social movements may be able to extract some leverage from this. This may be more likely at the level of the local state than the national one, because the opportunities for access to and communication with the former are greater, although its powers are more restricted. This possibility connects to Castañeda's argument, discussed in Chapter 3, that potential for the growth in influence of radical politics and popular empowerment is to be found, if at all, in the municipal and local dimensions of power.

Before continuing my consideration of the political significance of social movements, it is useful to examine one of their fundamental features which can be seen as having both positive and negative repercussions for their advancement and this is their diversity. I need to put some flesh on their bones and discuss the different kinds of phenomenon under scrutiny here. Popular movements are heterogeneous, with groups mobilizing around diverse agendas which may not always be compatible. Thus in Central America indigenous communities caught up in civil war and counter-insurgency responded by organizing around territorial concerns (the recovery of traditional land taken over by exploitative landowners), human rights issues (campaigns for the exhumation of victims of military massacres and the right of relatives to learn the fate of their 'disappeared'), defence of their local economies and environments and the creation of militant unions.[11] There has, however, been friction between indigenous and other social movements. Guillermo Delgardo has identified points of conflict, arguing that 'the indigenous movement has consistently rejected the overwhelmingly male-oriented and patronising attitude of leaders of the popular movements',[12] while the latter have accused indigenous activists of pursuing separatist programmes. Delgardo also castigates the clientelist intentions of both the Catholic Church and the Left with respect to indigenous movements. Thus the São Paulo Forum of Latin American left-wing parties has consistently claimed to represent indigenous groups, but its meetings have been conspicuous by the minimal attendance of their delegates.[13] Questions of differentiation by gender and ethnicity, as well as by class, clearly complicate relations between social movements and their dealings with other political actors. Their multidimensional profile, the lack of focus upon one determinant (such as class in the Marxist canon), is likely to inhibit the development of strategies which can encompass different kinds of mass movement. Some radical theorists tend to ignore these problems, adopting a simplistic 'take' upon the revolutionary potential of popular mobilization. Burbach and Nuñez refer to a 'third force' which they define as pivotal groups which have been radicalized by their experience of oppression and which are made up of 'diverse social groups . . . and movements that are more defined by their social and political attributes than by their relationship to the workplace'.[14] They fail to explain how this activism could be directed at transformative strategies by falling back to the position that the working class still remains at 'the core of the revolutionary process'.[15] A quite different perception is offered by Laclau and Mouffe, who contend that the working class is no longer revolutionary (questioning if indeed it ever was), and that its role within society has been undermined both by the effects of restructuring and de-industrialization and by the political Left's abandonment of socialist ambitions. In its wake, Latin American social movements provide the militancy often absent in the activities of traditional union politics, with their political engagement not being solely defined by their position within the production process. For Laclau and Mouffe, popular mobilization represents the activism of sectors with diverse identities and shifting positions within society, who engage in continuous and daily struggles rather than 'the Revolution' and whose ideal is egalitarianism rather than the elitism associated with the Left's historic relationship with 'the masses'.[16]

The most common activities associated with the new social movements have been grounded in community organization. One of the major consequences of authoritarian rule in Latin America has been the politicization of daily life (often referred to in Spanish as *lo cotidiano*, meaning 'the neighbourhood surrounding you'/'that which is closest to you'). Huge segments of populations – traditionally excluded both politically and spatially from public involvement – were drawn into the political arena, both negatively through their response to repression and economic recession and, in a process of evolution of consciousness, positively through their assertion that the state must acknowledge their status as citizens. Norbert Lechner has characterized this mobilization by saying that 'it is the concrete experiences of violence and fear, misery and solidarity that give democracy and socialism their meaning'.[17] Marginality in both its political and economic senses is at the heart of these social movements. Historically, Philip Oxhorn contends, 'state services in popular communities tend to be minimal to non-existent, the basic rights of their inhabitants receive little or no protection under the law and there is a dearth of opportunity for socio-economic advancement'.[18] Community organization arises because of the need for immediate problem-solving, the provision of water supply or sewerage, for example; such self-help initiatives highlight the state's failure to deliver both the means of collective consumption (infrastructure and services) and of individual sustainability (its management of the economy and the effect upon employment, wages and the cost and quality of living). David Slater maintains that the appropriation by popular groups of what should be the state's role as provider increases their recognition of it as illegitimate.[19]

The growth of community mobilization and organization around service provision has manifested itself in a variety of ways, including the setting up of collective kitchens and dining-rooms (*ollas comúnes* and *comedores populares*), allotments and food production and the establishment of food-supply networks both between communities and rural and urban locations. These have stimulated other activities such as health and nutrition education and environmental campaigns, as well as communities urging price controls and measures against speculators, employment programmes and improved service provision by both municipal and national government. However, as the latter have committed themselves to neo-liberal economic policies, communities have been forced to continue providing for themselves (under increasingly difficult conditions), as well as undertaking improvements of their physical environments by building pharmacies and clinics, schools and entertainment facilities. These activities have placed them in contact with a variety of external agents such as the Catholic Church and NGOs, both domestic and foreign. These relationships have developed in a complex fashion, often supportive, but also fraught with problems, particularly linked to the issue of clientelism.

During military rule, the Church (in a number of, but not all, countries) offered a strong critique of repression as well as providing material support for community organization. Inspired by liberation theology and its commitment to 'the preferential option for the poor',[20] many neighbourhood priests have worked closely with Comunidades Eclesiásticos de Base (CEBS, church base communities) which are grassroots lay organizations which combine spiritual study with practical development work. The CEBs have mushroomed: in Brazil by 1987, for example, it was estimated there were 80,000 of them, involving more than two million people.[21] Many base communities have turned to radical political positions, but even those regarding themselves as non-political 'can have long-term political consequences' because of their 'normal practice [of] critical discourse, egalitarianism and experiments in self-governance'.[22] Base communities participated in popular mobilization against military rule as well as supporting the Sandinistas in Nicaragua. An important example of the former was that of the Chilean Vicaría de la Solidaridad (literally, the Solidarity Vicarship), which embraced activities such as the legal defence of prisoners, human rights investigations, the provision of safe houses for fugitives from the Pinochet regime, care for their families, the running of educational classes and liaison with NGOs and foreign agencies. The Vicaría was acknowledged as representing the moral heart of resistance to institutionalized repression and the creation of a national climate of fear; 'it was more than simply an institution defending against authoritarian abuses of power. Although that was the reason it was founded, the organization evolved into one committed to strengthening the popular organizations and to searching for new ways to resist and denounce arbitrary abuses.'[23] It acted as a 'protective umbrella' for social movements at a time when orthodox political activity was prohibited;[24] this role instigated attacks upon it both by the regime and right-wing Catholics and upon the Chilean church hierarchy by the Vatican. The Vicaría was itself beset by internal tensions produced by those criticisms, and also by its ambivalent approach towards a proactive role in resistance to Pinochet (in the sense that it considered its activities to be essentially defensive). It had not envisaged a leading political role and, indeed, its commitment to human rights activism prevented it from occupying one, even if it had wished to do so. Fruhling argues that the Vicaría was vital in 'shattering [the regime's] monolithic image and undermining its legitimacy', but its capacities and vision were limited because 'the task of the human-rights organisations then was to do the groundwork [which] . . . paved the way to negotiations with those sectors within the Chilean regime that saw the need to initiate a political transition'.[25]

Through its engagement in grassroots pastoral work, the Catholic Church created a space for itself within a civil society fighting authoritarianism. Its role in political systems embarked upon pacted and consolidated transitions has been far more ambiguous. In Chile, for example, popular movements have complained that after the 1989 elections, the Church attempted to persuade them to abandon self-help initiatives in order to permit the state to resume its role as benefactor. The result has been the restoration of clientelistic approaches towards the poor and governmental attempts to co-opt and manipulate their organizations. Petras and Leiva have contended that: 'Built into the politicisation of the regime's poverty program is an antagonistic attitude towards autonomous social movements that are not part of its electoral apparatus. The scarce resources allocated towards poverty amelioration are used to segment the poor and to undermine local initiatives.'[26] Conversely, the Brazilian Church has been more progressive, as illustrated by its support of radical unionism, of landless peasants and its close co-operation with the PT. Castañeda notes that in neighbourhoods where CEBs were strong, they 'contributed decisively to the election of state or municipal authorities related to the grass-roots' in the 1989 presidential elections which Lula came close to winning.[27] Similarly, in Peru, CEBs were highly visible in the early to mid-1980s in supporting IU's national and municipal election campaigns, as well as in shanty-town organization. Despite the existence of a conservative hierarchy in Mexico, some bishops were insistent upon 'the preferential option for the poor' and CEBs flourished as socio-economic conditions deteriorated. Catholic bishops, priests and lay organizations supported Cuauhtémoc Cárdenas's candidacy in 1988, although in the aftermath of his fraudulent defeat and the general weakening of oppositional cohesion, the hierarchy redoubled its offensive against base community radicalism.[28] However, despite concerted Vatican attempts to rein in liberation theologists and grassroots opinion, the Latin American Episcopal Conference which met in Santo Domingo in October 1992 expressed trenchant criticism of neo-liberalism and its social consequences.

The radical Church has often joined forces with other political actors, be they parties or NGOs, in efforts to stimulate grassroots organization. The Brazilian Church's commitment to the struggle of landless peasants resulted in the creation in 1975 of the Church Land Commission, which subsequently developed contacts with popular groups, left-wing activists and other NGOs. Its pioneering role provided the model for non-church bodies concerned with a variety of developmental and social injustice issues and who acted as focal points for mobilization around critical issues such as land reform, human rights and the centrality of citizenship rights. Such NGOs tended to concentrate upon small-scale projects which, over time, encouraged their participants to move from material concerns to an emphasis upon empowerment through collective action. Anthony Hall believes that 'Combined pressure from religious and civil groups thus resulted in a gradual transition from a welfare orientation, considered paternalistic ... , to a more politicised and participatory style of intervention designed to encourage greater beneficiary independence and politicisation in the longer term.'[29] The relationship between other actors and popular organizations is not always positive. The dependency of the latter upon international funding agencies such as Oxfam, Christian Aid or United Nations (UN) outlets such as the UN Educational, Scientific, and Cultural Organization

(UNESCO) and HABITAT (the human settlements agency) may cause considerable tension both with respect to financial management and the setting of policy agendas. There has been a regrettably frequent tendency for such agencies to adopt what has been termed 'the wrong-headed assumption that modern technology could solve 'Third World' problems'.[30] The build-up of patron–client linkages between domestic and external NGOs can be mirrored in on-the-ground paternalist relations between NGOs and community groups. This may result in the latter having minimal input with respect to establishing priorities and involvement in day-to-day control over projects. This is not the way to stimulate sustainable development: 'If development organisations . . . are to make meaningful contributions towards alleviating poverty, then they must learn to follow the people, not expect the people to follow them. The poor themselves know the capabilities of their communities, and know what needs to be done. Development is done *by* people, not *to* people.'[31] However true this statement is, the achievement of development by the poor as the subjects rather than objects of the process is an extremely problematic and complicated undertaking. In order for small-scale, community-based projects to be successful, NGOs have to take the national socio-economic framework into account; in dealing with municipal and national governments, their working circumstances become ever-more complex. NGOs which pursue a radical agenda and disdain collaboration with the state risk marginalization, particularly with respect to funding. They are also vulnerable to political factionalism. Those willing to negotiate with the official political system risk co-optation, as governments attempt to manipulate the expertise and popular confidence NGOs enjoy in order to promote their own programmes, which may not have the best interests of the poor at heart. Hall appreciates the role that many NGOs have played in the growth of Brazilian social movements and their ability to understand the needs of poor communities often far better than official state organizations. He also understands their limited ability to influence the national political scene and the obstacles they face with respect to entering that 'official' politics in the light of their commitment to the de-professionalization of such politics and their emphasis upon a participatory ethos.

The greatest risk of the creation of a dependency culture within social movements rests in their interactions with political parties and, most acutely, with the state. Ton Salman pin-points the 1983 mass protests against the Chilean regime as a watershed in national politics and in intellectual recognition of popular activism. Although gathering in momentum and drawing in political parties, popular demonstrations were not able to bring down the military, which responded with great ferocity. After 1983, the nature of political activity shifted as the political parties focused their attention upon electoral strat-egies, culminating in the 1988 referendum campaign against Pinochet's efforts to remain in office and the 1989 election of Patricio Aylwin. The popular movement continued to mobilize, but its significance was underplayed by the parties which, in the post-transition period, have attempted to exclude it from political influence. Salman discusses what he terms the *movi-mentista* and *institucionalista* positions on the relationship between popular and conventional politics, which reflect the radical and pacted models examined in this book. The *movi-mentistas* applauded the empowerment participation in mass struggles was seen to breed whilst the *institucionalistas* down-graded them, pointing out the lack of sustainability and vulner-ability to co-optation and contending that only conventional politics could ensure democracy: 'The *institucionalistas* ... emphasised the uncoordinated nature of the participation and maintained that it was simply an act of desperation. The *movimentistas* ... insisted on the crucial role they (the popu-lar movements) played in forcing the military government to negotiate, implicitly accusing the parties of taking advantage of them.'[32]

There had been a long history in Chile of partisan inter-vention in grassroots politics. A highly politicized political cul-ture centred upon political parties and those of both Right and Left sought to manipulate popular organizations. The PCC began to work in the shanty towns in the 1950s, but it maintained a suspicious and disdainful approach towards what it regarded as the lumpenproletariat, which was incapable of assuming a revolu-tionary role and which was vulnerable to populist demagogy. However, during the period of military rule, the PCC was compelled to reassess its relationship with *pobladores* (that is, the inhabitants of shanty towns). Its traditional social base and its designated 'revolutionary class' – the industrial proletariat – had been severely damaged by Pinochet's economic policies and repression. Oxhorn argues that the PCC 'had to turn to the *poblaciones* (that is, the shanty towns) in order to maintain its importance as a political actor by claiming to represent a significant segment of Chilean society', and it directed its 1980 call for popular rebellion (discussed in Chapter 3) to them.[33]

The mass protests of 1983–86 in Chile were not spread evenly across poor neighbourhoods, but were concentrated in what Cathy Schneider terms 'the same "red" neighbourhoods that had been the centre of left-wing political activity years before the military coup'.[34] No matter how hard hit by economic depression, neighbourhoods did not mobilize unless they had a history of militancy. Those that did took on tanks with rocks. Schneider agrees that community organizations had always been managed by political parties, quoting Manuel Castells: 'Each settlement depended on the political leadership which had founded it . . . the participation of the settlements in the polit-ical process was narrowly linked to the political line dominant in each community . . . we must speak of a branch of *pobladores* in every party rather than a movement of *pobladores*.'[35] Dif-ferent experiences of militancy resulted in distinct types of popular mobilization. Schneider contrasts *poblaciones* (settle-ments) with links to the pro-Cuban MIR with those close to the PCC. The former party exhibited an elitist attitude towards inhabitants, whereas the Communists stressed a mass line based within popular culture. During the years of intense popular mobilization against the military, *mirista poblaciones* (pro-MIR settlements) tended to disintegrate, while the communist ones had the resilience to reorganize and to figure at 'the heart of the resistance movement'.[36] This is not to offer the PCC approbation with regard to its popular strategy. Internal polit-ical relations differed between communities; in some, the PCC's attempts to control events alienated inhabitants and reduced their capacity for mobilization, whereas when militants deferred to *pobladores* and worked in conjunction with them, commun-ity cohesion was at its strongest. This indicates how political parties operate differently at the local level as compared to the national one and, also, how specific conditions existing in particular locales determine political activity. The renewed interest of the PCC in shanty-town organization provoked other parties, including the PDC and those of the Renovated Left, to attempt to assert themselves in popular districts in order to pre-empt radicalism. This posed a challenge to the

independence of community organizations as the parties com-
peted to take control.

This danger – one which is experienced by all social movements – is captured by the case of the settlement of São Pedro
in the popular district of Vitória in the Brazilian state of Espírito
Santo, as documented by Geert Banck and Ana Maria Doimo
in their research undertaken in the mid-1980s. The community was formed after an illegal land invasion in 1977. Its survival owed much to the role of the Catholic Church, legal
commissions who became involved in its defence and the
activities of members of base communities living in São Pedro.
During the period of military rule, the Church was really the
only institution allowed to work with squatters; after the
abertura, other actors intervened, although the Church retained
an important presence as many lay Catholics performed a
double militancy as members of the PT. The situation was
complicated by the interplay of loyalties, with some inhabitants endorsing the PT and others the pro-military PDS and the
election of a pro-communist mayor in 1983. Various communal
projects, including an adult education campaign, were debilitated by personal animosities which mirrored 'the major ideological rift that was behind them'.[37] These inter-community
conflicts resulted in popular demobilization. They demonstrate
how social movements must contend with national political
processes, and whatever progress they make – in terms of local
development – is vulnerable to the evolution of the latter.
This can be demonstrated with reference to the relationship
between popular movements and the FSLN, following the latter's 1990 election defeat. The Revolution had received mass,
albeit sometimes critical, support through the years of *contra*
insurgency and economic adversity. However, this support
became increasingly ambivalent after 1990. Lacking state
power, the Sandinistas were in no position to manage or co-opt
popular groups. In the eyes of the latter, their legitimacy was
undermined by their tacit alliance with the Chamorro government, which led them to condemn protests against rising prices,
and peasants defending their land against former landowners'
attempts to repossess it.[38] Organizations such as the Asociación
de Trabajadores del Campo (ATC, Rural Workers' Union) and
the Unión Nacional de Agricultores y Ganaderos (UNAG,
National Union of Farmers and Ranchers), which had previously

accepted the FSLN's political leadership (although not always submissively), have moved to shed their partisan image and to represent the interests of their members against the interventions of both government and *frente*.[39] These efforts have been debilitated by the aggressiveness of the neo-liberal commitments of the post-1990 state and the absence of an alternative political project. While the mass organizations have rejected the vertical leadership they felt the FSLN imposed, its disappearance has left a political vacuum which may lead either to their fragmentation and inability to act as lobbyists or to their attempting an accommodation with the state.[40]

The local and specific concerns of social movements fit uneasily into the agendas of political parties, which are focused upon electoral politics and which, even at the municipal level, may appear to have little relevance to *pobladores*, poor women or ecological groups. Inter-party competition and internal divisions can exacerbate the factionalism and personal rivalries which are a common characteristic of social movements, and many organizations have disintegrated under the strain. As a consequence, there is widespread suspicion of the motives of parties of all ideological persuasions and a tendency for popular groups to guard their autonomy. A case in point is that of the Mexican *coordinadoras* (co-ordinating committees), which emerged in the early 1980s in response to the state's austerity policies. They are loosely structured organizations whose aim is to orchestrate the oppositional activities of peasants, workers and shanty-town inhabitants and to offer a platform for their criticisms of restructuring, privatization and the retraction of the public sector. They have been responsible for a series of *paros cívicos* (civic strikes), consisting of a variety of innovative activities including work stoppages, roadblocks, hunger strikes and boycotts, which have substituted for the industrial strike which, in times of deindustrialization, no longer has the same resonance it once might have done. The *coordinadoras*, although regarding themselves as 'of the Left', have maintained a healthy scepticism concerning the political Left's designs upon them. The latter – as was shown in the previous chapter – has been long susceptible to division, resulting in political immobility and its failure to exercise significant influence within national politics. Although many individual left-wing militants participate in the *coordinadoras*, the latter's objectives, style and patterns of activity are quite distinct from typical left-wing practice. Barry Carr identifies the major points of difference as being that the *coordinadoras* reflect the social movements' concentration upon consumption rather than production (that is, the *barrio* and the countryside rather than the factory), that relations between men and women within social movements are more equitable (although not equal) than in parties and, finally, that whilst the Left has always attributed priority to overtly political work which resulted in an explicit elitism, the popular movement is committed to mass activism and does not claim ideological hegemony.[41] Carr argues that the Mexican Left has still not understood the importance of respecting the autonomy of popular movements, nor the negative impact its desire for control over them has had. It is clear that as well as challenging the Left's assumption of leadership, the *coordinadoras* and the social movements they represent also challenge the PRI–state's corporatist management of Mexican civil society.

Joe Foweraker addresses what he calls 'the overwhelming presence of the state in the political economies of Latin America', but argues that this presence is 'a bulwark of social and economic exclusion' predicated upon a public space which neither welcomes the entrance of popular movements nor satisfies their demands. The result has been that 'social movements have mainly sought local and immediate solutions to concrete problems' which the inefficient and anti-popular state neglects.[42] This realization notwithstanding, the social movements still have to operate within the institutional context over which the state presides and, thus, must negotiate with it. The other side of the state's efforts to exclude large segments of populations, whether it be through repression or policy decisions, has been what Foweraker terms the 'parallel politics of . . . inclusion' through co-optation with the aim of demobilizing social radicalism.[43] This strategy has had various manifestations.

In Peru, after 1968, the reformist military regime led by General Velasco Alvarado was responsible for stimulating mass mobilization through a pseudo-revolutionary rhetoric of participation and egalitarianism and the establishment of officially controlled parallel organizations, which sought to challenge the political influence of parties, unions and community groups. This strategy backfired in that the participatory ethos combined with mounting opposition to deepening economic crisis, and the resultant introduction of restructuring packages ignited the mass mobilizations of the 1977–80 period, which included six general strikes and other forms of protest, such as regional defence fronts.[44] The general strike of July 1977 was the decisive factor in the military's decision to begin the process of transition which concluded with the 1980 general election. It signalled that the regime was no longer in control of either political events or of once 'tame' mass organizations; for Eduardo Ballón, 'la dinámica abierta por las reformas velasquistas posibilita [sic] el desarrollo de nuevas y antiguas organizaciones populares'[45] ('the dynamic opened by the *velasquista* reforms implemented during the first phase of military government under General Velasco facilitated the development of old and new popular organizations'). Popular mobilization compelled the Peruvian Left to become more involved in union, peasant and neighbourhood struggles and launched its electoral career. It also transformed the complexion of the Left as traditional Stalinist communist control was challenged by Trotskyist and Maoist parties, and radical union militants disputed reformist management of labour federations. The renewal of the Left was reflected in its considerable success in the 1978 Constituent Assembly elections, although its continuing factionalism after 1980 and its embrace of increasingly reformist positions dissipated the vigour that popular mobilization had injected into national politics, as well as causing a growing distance between the parties and their erstwhile supporters.

The Mexican PRI–state is possibly the best historical example of governmental attempts to co-opt popular movements, although this policy has been beset with serious problems in recent years. Foweraker suggests that 1968 was significant in that it saw a 'shift from the politics of class . . . to the politics of popular–democratic struggle':

> Before 1968, Mexican civil society found political expression largely through class interests, most of which were successfully mediated through the sectoral syndical organisations of the ruling party or repressed. After 1968, the struggles of civil society, directed to a broader and implicitly democratic set of demands, discovered organisational forms and strategic capacities which the state has found more difficult to counter and contain.[46]

The breakdown of PRI-orchestrated demand management was accentuated by the 1982 debt crisis and the application of

austerity measures, accompanied by growing political opposition from the PAN and the PRD and by internal rifts between
modernisers and old-style party bosses within the governing
party. The rise of oppositional electoral politics has produced
some abatement in popular mobilization, but it maintains a
significant presence within Mexican politics. However, although
the PRI's monopoly of power has been challenged, it has not
yet been broken and popular groups have to make important
decisions with respect to their relations with it. President
Salinas's Programa Nacional de Solidaridad (PRONASOL, Programme of National Solidarity) channelled state funds to 'loyal'
organizations in an attempt to defuse the discontent caused
by the de la Madrid administration's restructuring policies.
Independent community organizations did not receive such
largesse, prompting their members to put pressure upon their
leaders to move towards an understanding with the regime.
Judith Adler Hellman has argued that the relationship between
popular organizations and the state is highly complex.[47] She
cites the research undertaken by Paul Haber on the Comité de
Defensa Popular General Francisco Villa de Durango (General
Francisco Villa of Durango Popular Defence Committee), which
charts the evolution of the organization from an experimental
and independent *colonia popular* (popular colony) which enunciated a radical critique of the PRI's political economy from
the late 1960s, to its *convenio de concertación* with Salinas in
1989 and its subsequent relaunching as a political party with
responsibility for managing huge developmental and environment programmes which are financed by the state.[48] Community organizations have also had to carefully weigh up their
closeness to opposition political parties, pre-eminently the PRD.
Open identification with the latter would curtail any short-
term material benefits they could hope to receive from the PRI
and, thus, support for Cárdenas has had to be speculative (based
on the belief that he was both capable of winning the Presidency and that he would offer the popular movements a space
within the state). It will come as no surprise that many groups
have chosen the devil they know rather than the one they do
not. This has led the PRD and parties of the Left to accuse
them of selling out. This critique ignores the immediate
needs of communities, which popular organizations are in
no position to neglect. It also forgets the fact that opposition
parties are not immune to the temptations of clientelism or the

possibility that, once in power, the PRD would not remember its erstwhile friends.

An example of a more positive although still problematic partnership between social movements and political parties has been that of the links between popular groups and the PT in Brazil. The latter emerged in 1980 from the new unionism based in the car factories around Sâo Paulo; these newly militant unions stressed grass roots decision-making with direct voting on strategy. Receiving support from the Church and left-wing activists, the unions' illegal strike movement spread rapidly throughout 1978 and 1979. Although subject to strong state repression, the strikers had undoubtedly won a moral victory, which provided the momentum for the PT's entry into public life and which also laid the foundations for the creation of the Central Unica dos Trabalhadores (CUT, Unified Workers' Central, the general confederation of trade union) in 1983. The CUT brought together left-wing militants, independent unions and CEBs, thus representing a perfect example of the multiple identities inherent in a new social movement. Given the different agendas that such diverse constituencies pursue, the CUT campaigned on a wide platform of political and economic demands as well as more narrowly labour concerns. By 1994, it led a movement of some 18 million urban and rural workers (the latter in conjunction with the Movimento dos Sem-Terra, or Landless Workers' Movement).[49] However, in the 1990s the profile of the CUT has been changing, with the Central becoming institutionalized and bureaucratic and activists finding that their role in decision-making has been reduced and that of the generally middle-class leadership expanded. The result has been increased factionalism – what has been termed a 'democracy of tendencies' – which hampers the CUT's effectiveness. Iran Jácome Rodrigues has drawn attention to what he sees is a fundamental paradox, which is that 'at the very peak of its influence in the broader political process', both through its own efforts and its relationship with the PT, the CUT may be losing its authentic workplace presence.[50] The general conclusion which the CUT's evolution may suggest is that in carving out a position within the official political system, popular movements sacrifice their commitment to participatory democracy. The same process of de-radicalization may also apply to political parties which, like the PT, have aligned themselves to popular movements.

One must ask whether the cost of winning electoral office and possibly challenging for state power must be estrangement from their original bases of support and their wide-ranging, transformative demands. Such a question has perhaps even more resonance if it is applied to socialist governments, which theoretically could be expected to generate mass participation and control over the state. I turn now to a brief consideration of the Cuban and Nicaraguan Revolutions and the role of popular movements within them.

The process of instutionalization of the Cuban revolutionary government in the post-1959 period has already been covered, as has the notion of 'popular hegemony' to which the Revolution claimed allegiance. It is certain that there was a high degree of politicization of social relations, and also strong expectations of the state's commitment to delivering job security, health services, education and infrastructure. The latter remained a constant for many years, although the government's ability to honour this was undermined by growing economic crisis. This, it could be argued, would likely lead to a weakening of the legitimacy of the ruling elite. The Cuban revolutionary discourse has been based upon the notion of a culture based upon equality of a wide socio-economic and political nature – in sum, the radical model of substantive democracy. Popular organizations were regarded as the instruments of socialization through their participation in governance at the workplace and in the community, as well as their involvement at various levels of state structure. Thus the *comités de defensa de la Revolución* (revolutionary defence committees) have responsibility for activities in health care, education and voluntary work, whilst the *organos locales del poder* (local power agencies) are concerned with the selection of local government representatives and the evaluation of their accountability and performance. It has been estimated that by the late 1980s, approximately 70 to 80 per cent of the Cuban population were represented by such popular organizations whereas, in contrast, less than 20 per cent were politically active in the Communist Party and the Unión de Jóvenes Comunistas (UJC, Communist Youth Union).[51] However, as political power in Cuba is concentrated in these two bodies, the idea of popular hegemony may be seen as no more than a veneer on the surface of an authoritarian rather than participatory culture. As Hernández and Dilla comment: 'To participate is not simply to have access to multiple areas of discussion but to contribute to decision-making in these areas. Participation in discussion and execution is relatively high; in political decisions and their control it is considerably less.'[52] In defence of the Cuban experience, they contend that the external threats it has faced have made the 'centralisation of a number of important aspects of policy-making' a regrettable necessity, but that the inception of the 1986 rectification strategy was an attempt to make popular participation and control more central to the political project.[53] Cynics could argue that this was merely a public relations manoeuvre by a hard-pressed regime to maintain its political legitimacy.

There is much evidence pointing towards the positive achievements of the Nicaraguan Revolution with respect to the enhanced status accorded the poor, as well as considerable progress made (at least in the early 1980s) in terms of literacy, health and welfare. It certainly represented a cultural transformation, as well as focusing upon the idea of citizenship as universal rather than exclusive.[54] The Sandinistas advocated political pluralism and popular participation and their government endorsed the appearance of a variety of mass organizations with direct relationships to the state. These included the labour confederation, the CST, and the rural unions, the ATC and the UNAG, as well as the Comités de Defensa Sandinista (defence committees based within neighbourhoods) and the Asociación de Mujeres Nicaragüenses Luisa Amanda Espinoza, the women's organization which is discussed in Chapter 5. However, it has been argued that the FSLN replicated Cuban practice by inverting their ideological commitment to popular democratic control and replacing it with a deepening authoritarianism. As Luciak phrases it, 'popular hegemony was . . . mediated by the FSLN's control of power'.[55] The decline in influence of the popular organizations accompanied the intensification of the *contra* war. The argument that national security concerns were accorded privilege whilst popular demands were marginalized is pertinent to both the specific experiences of women and ethnic groups and to the broader experience of the Nicaraguan people. The general consensus seems to be that the hierarchies of the mass organizations were loyal to and dependent upon the FSLN, but were not accountable to their grassroots memberships. The latter, disenchanted with this situation, became increasingly restive with both their own and national leaderships. Thus the defence committees, which were the largest of the mass organizations and initially central to the political system, found their influence declining from the mid-1980s. In 1984, they lost their seats in the National Assembly as part of the process of constitutional 'reform'. This provoked rebellion within the committees against the top-down approach of leadership, beginning a gradual disengagement from the FSLN. By the late 1980s the committees were publicly identifying themselves with the popular community rather than the state. Generally, the government's adoption of economic austerity measures in 1988, with resulting cutbacks and restrictions on public expenditure, contributed to a growing dissatisfaction with, and, ultimately, alienation from, the FSLN. Daniel Ortega's speech of June 1988, in which he argued that although the austerity policy was anti-popular it was nevertheless necessary in order to prevent economic collapse, may have appeared rational to the government but heralded the final destruction of the notion of popular hegemony.

In a study of the state's attempts to transform the political economy of the Nicaraguan countryside, Ilja Luciak points to the paradox that although rural grass roots movements strengthened after 1979, their relationship with the Sandinistas was complicated by the latter's commitment to make concessions to landowners in order to gain their political support. The government's efforts to create a distinctive policy with respect to the rural poor were further hindered by the complexity of class relations in the countryside. The ATC, the officially recognized Sandinista rural mass organization, made strong progress during the early 1980s, but it represented a diverse constituency which included seasonal workers, small farmers and landless rural workers. Conflicting interests between the small farmers and the others resulted in the former's' 1981 breakaway and the constitution of the UNAG. The latter adopted a more critical stance vis-à-vis the Sandinistas' policies at the local level and, specifically, acts of indiscriminate authoritarianism which affected peasant communities. It was responsible for promoting the creation of agricultural co-operatives which doubled as self-defence committees, attempting to defend communities from the vicissitudes of civil war. The UNAG managed, nevertheless, to maintain a reasonably close if sometimes prickly relationship with the FSLN at the state level. The ATC suffered from its close identification with a government which was also the employer of many of its members working in state farms and which was unwilling to accept criticism of its official policies. Additionally the ATC, as with the other mass organizations, was not given organizational independence. Its leadership was chosen from above and there was a failure to institutionalize internal democratic procedures. Over time this reduced the ATC's credibility in the eyes of its members. Luciak argues that the FSLN's 'authoritarian potential was in turn replicated within the mass organisations'.[56] As discussed earlier in this chapter, the situation changed dramatically after 1990 as the ATC and other mass organizations lost the state's protection. The ATC moved to shed its partisan alignment with the Sandinistas and to defend its falling membership against the anti-popular policies implemented by the Chamorro government (these included increasing price rises, reduced social services and the end of protective legislation). The irony was that popular militancy developed as a response both to the hostile political economy of the 1990s *and* to the failure of the FSLN to create an authentically democratic and equal relationship with the popular movement.

How, then, may one evaluate the present and future political strength of the new social movements in Latin America from the liberal pacted and radical participatory perspectives? There is diversity of opinion between and within these models, with commentators offering positive and negative prognoses. Manuel Castells, in his influential work in the 1970s on Chilean *pobladores*, accorded them a significant role, but by the following decade was referring to their 'political dependence', arguing that they were not 'agents' of structural change but 'symptoms of resistance . . . to social domination' and, as such, 'reactive utopias'.[57] This negative reading suggests that poor people mobilize through necessity but expend their energies on projects which lack coherence and permanence. The fragmented, defensive and vulnerable character of much popular organization is recognized by most authors, as are the external constraints that social movements work under and the changing political contexts they have to engage with. Thus Cathy Schneider writes that 'they reflect social inequalities, cleavages, changes, impoverishment, endemic lack of perspective', but then takes a positive position by stating that 'what we have observed may be a far cry from a movement but in the end these are the processes and building blocks that movements

are made of'.[58] In itself, a well-organized participatory movement cannot insure against fragmentation, co-optation or
demobilization. It is part of a progress towards democracy
rather than its achievement, its affirmation rather than its con-
firmation, and success is certainly not guaranteed. Popular
movements are not radical *per se*. Some radical theorists have
wanted to romanticize popular movements, seeing them, as
Foweraker has described, 'in uniform teleological terms as
progressing inexorably from daily resistance to political protest
to democratic project'.[59] Putting this kind of gloss upon the
political and social activities of the poor is commensurate
with the objectification of the proletariat by many on the Left,
old and new. It does not offer any insights into the problems
social movements face, nor how they may surmount them. A
more realistic approach by radicals will accept the humanity
of popular movements rather than proposing their reification.

Tilman Evers endorses a positive reading of Latin American
social movements as aiming 'at appropriating society from the
state'.[60] This notion of the resurgence of civil society is at the
heart of much of the radical model's literature. Evers proposes
that the social movements cannot be understood as exclusively political because they possess sociocultural and ethical
resonances which are grounded within the concept of participation as both methodology and vision of the future. Critics
from the liberal pacted school identify this preoccupation as
utopian, contending that the religion of participation is the
cause of the frailty of social movements in that, in their
view, sustainability is built upon leadership, organizational
resilience and discovery of the most advantageous routes into
the realm of 'official' politics. It will be apparent from my
discussion in Chapter 3 that this view would be shared by
many on the Left. Even if one adheres to the realistic radical
model and argues for Schneider's 'building blocks' theory, one
cannot ignore the massive obstacles popular organizations confront in terms of the pursuit of their aims and their dealings
with outsiders.

Politics is, of course, about power, and the new social movements operate in the sphere of everyday life (*lo cotidiano*),
which has historically been excluded from the world of power
relations in Latin America and denied meaning and significance.
Evers questions whether their marginalization by the official
political system renders the poor's experience irrelevant. In a

sense this is a ridiculous question, given that millions of poor Latin and Central Americans are continuously engaged in activities of a daily and consistent nature which can be labelled popular mobilization. The question, however, is important in terms of the intellectual and political debate which attempts to come to terms with this activity. Simply put, receptivity to the significance of the new social movements depends upon the parameters of debate to which observers subscribe. By parameters, I understand the following strictures: who controls what is defined as being political, who sets political and intellectual agendas, and the contested issue of the neutrality of the state. Both the liberal – pacted and consolidated – and radical models of democracy have developed their own mindsets and suffer their own forms of myopia. The former consistently wishes to undervalue and minimize popular political activity (unless it has been incorporated and so sanitized), while the latter has vacillated between emphasizing leadership and control and advocating bottom-up democracy.

Depicting the social movements as champions of participation, egalitarianism and democracy and, as such, the cornerstones of a civil society resisting an elitist and authoritarian state, may be regarded as idealizing them but may still contain an element of truth. The internal politics and levels of consciousness within any social movement will be more complex than an idealized reading would suggest. Philip Oxhorn makes the point that Chilean shanty-town organizations pursue the interests of their own members rather than of all shanty-town inhabitants. It has proved very difficult to create linkages between such organizations because of their localized demands and natures. Despite their high visibility in recent years, they remain embryonic social movements, as the latter 'knowingly pursue goals whose benefits are not limited exclusively to ... (their own) members'.[61] The conclusion seems to be that even if shanty-town organizations achieve a great deal in terms of their own needs and acquire cohesiveness and solidarity, nevertheless their influence is inevitably limited because they do not have national political weight. Susan Stokes, in her study of the popular neighbourhood of Independencia in Lima in the mid- to late 1980s, addresses another major constraint upon popular mobilization. She analyses the heterogeneous political cultural profiles of Independencia's inhabitants, which she places along a spectrum of clients and radicals. She does this within the context of the development of Peru's political history, attempts by successive governments to control communities (what she terms the creation of 'a manipulated consent'[62]), and the impact of the evolutionary nature of settlement growth upon *pobladores*. With respect to the wider political process, the emergence of a critical discourse on the part of the poor depends upon their ability to challenge the dominant culture and their reception of it through the socializing mechanisms of the state, religion and education. Stokes describes the politics of clientelism exercised by the state and parties of both Left and Right which has been a resilient leitmotif of Peruvian public life. Since the 1950s, emerging squatter groups looked to government to address their needs; the latter responded in paternalistic fashion, employing the traditional devices of huge promises and meagre outcomes. Politicization and the beginnings of independent organization began following the 1968 Revolution of the Armed Forces, when that regime's attempted corporatism – with its talk of popular empowerment and structural transformation – backfired as it imploded with the onset of economic crisis.

In Independencia, Stokes found a local political culture characterized by a shifting and frequently ambiguous dichotomy between passive and dependent clientelism, and assertive radicalism, with both positions incorporating many gradations with respect to changes in time and situation and the specific rites of passage of individuals. Typically, clientelists tended to look upwards, acknowledging the power of their 'betters', whereas radicals were more confrontational, conscious of themselves as poor, and dominant politics as inhabited by the wealthy. They were also aware of the state as the site of struggle and of the relationship between local conflicts and national power relations. This awareness stimulated a fresh perception of how they could engage in political and social change. Differences between the two positions influenced their attitudes towards neighbourhood organization, with clientelists tending to be more hierarchical and radicals stressing internal democracy. Clientelists believed that they could draw concessions from government, while radicals felt they had to be fought for through hard bargaining and, when necessary, militancy. Stokes identifies the emergence of a 'counterhegemonic ideology' amongst some Independencia – and, by implication, other shanty-town – residents during the 1970s which was cultivated and augmented by what she terms 'the intermingling of the poor and "the outsiders" (party militants, NGOs, church lay communities), whose daily lives became intertwined'.[63] This radicalism was moderated by the decline in oppositional politics by the Left through the 1980s and the authoritarian bent of government from 1990. The consequence has been disillusionment with the 'democratic' experience and a dilution of activism, with the accompanying possible corollary of a return to the managed mobilization of the past and, in the most extreme scenario, military repression.

Without diminishing the intensity of the difficulties social movements face, I wish to conclude this chapter on a more positive note by referring back to the idea of these movements, providing at least a skeleton of an alternative model of social and political activity which is embedded in the idea of a resurgent civil society. Carlos Vilas argues that Latin Americans are organizing under multiple although overlapping identities, which has resulted in the 'broadening of the socio-cultural reference points for collective action', and that such mobilizations involve 'at least implicitly an alternative notion of justice',[64] which endorses gender equality, is against racism and calls for constitutional guarantees, equitable economic policies and the safeguarding of human rights. Such demands will not disappear, no matter how much the world of official politics attempts to ignore them. Social movements may never achieve hegemonic status within Latin America but in their variety and dynamism, they constitute a form of collective cultural resistance which builds both upon memories of earlier struggles and present experience.[65] The imagery of dissent is symbolized by the figure of Superbarrio (a man dressed as Superman who made frequent appearances in the barrios, the shanty-town neighbourhoods of the capital), who emerged as a champion of the poor and social justice following the 1985 Mexico City earthquake.[66] For Brazil, Rowe and Schelling argue, 'the samba schools and football clubs articulate a more genuine although "unofficial" citizenship than the formal institutions modelled on European and US paradigms'.[67] Popular mobilization in Latin and Central America offers a more authentically democratic trajectory than does the constrained pacted model, and is infinitely more complex and problematic than the idealized vision projected by the radical school.

Notes

1 A. Gilbert and J. Gugler, *Cities, Poverty and Development. Urbanisation in the Third World* (Oxford, Oxford University Press, 1982) offer a general account whilst Brian Roberts, 'The Poor in the City. Urban Careers and the Strategies of the Poor', in E. P. Archetti, P. Cammack and B. Roberts (eds), *Latin America* (London, Macmillan, 1987), discusses the options open to new urban dwellers. There are many reasons for rural to urban migration; for example, Castañeda describes the massive exodus in Colombia as peasants fled from *la violencia* and the demographic shift this produced (from 30 per cent of the population living in urban areas in the 1950s to 70 per cent in the 1980s) (*Utopia Unarmed: The Latin American Left After the Cold War*, New York, Vintage Books, 1994), p. 223.

2 A good historical account is to be found in D. Collier, *Squatters and Oligarchs: Authoritarian Rule and Policy Change in Peru* (Baltimore, Johns Hopkins University Press, 1976).

3 O. Lewis, *Five Families: Mexican Case Studies in the Culture of Poverty* (New York, Basic Books, 1959). Lewis later acceded that the Cuban Revolution had succeeded in abolishing the state of consciousness which nurtured a culture of poverty (quoted in Gilbert and Gugler, *Cities*, p. 130).

4 S. Stokes, *Cultures in Conflict. Social Movements and the State in Peru* (Berkeley, University of California Press, 1995).

5 J. Adler Hellmann, 'Mexican Popular Movements, Clientelism and the Process of Democratisation', *Latin American Perspectives*, 81: 21 (Spring 1994). Adler Hellmann describes these movements as being 'deeply enmeshed in clientelistic patterns from which they escape only very rarely' (128), with many having very hierarchical structures and minimal rank and file input into decision-making. The internal cultures of popular organizations will reflect their subordinate position within society, thus making attempts to make them more independent and radical difficult.

6 Quoted in M. Quandt, 'Unbinding the Ties that Bind: The FSLN and the Popular Organisations', in M. Sinclair (ed.), *The New Politics of Survival. Grassroots Movements in Central America* (New York, Monthly Review Press, 1995), p. 268. The CST had co-operated with government austerity measures and the *comités de defensa civiles* (civil defence committees) carried out unpopular food rationing and military recruitment, but their patience ended after 1990, when the Sandinistas lost state power.

7 G. Waylen, 'Democratisation, Feminism and the State in Chile: The Establishment of SERNAM', in S. M. Rai and G. Lievesley (eds), *Women and the State. International Perspectives* (London, Taylor & Francis, 1996), p. 114.

8 M. Barrig, 'The Difficult Equilibrium between Bread and Roses: Women's Organisations and the Transition from Dictatorship to Democracy in Peru', in J. S. Jaquette (ed.), *The Women's Movement in Latin America* (Boston, Unwin Hyman, 1989), p. 115.

9 W. Assies, G. Burgwal and T. Salman, *Structures of Power, Movements of Resistance. An Introduction to the Theories of Urban Movements in Latin America* (Amsterdam, CEDLA, 1990), p. 72.

10 J. Foweraker, *Theorising Social Movements* (London, Pluto Press, 1995), p. 63. The result, he argues is that 'the politics of social movements is a politics of incremental advance and disguised retreat, of frequent failures and partial successes' (*ibid.*), which must sap the vitality and determination of such groups to proceed.

11 In 'Uncovering the Truth: Political Violence and Indigenous Organisations', in Sinclair (ed.), *The New Politics*, Rolando Alecio describes how the appearance of the *sectores surgido por la violencia* (groups arising out of violence) in Guatemala has reinvigorated communal life despite the devastation wrought by the war. Rigoberta Menchú has documented the evolution of the Comité de Unidad Campesina (CUC, Committee of Peasant Unity) in her autobiography, *I, Rigoberta Menchú. A Peasant Woman in Guatemala* (London, Verso, 1984). Militant peasant unions have also organized the armed defence of communal lands in El Salvador, Panama and Mexico (explicit in the Chiapas rebellion has been the claim that the Mexican state has reneged upon the Revolution's promises to safeguard the rights of its indigenous citizens).

12 G. Delgardo, 'Ethnic Politics and the Popular Movement', in S. Jonas and E. J. McCaughan (eds), *Latin America Faces the Twenty First Century. Reconstructing a Social Justice Agenda* (Boulder, CO, Westview Press, 1995), p. 82.

13 *Ibid.*, p. 85.

14 R. Burbach and O. Nuñez, *Fire in the Andes. Forging a Revolutionary Agenda* (London, Verso, 1987), p. 64.

15 *Ibid.*

16 E. Laclau and C. Mouffe, *Hegemony and Socialist Strategy. Towards a Radical Democratic Politics* (London, Verso, 1985).

17 Quoted in A. Escobar and S. Alvarez (eds), *The Making of Social Movements in Latin America* (Boulder, CO, Westview Press, 1992), p. 44.

18 P. Oxhorn, 'The Popular Sector Response to an Authoritarian Regime: Shantytown Organizations and the Military Coup', *Latin American Perspectives*, 68: 18: 1 (Winter 1991), 68.

19 He contends that 'the steadily eroding legitimacy of the state' felt by social movements includes increasing public cynicism about political parties and their commitment to articulating mass demands. D. Slater, 'Social Movements and Recasting of the Political' in D. Slater (ed.), *New Social Movements and the State in Latin America*, Amsterdam, CEDLA, 1985, p. 8.

20 David Lehmann traces the development of radical Christianity in Latin America under the influence of such theorists as Paulo Freire and Gustavo Gutierrez and the central position assigned base communities in *Democracy and Development in Latin America* (Cambridge, Polity Press, 1990), ch. 3.

21 *Ibid.*, p. 135.

22 D. H. Levine and S. Mainwaring, 'Religion and Popular Protest in Latin America: Contrasting Experiences', in S. Eckstein, *Power and Popular Protest. Latin American Social Movements* (Berkeley, University of California Press, 1989), p. 214.

23 H. Fruhling, 'Resistance to Fear in Chile: The Experience of the Vicaría de Solidaridad', in J. E. Corradi, P. Weiss-Fagan and M. A. Garretón (eds), *Fear at the Edge. State Terror and Resistance in Latin America* (Berkeley, University of California Press, 1992), p. 128.

24 Oxhorn, 'The Popular Sector', 75.

25 Fruhling, 'Resistance', pp. 138–9.

26 J. Petras and F. I. Leiva, *Democracy and Poverty in Chile. The Limits to Electoral Politics* (Boulder, CO, Westview Press, 1994), p. 150.

27 Castañeda, *Utopia*, p. 209.

28 *Ibid.*, p. 212.

29 A. Hall, 'Non-Governmental Organisations and Development in Brazil under Dictatorship and Democracy', in C. Abel and C. Lewis (eds), *Welfare, Poverty and Development in Latin America* (Basingstoke, Macmillan, 1993), p. 426.

30 L. MacDonald, 'A Mixed Blessing. The NGO Boom in Latin America', *NACLA. Report on the Americas*, XXVIII: 5 (March–April 1995), 31.

31 John Clark, formerly of Oxfam UK, quoted in *ibid.*, 35.

32 T. Salman, 'The Diffident Movement. Generation and Gender in the Vicissitudes of the Chilean Shantytown Organisations, 1973–1990', *Latin American Perspectives*, 21: 82: 3 (Summer 1994), 10.

33 P. Oxhorn, *Organising Civil Society. The Popular Sectors and the Struggle for Democracy in Chile* (Philadelphia, Pennsylvania State University Press, 1995), p. 213.

34 C. Schneider, 'Mobilisation at the Grassroots. Shantytowns and Resistance in Authoritarian Chile', *Latin American Perspectives*, 18: 67: 1 (Winter 1991), 92.

35 *Ibid.*, 95.

36 *Ibid.*, 98.

37 G. Banck and A. M. Doimo, 'Between Utopia and Strategy: A Case Study of a Brazilian Urban Social Movement', in G. Banck and K. Koonings (eds), *Social Change in Contemporary Brazil* (Amsterdam, CEDLA, 1988), p. 81.

38 Thus in 1992, Tomás Borge attacked the sugar workers' strike, which was endorsed by the Sandinista Workers' Central, for undermining national stability. (Discussed by M. Quandt, 'Nicaragua: Unbinding the Ties that Bind', *NACLA. Report on the Americas*, XXVI: 4, February 1993.)

39 Prior to 1990 'the farmers' movement demonstrated a greater degree of independence from the FSLN than ... observed in the case of the other mass organizations. Its leaders were not afraid to oppose Sandinista policies when they ran counter to the interests of the farming community' (I. A. Luciak, *The Sandinista Legacy. Lessons from a Political Economy in Transition* (Gainesville, University Press of Florida, 1995), p. 113. This pragmatism combined with the fact that its rank and file were politically heterogeneous has facilitated the UNAG's recent moves to drop its previous loyalties and pursue a legitimate position in the new political climate. Luciak observes that UNAG is now working with both the World Bank and the USA Agency for International Development (USAID) in projects aimed at improving farmers' fortunes (*ibid.*, 122).

40 A succinct analysis of the alienation between the FSLN and popular organizations is offered by Quandt, 'Unbinding', pp. 265–88.

41 B. Carr, 'The Mexican Left, the Popular Movements and the Politics of Austerity, 1982–1985', in B. Carr and R. Anzaldúa Montoya, *The Mexican Left, The Popular Movement and the Politics of Austerity* (San Diego, University of California Center for US–Mexican Studies, 1986), pp. 16–17.

42 Foweraker, *Theorising*, p. 31.

43 *Ibid.*, p. 65.

44 A good account of popular struggles during these years is found in T.Tovar Samanez, *Movimiento popular y paros nacional – historia del movimiento popular, 1976–80* (Lima, DESCO Biblioteca Popular 5, 1982).

45 E. Ballón, 'El proceso de constitución del movimiento popular peruano', in D. Camacho and R. Menjívar, *Los movimientos populares en América latina* (Mexico, SigloVeintiuno Editores, 1989), p. 318.

46 J. Foweraker, 'Popular Movements and the Transformation of the System', in W. A. Cornelius, J. Gentleman and P. H. Smith (eds), *Mexico's Alternative Political Futures* (San Diego, University of California Center for US–Mexican Studies, 1990), p. 109.

47 Adler Hellman, 'Mexican Popular Movements'.

48 P. Haber, 'Cárdenas, Salinas and the Urban Popular Movement', in N. Harvey (ed.), *Mexico – Dilemmas of Transition* (London, Institute of Latin American Studies and British Academic Press, 1993).

49 I. J. Rodriguez, 'The CUT: New Unionism at a Crossroads', *NACLA. Report on the Americas*, XXVIII: 6 (May–June 1995), 32.

50 *Ibid.*, 34.

51 R. Hernández and H. Dilla, 'Political Culture and Popular Participation in Cuba', *Latin American Perspectives*, 69: 18: 2 (Spring 1991), 45.

52 *Ibid.*, 53.

53 *Ibid.*

54 J. Brentlinger, *The Best of What We Are. Reflections on the Nicaraguan Revolution* (Amherst, University of Massachusetts Press, 1995) offers extensive testimonies by individual Nicaraguans on their experience of the Revolution.

55 Luciak, *Sandinista Legacy*, p. 42.

56 *Ibid.*, p. 9.

57 M. Castells, *The City and the Grassroots* (London, Edward Arnold, 1983), pp. 328–9.

58 Schneider, 'Mobilisation', 26.

59 Foweraker, *Theorising*, p. 90.

60 T. Evers, 'Identity: The Hidden Side of New Social Movements in Latin America' in Slater (ed.), *New*, p. 149.

61 Oxhorn, *Organising*, p. 20

62 Stokes, *Cultures*, p. 5.

63 *Ibid.*, p. 125.

64 C. Vilas, 'The Hour of Civil Society', *NACLA. Report on the Americas*, XXVII: 2 (September–October 1993), 39, 41.

65 The variety of contemporary social mobilization is impressive, including as it does the organization of gays and lesbians, debtors' activism in Mexico, the creation of alternative media networks which offer even the most marginalized communities access to information and the possibility of collaborative undertakings, and the mammoth treks undertaken by the Sem-Terra movement in Brazil to press for land redistribution. The El Barzón debtors' alliance, which was formed in Mexico in 1993, is an interesting example. Farmers and ex-*ejido* members pressurize banks to adopt more tolerant and flexible attitudes towards their repayments. Their remit has broadened to include attacks on NAFTA, neo-liberalism and corruption amongst government members. The debtors have established links with the EZLN, as indeed have environmentalist groups protesting against oil and lumber companies (A. Senzek, 'The Entrepreneurs Who Became Radicals', *NACLA. Report on the Americas*, XX: 4, January–February 1997, 28–9).

66 In the person of 'Superbarrio', 'the popular struggle is raised to epic level within an imagination shaped by the comic strip' (W. Rowe and V. Schelling, *Memory and Modernity. Popular Culture in Latin America*, London, Verso, 1991, p. 103). They make a similar point concerning the immense influence of the *telenovelas* (soap operas) in Latin America, arguing that the popular reception of the melodrama and crisis on screen is 'received by people who are living the actual conflicts of a society and who bring the strategies with which they handle these conflicts into the act of reception' (p. 107).

67 *Ibid.*, p. 141.

5

The political power of women

Having examined official and unofficial political processes in contemporary Latin America in a non-gendered manner, I wish now to turn to the question of women's involvement in politics and the challenges they pose to orthodox forms of political expression and activity. Women played a prominent part in the opposition to military regimes and mobilization for democratic transitions, but how influential have they been in the consolidation of those transitions? Women participated in nationalist struggles in Cuba and Central America, but how were their interests represented within left-wing cultures and in post-revolutionary societies? Women's movements constitute the single most important element of the 'new politics' which I have linked to grassroots mobilization and the model of radical democracy. However, in post-transition regimes generally, official, male-dominated politics has attempted to ease women out of the public sphere and to minimize their impact upon decision-making and political agendas. This chapter assesses how women organize in order to repudiate this marginalization. This necessitates considering the relationship women have with the state and other institutions, discussing what democratic forms most promote women's presence in public life, and evaluating the different strategies women pursue. It will also involve a consideration of how women, differentiated by class, ethnicity, wealth, education and political experience, relate to each other.

There appears to be a paradox that under conditions of authoritarianism women had expanded opportunities to enter the public arena, whilst post-transition governments (including post-revolutionary Cuba and Nicaragua) have either attempted to return them to the private sphere or, at best, have sidelined their demands. Let me elucidate. Military regimes, for example, made strenuous efforts to paralyse traditional political activities by banning parties, trade unions and professional associations, through attempts to manipulate and co-opt civilian politicians, through the creation of their own tame parties and mass organizations and through varying degrees of repression. However, as Foweraker has pointed out, 'the state ... set out to suppress all conventional channels of political representation and so suffocate the public sphere. But in attempting to "privatise" political life it effectively politicised private life'.[1] The main target of this offensive was the male-populated public arena. Male activists were imprisoned, tortured, exiled, murdered. Women also suffered repression, but theirs was seen to be of a more indirect nature as they were not regarded as public actors. Women had typically perceived themselves as 'invisible' politically, but this was to change under military rule. In her study of women shanty-town inhabitants in São Paulo, Teresa Pires de Rio Caldeiro shows how women believed themselves to be outside politics, thinking that what they did at the community level was different from party politics, which was not linked to their own lives. She quotes one woman as saying: 'This interview is all about politics but I don't understand anything about politics ... it's something that doesn't affect me.'[2] The isolated environment of the home and the drudgery of the tasks women faced therein reinforced such attitudes. However, the experience of persecution, the loss of husbands, relatives and children and the removal of male breadwinners compelled women to move into the public sphere both in terms of income generation and political protest.

The military state made a direct attack upon women in terms of the economic survival of themselves and their families. Under the constraints of indebtedness and the application of restructuring programmes, male unemployment and family impoverishment deepened. This led to many women joining the labour force, albeit in unskilled, poorly paid work in the informal sector, particularly in domestic service, street selling and laundry work.[3] There was a growing number of women single-headed households in the poorest urban districts. The increasing incidence of working women caused a shift in marital relations. The military had set in motion significant changes in the domestic political economy of the lower classes which was ironic, given their ideological commitment to the virtues of 'the traditional family'.[4] A central military discourse – and, indeed, of authoritarian regimes generally – has been the role of the family as the cornerstone of the nation and women's important role as obedient wives and caring mothers. However, while idealizing 'woman' and 'motherhood', the military showed no compunction in degrading individual women through orchestrated sexual violence. There was systematic use of the rape and torture of women and their children, with the authorities apparently believing that 'passive' women would submit and not fight back.[5] This image of passivity actually gave women what Alvarez has called 'opportunity spaces' in that the economic and sexual repression experienced by women had the opposite effect intended by the military: it politicized them.[6] Foweraker argues that 'defending the family by violating its sanctity clearly contributed to politicise women'.[7]

Women from diverse social backgrounds mobilized in response to the repressive practices of military governments, including the detainment, torture and sometimes execution of political, union and grassroots activists. They were also concerned by the widespread use of 'disappearances' where the victims' families would have no knowledge of their fate. Organizations of women such as the Argentinian Madres de la Plaza Dos de Mayo, the Co-Madres of El Salvador, the CONAVIGUA (Coordinadora Nacional de las Viudas Guatemaltecas, National Coordinator of the Widows of Guatemala)[8] and the Chilean Agrupación de los Familiares en Defensa de los Desaparecidos (Organization of Relatives in Support of the Disappeared)[9] initially emerged as informal groups of women who met as they travelled between law courts, government offices and prisons in an effort to find their loved ones. Their frustration at state indifference and obfuscation led them to employ imaginative tactics, including the publication of photographs and life histories of the disappeared, chaining themselves to court gates and the public, silent testimony of the Madres and others. The women received support from the Church in a number of countries, such as the Vicaría in Chile. Over time they became increasingly visible and intransigent. Thus the Chilean Agrupación, which had formed in 1974, had by 1985 five linked organizations (relatives of the disappeared, the relegated, or those sentenced to internal exile, the executed, the exiled and the imprisoned). Many left-wing activists joined the *agrupaciones* (groups), which caused some tension, although it contributed to widening the organizations' objectives in that they became part of the wider campaign for democracy. The Madres, on the other hand, rejected any political affiliation or, indeed, a feminist agenda ('We are mothers not women'[10]). They argued that feminists stressed separatism from and struggle against men, whereas they believed that there should be equality of rights for men and women, all of whom suffered from abuse of their human rights.

The Madres are the most famous of the women's human rights groups; their campaign to discover the fate of their children and grandchildren, begun in 1977, continues to this day, emphasizing the failure of civilian governments to bring the Argentinian military to justice. The Madres captured the public imagination by their weekly symbolic protests in the square outside the presidential palace in Buenos Aires – that is, the physical centre of public life and one which was forbidden to male political demonstration under martial law. The Madres insisted that they were not making a political statement, but rather challenging the moral legitimacy of the regime. The *junta*, originally caught off balance by the women, was by 1979 subjecting them to intense harassment and violence (some Madres were themselves 'disappeared'). After the collapse of the military and the election of Alfonsín, the state appeared to acquiesce to the Madres' demand that military crimes be investigated through its creation of a National Commission on the Disappeared.[11] However, whilst the Madres wanted an admission that the disappearances were part of a systematic policy of state repression, arguing that not only the military but all those who had collaborated with it (political parties, the Church and the judiciary) should be judged, the government limited its activities to individual cases and was loath to allocate blame and bring those responsible to trial. Their continued campaigning was an annoying thorn in the flesh for the Alfonsín administration, which accused the Madres of endangering the democratic transition by risking a military backlash. The official line was that the crimes of the past should be forgotten in order to allow for national reconciliation. When General Videla and Admiral Massera were sentenced to life imprisonment and General Viola to 18 years in December 1985, whilst other high-ranking officers were acquitted, the Madres furiously accused Alfonsín of timidity and occupied Government House.[12]

From the late 1980s, the Madres experienced serious divisions, with some members criticizing their methods as too abrasive and calling for a more conciliatory approach towards government. The more militant Madres continued to press for more judicial assertiveness, but the opportunity for this was foreclosed by the Punto Final law, which effectively prohibited further prosecutions of military personnel. Their campaign suffered another severe setback when Carlos Menem assumed the Presidency in 1989; despite the fact that he had suffered five years' imprisonment under the generals, he amnestied junior officers and civilians serving prison terms for human rights abuses. Thus, only senior officers and *junta* members remained incarcerated. Those Madres who maintained a critical stance vis-à-vis the government embraced a wider, more embracing political perspective, which endorsed the idea of a transformative politics based upon prescriptive values such as non-violence and social justice. They looked to cultivate links with other grassroots movements. By becoming more overtly political, the Madres lost a great deal of their sympathy appeal. Fisher contends that 'as the Mothers ... moved further from the image of "the weeping mother", so the public support that was based on the powerful emotional appeal of their campaign ... slipped away'.[13] As noted, the Madres were committed to citizenship rights for all, regardless of gender. They shared this conviction with the Co-Madres of El Salvador and the CONAVIGUA widows of Guatemala. The former – galvanized by the liberation theology of Archbishop Romero of San Salvador before he was assassinated in 1980, and representing both urban and peasant women – grew increasingly assertive in their efforts to compel the Salvadorean regime to investigate and punish those responsible for disappearances and massacres. They found themselves subject to the attention of the death squads, but despite individuals being harassed, raped and murdered, they remained firm in their very high-profile opposition. The CONAVIGUA widows had lost their husbands during the counter-insurgency. The majority were indigenous peasants who were forced not only to deal with bereavement, but also to take over food production and household subsistence. Their activism acquired a double focus: to make the Guatemalan regime admit responsibility for the years of repression (which embroiled them in years of legal wrangling) and to initiate self-help organizations, including literacy, skills training units and small business start-ups. The latter aim extended their range over and above human rights to a more general empowerment for poor women.[14]

Women involved in human rights movements insisted on their fundamental right to know about lost relatives because of their identities as mothers and wives. Their movement into the public sphere of hitherto masculine politics can be read as a politicization of the notion of motherhood, a recognition by women that the private sphere of life had been violated. Rather than being defined as conservative women, preoccupied with child-rearing and submitting to their husbands' – and, by implication, the state's – authority, these 'motherist' groups were reconstructing their traditional identity through acting radically and making direct demands upon the state. From their initial anxiety about their husbands, sons, daughters and grandchildren, many women experienced a development of awareness as they repudiated the label of passivity attached to them, and in so doing challenged the state's hegemony. To employ Maxine Molyneux's terminology, their mobilization around pragmatic concerns might become strategic, that is, through personal experience they might come to a realization of women's position within society and the need to change it.[15] The 'motherist' approach has been criticized by some feminists as essentialism in that it appears to confirm the stereotypical image of women as being only concerned with bringing up their children. Certainly, women in such organizations entered politics precisely because they were mothers (or widows precisely because they were widows), but once engaged, many began to criticize conventional notions of what motherhood and womanhood constituted. Involvement in human rights movements highlighted how women were disadvantaged economically, sexually and legally (in Chile and Argentina, for example, *potestad marital*, marital power, gave husbands absolute legal authority over their wives). Women in human rights and community politics were rethinking relations with their partners, some were questioning unequal power relations between the genders and the state's role in perpetuating them and many were choosing activism over subordination. To take one example, in 1980 Señora Belaúnde (wife of the new Peruvian president) toured the shanty towns of Lima in time-honoured clientelist fashion. She paid homage to the sacred role of women within the family and the nation. With the economy in a state of chaos, poor mothers responded by preparing a programme of demands with respect to employment, childcare, community health and food prices. This received no official response. Subsequently, Mother's Day became a demonstration of protest rather than reverence.[16]

Individual tragedies had intense and varied personal consequences for women. Not all moved towards a feminist perspective, but all experienced a political education. As Molyneux has expressed it: 'However limited in practice, essentialising movements based in motherhood are not by definition incompatible with all forms of feminism – it depends on their goals and whether in defending ... motherhood, they challenge the social devaluation and subordination associated with it.'[17]

Social movements mobilize as a direct result of the precariousness of daily life and the threats made to community and individual survival. Over recent decades, they have had to respond to the consequences of neo-liberal economic programmes implemented by all types of political regime. Women – in their traditional role as providers – have been at the forefront of such mobilization. They have faced a multiplication of domestic tasks, balancing informal economy work with tending vegetable plots, making and washing clothes, queuing for food, travelling for free milk or medical treatment, childcare and general household management. Poor women do not organize – at least initially – out of any avowedly feminist conviction. Rather, they address essential issues such as the withdrawal of food subsidies, the spiralling cost of living, the lack of basic amenities such as sewerage, clean water and health and educational services. These demands have propelled women into the public – albeit local – realm, as they first learn to work together and then with male colleagues in order to organize themselves, and then to negotiate with state institutions at the municipal and regional levels. These processes cannot help but lead to a widening and deepening of women's experiences and confidence. They also lead to a change in the domestic environment, with women leaving the home to attend evening meetings, go on demonstrations and speak in public, and with their partners being called upon to assume more responsibility for housework and children as a consequence. Women's increased intervention in community politics has antagonized many men, who have been accustomed to male-dominated organizations with male-set agendas. They have felt threatened by women's demands for parity and for hitherto neglected issues to be addressed. Men have often responded negatively to women's calls for them to transform their own roles with respect to family commitments. While common activism with respect to housing and environmental needs is regarded as acceptable, cooking and cleaning are still regarded as 'women's work'.[18] Women are, therefore, compelled to face a series of obstacles in the way of their mobilization and organization at the personal, community and state levels. Community organizations will frequently attempt to block their movement into leadership positions, whilst the threat of state violence is ever present. Women, additionally, have to confront what Caroline Moser has called the 'triple burden' of caring for their families and managing their households, seeking paid work and supporting community initiatives.[19]

Despite these constraints, one is struck by the diverse nature of women's efforts to deal with the tremendous problems created by austerity. For example, widespread looting (known as 'sacking') erupted spontaneously in São Paulo in 1983 and eventually led to the formation of the Brazilian unemployed movement. 'Sacking' was undertaken almost exclusively by women, who organized swoops on supermarkets in order to collect basic foodstuffs.[20] An extremely common activity was the creation of *ollas comúnes* and *comedores populares* as individual resources were inadequate to guarantee sufficient food for families. Thus the preparation and serving of meals moved symbolically from the private to the public sphere; the state, which idealized the family in its ideology, was seen to be attacking its survival in reality. The *ollas comúnes* did not just provide food, they also served as a site of protest with respect to food supply and distribution and the paucity of the state's safety-net facilities. More fundamentally, they challenged the gendered notion of men – and, again, by implication the state – as providers. Initially the *ollas* and *comedores* were not regarded as political, but over time their organizers joined in general critiques of governments. Thus, for example, in 1986 in Santiago the *ollas* joined other grassroots organizations, trade unions and political parties in the Asamblea de Civilidad (Civil Assembly), which held a two-day general strike. The Pinochet regime's response – in the wake of an assassination attempt on the general – was to impose a state of siege and launch a massive military occupation of the shanty towns. By 1990, the

Chilean *ollas* held their first National Congress, with an estimated membership of 80,000. Participants developed links with feminist groups and left-wing parties, although they complained that both often treated them in a patronizing manner.[21] Another response to the state's pursuit of neo-liberalism was the establishment of *organizaciones económicas populares* (popular economic organizations). Women dominated the two most important types, the production of goods, including artisan work, and services, and the setting up of alternative food-buying committees (*comprando juntos*) and distribution networks.[22]

Under military rule in Argentina, collective survival strategies were initially far less significant than in other countries, although this changed as the impact of a series of shock adjustments worked its way through the economy. By 1988, it was estimated that about one-third of the population were unable to meet basic needs and 15 per cent were destitute.[23] While middle-class women were active in traditional charitable movements such as the Women's Union, poor women of the MACP (Movimiento de Amas de Casa Populares, National Housewives' Movement) adopted a more radical stance. Their tactics included boycotting targeted supermarkets, the 'don't buy on Thursdays' campaign and demonstrations, whilst the MACP's 1983 programme demanded price controls on basic foods, and cheap housing.[24] Establishing links with both the trade unions and the Madres de la Plaza Dos de Mayo, the MACP extended its public profile by linking its demands for affordable food and adequate social services with a defence of democracy as the transition elections approached. It also made contact with the feminist Multisectoral de la Mujer (Women's Multi-Sectoral Alliance) and expressed its concerns about issues such as domestic violence although – like the Madres – always stressed that it was not feminist itself.

An important by-product of poor women's pursuit of survival strategies and the parallel development of community organization has been their growing concern with health and environmental matters. This has been linked to what García Guadilla has termed the ' "environmentalisation" of economic problems'.[25] In Venezuela, this was caused by the crisis of the 1980s when the bottom fell out of the oil market, bringing to an end the economic growth it had generated since the 1960s. Economic restructuring and the collapse of the Bolivian tin market in the mid-1980s coincided with severe drought, which meant Bolivia was no longer self-sufficient in wheat. Peasants became dependent upon food donations from aid agencies, which caused a deterioration in morale and an increase in rural to urban migration. Peasant women played a prominent role in emergency food distribution and also built solar-powered greenhouses to produce food for their communities and constructed sanitation and drinking-water installations.[26] In Brazil, the military's programme of rapid industrialization and agricultural modernization (the era of 'savage capitalism') resulted in massive migration to the cities and a persistent decline in the living standards of the poor. The management of daily life was dominated by consumption issues. Food price-hikes inevitably led to malnourishment, which was aggravated by poor environmental conditions such as the lack of running water. The Health Movement of the Jardim Nordeste neighbourhood in São Paulo emerged in 1976 in order to campaign for a health centre. Supported by church base communities, this project influenced others, which also sprang up in the city and elsewhere. The Church wanted to concentrate upon practical relief and the improvement of poor women's practical and domestic skills, hoping to prevent them from discussing either political or sexual matters. This produced tensions, as many women rejected this attempt at censorship; the movement eventually split, with the radicals creating an independent organization. Although they made contact with feminists and participated in workshops and congresses, they also resisted – in what was a common characteristic of popular women's groups – the label.[27] Their justification was that feminism had a national agenda, while their demands were local. This notwithstanding, Machado makes the point that feminism was influential in that the diffusion of its ideology into social discourse had made it more 'acceptable for . . . women to organise collectively and to demand what they saw as their rights'.[28]

Privatization and economic restructuring policies have not only led to growing income differentiation and increasing health problems, but also to a reduction in state regulation of industrial pollution and a deterioration in the quality of the physical environment. The notion of 'eco-feminism' rests upon the perception that women identify themselves as being closer to nature as a consequence of their nurturing and protecting functions within the family. Here again the feminist critique of essentialism surfaces, contending that women's preoccupation with the quality of life is seen as part of the domestic sphere of life, the politics of the 'everyday', thus reinforcing stereotypical femininity and the contrast with masculine public-sphere politics. García Guadilla found that Venezuelan women were most prominent in 'symbolic–cultural' organizations, whereas male activists applied pressure through traditional party and institutional channels.[29] Women have found that governments have tended to ignore their activities, and this indifference has led many to draw back from activism. This has been particularly evident following military to civilian transitions, when the suspension of traditional party politics was lifted.

Maruja Barrig, in her study of popular women's mobilization in Peru, made a general observation on the marginalization which popular organizations have experienced once civilian political systems are re-established: 'By not being linked consistently with other demands and actions in the public sphere, the political dimension of everyday life remained separate from local and municipal politics further accentuating false dichotomies: political power is man's discourse and the domestic sphere and the quality of life is women's concern.'[30] Poor women's mobilization, whether it be around communal kitchens, the cost of living or the environment, is not regarded as having political weight. The issues with which women have been most concerned have been 'feminized' and thus downgraded. Women's frustration at this neglect may lead them to cease their own organizational efforts and, instead, look for representation within conventional politics, leaving them open to co-optation by the state and political parties. In the previous chapter, I discussed the Mexican state's attempts to curb popular mobilization through its *convenios de concertación* with community leaderships. Other strategies have focused upon temporary work schemes and food relief projects which have had negative consequences for the autonomous organization of the poor. Thus, in 1986, Alan García's government introduced the Programa de Apoyo al Ingreso (PAIT, Temporary Income Support Programme) to Peru. Its brief was to offer the unemployed three months' work in road building and repair projects. This work was unskilled, non-unionized and with no prospect of permanent employment. However, its promise of immediate income attracted many women single heads of household, causing them to leave *ollas*, *comedores* and other forms of collective activity.[31] A similar aim of breaking up communal groups and reverting to traditional patron–client relations lay behind the government's sponsorship of networks of mother and child clubs, which offered loans and help in setting up small businesses. Both state and churches (including Peruvian Seventh Day Adventists, using US surpluses) organized food relief distribution but only to those women whom they considered non-radical.[32] Survival strategies have highlighted the class differences between women; although the middle classes have certainly encountered impoverishment, theirs has not been the experience of total privation borne by the poor. Rather, they have agitated against their lack of parity with men in terms of educational, employment and public-office opportunities. Their progress in these areas has been hampered by the glass ceilings which exist – particularly in terms of governmental and party political appointment and discriminatory legislation – in Latin America as elsewhere.

It is generally true that once civilian government is established, whether it be in consolidated systems, military to civilian transitions or after revolutionary upheavals, mobilized women have found themselves and their interests excluded. Both middle-class and poor women constituted important elements of opposition movements demanding the withdrawal of authoritarian rule. Alvarez has linked the parallel processes of democratization and 'the politicisation of gender'; gender-specific agendas were drawn into public debate as a result of women's physical presence demonstrating and organizing in squares, streets and shanty towns. However, post-transition, the objective of what she calls 'the prevailing pacts of domination' was to sideline women.[33] If women choose to compete against men in the conventional politics of the public sphere, they enter a culture which is prejudiced against them and their policy priorities. Given women's electoral weight, neither parties nor the state can afford to ignore their demands, but they have been intent on sanitizing them. The aim has been to manage women by appropriating the language of the women's agenda, incorporating their concerns into party and government programmes, promising legislation, setting up women's commissions and departments (which have, however, functioned as appendices, not foci, of power) and enabling individual women to rise to political prominence, albeit in order to control them. To take one example, the Brazilian military regime permitted women's organizations because it considered them apolitical and, therefore, non-threatening. As the regime liberalized and the *abertura* widened, so the women's movement grew. Women were prominent in the agitation for direct elections and, when that failed, campaigned for Tancredo Neves's presidential candidacy. Parties of Left and Right hoped to control women and define the parameters of their activities. Thus the conservative PDS and the centre-right PMDB gave women 'special places' within their organizational structures, but by identifying them with safe *women's* concerns (welfare, health, education), aimed to preserve their stereotypical identity. The radical PT, although it enjoys a high percentage of women activists and has been one of the more progressive Latin American parties with respect to gender equality, has nevertheless resisted highlighting controversial issues such as abortion.[34] The new civilian government of Raul Alfonsín in Argentina created the National Women's Agency, but regarded it as a palliative designed to demobilize women. It was eventually disbanded in 1989 by his successor, Carlos Menem, on the basis of economic rationalization.[35] When it has come to the need to 'rationalize' public expenditure, in terms of the ending of programmes and the disbanding of institutions, the experience of women's marginalization in the different forms of political system in Latin America (whether it be Argentina or Nicaragua, for example) has been very similar.

Despite the fact that women's party membership has been increasing and there is pressure from women's organizations outside party boundaries, Valenzuela has noted that women activists continue to be 'confined to segregated spaces and kept out of power positions'.[36] In government, in the state apparatus, in parties of both Left and Right and in other institutions such as trade unions, the convention is to exclude women from high office and to favour the perpetuation of hierarchical and elitist male structures and power relations. Obviously, differences of degree exist between countries as a result of historical developments. Thus, Uruguayan women have traditionally enjoyed progressive social legislation (for example, the right to divorce in 1907 and to vote in 1933) and have occupied a strong presence in party and union politics; the downside is that moral and cultural values remain highly conservative.[37] It is perhaps surprising that left-wing parties and trade unions, which might be expected to be in the business of endorsing the claims of the oppressed, have not been better champions of women's rights. Many on the Left have adhered to the orthodox Marxist position on female emancipation, which stressed class struggle and believed that gender issues sapped energy from this priority. The Left's ability to engage with the politics of poor women's and feminist movements has been as problematic as its relationship with popular democracy. The disdainful, frequently contemptuous attitudes of socialist men have created a serious dilemma for socialist women. Female militants – tired of being relegated to mundane organizational tasks and frustrated by the distinctly *machista* behaviour of their male counterparts – have pressed for change. Thus, in Peru in the 1970s, women members of the eclectic Vanguardia Revolucionaria (Revolutionary Vanguard) called for the disbanding of undemocratic and non-participatory processes and an end to the male leadership's 'sterile and arrogant intellectualism'. They made a direct connection between the Left's alienation from popular struggles and its failure to acknowledge the importance of women's rights. They argued that the Left had to reject its own authoritarianism and sectarianism, democratize itself and rediscover its mass roots if it were to have any relevance in the new political climate.[38] Alvarez narrates a similar story for Brazilian women activists. In the late 1960s and early 1970s they were linked to the PCB and to guerrilla groups. However, over time, their commitment to a singular class struggle ended as they argued that class and gender-specific demands should be complementary rather than antagonistic. For Alvarez: 'women's movements . . . not only had to contest the reactionary gender ideology of a military authoritarian regime but also had to contend with less than progressive gender ideologies adhered to by sectors of the radical opposition'.[39] Women's campaigns for the transformation of their parties were generally fruitless. Peruvian male militants talked disparagingly of their female colleagues, labelling them *las locas* (the mad women).[40] The consequence was that women reacted in two distinct ways: some decided to remain within parties and work for change (the *políticas*), whilst others repudiated the male world of politics and opted for autonomous activity (the *independientes*). Political women criticised independents for isolating themselves from ongoing political and social struggles and from the popular movement and consequently from poor women. They maintained that it was possible to pursue a double militancy – of feminism and socialism – but only if women remained within the system. Independents attacked what they saw as the politicals' naive belief in the system's capacity for change; they maintained that a patriarchal, capitalist society would always marginalize women. It has been argued that each kind of activist required the existence of the other in order to survive. For Georgina Waylen, 'engagement in the conventional political system can only occur within the context of an autonomous movement'.[41] Political women, caught up in ongoing, immediate struggles, could use autonomous feminists as a resource, a hinterland to fall back upon; independents could offer them longer-term perspectives and a counter-logic as they grappled with the state (what Elisabeth Jelin has called a 'critical consciousness'[42]). However, many women have not accepted such an approach, and differences over correct strategies have caused schisms and the subsequent weakening of Latin American women's movements.

Trade unions have been equally resistant to women's demands and women unionists have made slow headway with respect to recognition of their rights and in terms of their upward progress within union structures. These constraints have been compounded by general neo-liberal imperatives which have endorsed policy commitments to export-directed investment, which has led to de-industrialization and to a subsequent decline in union influence and its bargaining power. Despite these circumstances, women are an increasing presence within the labour force and have become increasingly visible in labour struggles,[43] although their efforts face innumerable obstacles. The source of the problem lays in the gendered political roles assigned to men and women. In her study of peasant unionists in Peru, Sarah Radcliffe has shown that women who believed that class interests subsumed gender ones (that is, they accepted a 'masculine' viewpoint upon politics) were more likely to have greater influence within their organizations, although they would be given positions seen as being associated with domestic issues. On the other hand, women espousing gender-specific viewpoints were less willing to compromise and their political interventions, accordingly, carried less weight.[44] Thus, women willing to adopt a more traditional view may rise within male-structured hierarchies, but their elevation will contribute to a continued exclusion of women from the sphere of power.

Women engage with government in a number of ways. They can, of course, compete for political or administrative office. In recent years, some high-flyers have emerged, such as presidents Laura Gueller in Ecuador and Violetta Chamorro in Nicaragua. Some women, such as Zulima Menem and Susan Higuchi, in Argentina and Peru, respectively, acquired high, and controversial, profiles as presidential wives, although their notoriety was due to marriage problems rather than political conviction.[45] Such examples are rare; the norm is for political wives to immerse themselves in non-threatening, charitable roles which serve to confirm one stereotypical image of women. Women who do gain governmental or legislative office typically share a narrow social profile – white, middle-class and professional – and many share the values of the male political elite. It is difficult to go against the tide of the dominant culture. If women are unable to influence the definition of political and governmental agendas, their role may be little more than cosmetic. Their position within official power structures and their class background will distance them from the experience and concerns of the majority of women. This is not to dismiss the impact of such political women out of hand. Any legislative changes which improve women's status, the expansion of educational and employment access and the general publicizing of women's issues must all be welcomed. However, constraints upon these initiatives continue to hinder women's empowerment. In 1988, for example, the Brazilian Constitution acknowledged feminist lobbying by including clauses which prohibited domestic violence, permitted family planning, allowed for female property rights and committed the state to equal pay for equal work (including women home-workers as well as those in the formal labour market). On paper, this seemed a huge advance, but these promises have remained largely symbolic, with legislation lacking enforcement.[46] Such potential advances must also be seen within their proper context in that they neither challenge underlying structures of oppression and discrimination, nor do they transform the 'images' women are given through the state's ideological and socializing discourses.

An interesting example of the difficulties women in government face – both from within its institutions and in terms of their relationship with women outside it – is that of the Servicio Nacional de la Mujer (SERNAM, National Women's Agency), which was created by the incoming centre-left Concertación government of Chile in 1990. Its foundation can be attributed to the lobbying of the Concertación de Mujeres (Women's Caucus), who regarded the new government as gender-neutral and were confident that it would enact extensive legislation and facilitate women's participation in politics and the economy. SERNAM's brief was to encourage women's programmes and to scrutinize the activities of other government departments. In practice, its job has been very difficult. Given neither adequate powers nor funding, its ability to intervene in the affairs of other agencies is circumscribed and it has faced considerable resistance from within government, from the parties and the Church. Its achievements – starting training programmes, research and campaigning for a domestic violence bill which was finally passed in 1994 – have been overshadowed by internal divisions stimulated by party political arguments, and any attempt to bring controversial topics – such as abortion – on to its agenda have been blocked. Additionally, SERNAM has been criticized by both feminists and popular women's groups. For the former, it acts as an instrument of the state and is thus antithetical to women's interests. The latter have accused it of creating a dependency culture, regarding them as objects of its policies rather than offering them representation within its decision-making structure. Waylen has argued that its management of funding (in itself insufficient) has created a hierarchy of women's groups, with the middle class – who know how to work the system – having the advantage over poor women who do not. Apparently unable to please anybody, SERNAM has also jeopardized its own survival: 'SERNAM loses potential power through any reduction in the strength of the autonomous women's movements outside the state as its existence is due in part to their strength and the pressure that they bought to bear on the political parties which . . . form government.'[47]

So far, my discussion of women's political participation has been confined to political systems committed to a liberal democratic (albeit narrow) conception of politics. I wish now to extend my scope to a consideration of how women have fared under socialist governments. Many women participated in the revolutionary struggles in Cuba and Nicaragua and some, such as Celia Sánchez, who was Castro's confidante, and Vilma Espín, the wife of Raúl Castro, who headed the FMC from its inception in 1960, occupied high government office. As an arm of the state, the FMC's brief was to mobilize Cuban women in support of the Revolution. Margaret Randall has acknowledged the tremendous progress made in terms of women's health, education, access to employment and day care and enhanced legal and social status (including the attempted elimination of prostitution, divorce and abortion), but she argues that these have been won at the cost of a total lack of autonomy for the Cuban women's movement. The FMC took the orthodox Marxist position that women's emancipation would be achieved with the transformation of the relations of production and by women entering the labour market. Socialism would solve all women's problems. Thus women who argued for a specific gender agenda were regarded as working against the Revolution and harbouring bourgeois values.[48] The FMC was funded generously, but the paternalistic state 'decided what was and was not necessary and appropriate concerning women's rights and needs'.[49] Julie Marie Bunck argues that by the late 1970s, it was apparent that Cuban women had not secured equal status with men in terms of employment (although increasing numbers were working, they tended to cluster at the low-income end and experienced a high turnover rate, particularly as economic pressures intensified and their domestic burdens grew), in political power or in the eradication of *machismo*.[50] Despite a progressive family law and a strong emphasis on men sharing familial responsibilities, a gendered division of such activities has persisted. The persecution of homosexuals reinforced the cultural attitudes that the legislation appeared to be fighting. Recently there has been greater tolerance, although still not acceptance of homosexuals, but the re-emergence of prostitution (accepted as part of the drive to boost tourism) reinforces traditional attitudes. After the Rectification campaign began in 1986, it was increasingly apparent that women's concerns had been marginalized. At the FMC's 1990 Congress, Fidel Castro stated that 'irrelevant women's issues' such as job opportunities and equal pay would 'be postponed because of other issues of pressing national concern'.[51]

A similar account can be given of the experience of Nicaraguan women during the FSLN's government. Women were highly visible in the FSLN during the fight against Somoza, constituting approximately one-third of the combat force and playing a significant role in logistical services and grassroots mobilization. Their activities were co-ordinated by the Asociación de las Mujeres Interesado en la Problema Nacional, (AMPRONAC Association of Women Concerned with the National Problem) which was the first mass women's organization in the country's history. After 1979, the Sandinista government appeared to have recognized this contribution by enacting a series of laws which included equal pay for equal work, a prohibition on the use of women's bodies in advertising, child support, a Family Relations Law (giving parents equal responsibility for their children) and an Agrarian Reform which recognized the owner-ship rights of women.[52] Women participated in and benefited from the FSLN's mass literacy, health and infrastructure cam-paigns, were encouraged to join the labour force, and many were promoted to government and party posts. In 1979, AMPRONAC was reborn as the Asociación de Mujeres Nicaraguenses Luisa Amanda Espinoza (AMNLAE, Luisa Amanda Espinoza Asso-ciation of Nicaraguan Women, named in honour of the first woman killed in the fight against Somoza), its task being to work for women's political, economic and educational empower-ment. It was apparent that there was considerable support amongst Nicaraguan women for a government which com-mitted itself – in numerous policy statements – to gender equality. However, it remained to be seen how successful these initiatives would be and, most importantly, 'how women's interests would be represented in the Sandinista state',[53] and whether AMNLAE could function as an independent body pursuing a women's agenda rather than functioning as a potentially restrictive arm of the state.

Those writers who have criticized the progress made towards women's empowerment during the 1980s have acknowledged the tremendous problems of underdevelopment which the Sandinistas inherited and which were compounded by the escalation of the *contra* war and the belligerent attitude adopted by the Reagan and Bush administrations. The militar-ization of civilian life, the loss of partners and family members, forced migrations to escape war zones, scarcity and privation both undermined the government's reform programme and placed a huge burden upon women. Widowed, left as single heads of households, they were still expected to sustain their families, work and remain politically active. The government's focus centred upon winning the war and its efforts with respect to women were subsequently scaled down. Women's specific needs were subsumed under the exigencies of the broad, national agenda and women who protested ran the risk of being labelled anti-patriotic and pro-*contra*. Indeed, Maxine Molyneux has contended (writing before the fall of the FSLN government): 'The policies from which women have derived some benefit have been pursued principally because they have fulfilled some wider goal or goals, whether these are social welfare, development, social equality, or political mobilisation in defence of the revolution.'[54]

The promises of 1979 often went unfulfilled or, at best, were poorly implemented. Thus although women were encouraged to join the labour force, their employment was mainly restricted to the informal sector or to poorly paid, unskilled factory work (where managers ignored protective legislation and the FSLN, in line with its policy of wooing the middle class, turned a blind eye or found itself too weak too impose its authority). Although promised, childcare facilities were inadequate; resources were required more urgently elsewhere. Despite early legislation and under pressure from women's organizations, the government was not willing to confront the Catholic Church and no progress was made on the question of reproductive rights and abortion. The Church also resisted such innovations as weekend work for women and technical training. This reflected an ideological confusion on the part of the Sandinistas, who appeared to have an instrumental view of women's emancipation, regarding access to the labour market as the key. Consequently – despite protestations to the contrary – there was very little examination of concepts of male power, of masculinity and of sexual oppression and, instead, a perpetuation of traditional male gender approaches. Nicaraguan society was infused with *machismo*. Although Daniel Ortega pledged to eliminate sexism in 1986, he campaigned in 1990 as a typical Nicaraguan man – that is, on horseback. Criquillon has suggested that the fact that many women voted for Violetta Chamorro can be accounted for not only because of their desire to end the war but also their repudiation of such posturing.[55] Women's circumstances have, however, rapidly deteriorated in the 1990s with the reprivatization of land, the elimination of sex education, the return of prostitution and a general and deepening economic malaise. The relationship between the FSLN and AMNLAE and between both and independent women's groups has deteriorated rapidly. The FSLN constantly interfered in the management of the agency, and in 1989 froze its internal electoral mechanisms and imposed its own hand-picked leadership. AMNLAE has become increasingly conservative and isolated, with many women leaving to join autonomous groups, including a burgeoning lesbian movement. As with the case of the Cuban FMC, it appears that AMNLAE's objective was not to empower women but to ensure women's support for the Revolution. However, in failing to support the existence of an independent women's movement which could have provided a critical voice and campaigned for a more democratic and participatory culture, both institutions contributed to the loss of women's confidence in these revolutionary processes.[56]

I turn now to a consideration of the contemporary feminist movement in Latin America. This has attempted to maintain its independence with respect to male-dominated conventional politics although, inevitably, coming into contact with it, and has also enjoyed a complex and occasionally troubled relationship with popular women's groups. Feminism experienced a tremendous surge in the 1970s, particularly after the start of the UN's Decade of Women in 1975 which offered publicity and funding possibilities, but it has a much longer history. Thus the Partido Cívico Femenino (PCF, Feminine Civic Party) was formed in Chile in 1919 and upper- and middle-class women campaigned for the franchise throughout the 1920s (the right to vote in municipal elections was won in 1934, but not in national contests until 1949). Left-wing and working-class women founded the Movimiento de Emancipación de la Mujer Chilena (Movement for the Emancipation of Chilean Women) in 1936 and a Feminist Party existed between 1945 and 1953. However, these independent groups were gradually subsumed by the party system which dominated Chilean politics of both Right and Left,[57] although their increased educational opportunities and entrance into professional employment meant that women were acquiring a greater public presence.[58] Similar struggles for the right to vote, to enter higher education and greater access to employment occurred in many countries. In Peru, the feminist movement was born within the literary circles and journals of the late nineteenth century. Literary activities were the first professions open to women outside the home; the circles discussed broad social problems, including the exploitation of indigenous communities and peasants as well as the plight of women. During the second decade of this century and into the 1920s, feminists worked with the socialist newspaper *La Razón* and the *Amauta* group led by the founder of Peruvian Marxism, José Carlos Mariátegui. In Argentina, there was a fragmented struggle around civil, political and labour rights in the early twentieth century; it was left to the first Peronist government (1944–54) under the aegis of Eva Perón to legislate for female suffrage and divorce (this contributed to the Catholic Church's opposition to Juan Perón and the coup which deposed him).[59] The Frente Unidad por las Derechos de las Mujeres (FUPDM, United Front for Women's Rights) mobilized Mexican women from different social classes and with different political views from the 1920s until the 1940s, but women's voices were taken over by the corporatist management of the PRI and they found it difficult to develop a distinctive identity. However, involvement in the 1968 student movement and increasing contacts with left-wing parties led to the formation of small feminist groups.[60]

The launching of the Decade of Women in Mexico City in 1975 acted as a stimulus both for the emergence and growth of feminist groups and also for linkages across national boundaries. The first Encuentro Feminista Latinoamericano y del Caribe (Latin American and Caribbean Feminist Meeting) was held in Bogotá in 1981, introducing a forum which has since been held every two years; the Encuentros have spawned a flourishing network of institutional, academic and cultural interactions.[61] The first Lesbian Encuentro was held in Cuernavaca in Mexico in 1987, while indigeneous women have created their own transnational contacts. The growth in the women's movement was reflected in the fact that 250 Latin and Central American organizations were represented at the Fourth World Conference on Women which took place in Beijing in 1996.[62] However, this evolution has not been a smooth and trouble-free process. There have been debates, often of a very fierce nature, between independent and political feminists and between popular and middle-class groups, and accusations by indigenous women that they have been accorded second-class citizenship within the movement. At the Cartagena Encuentro (held in Colombia in 1996), autonomous feminists attacked women working in NGOs for acting as lobbyists and advisers to government, which they saw as a form of selling out. These divisions represent the heterogeneity of the Latin American women's movements which, as with other social movements, is both their greatest strength and largest weakness.

Feminist movements in individual countries have developed within the context of changes in national political circumstances and in response to shifting relationships between different kinds of women's group, their agendas and their priorities. The latter have included both what may be termed the more narrowly political (and economic, legal and educational) opportunities open to women, their attempts to influence legislation and government policy and also broader gender issues grounded in questions of sexual identity and difference, reproductive control, domestic violence and pornography. In Chile, the first Círculo de Estudios de la Mujer (Circle for Women's Studies) was founded in 1977 and aimed to generate research into women's lives. Originally operating under the aegis of the Church Academy of Christian Humanism, it was expelled in 1983 for discussing abortion and sexuality. It was joined in 1980 by the Comité de Defensa por los Derechos de la Mujer (Defence Committee for Women's Rights). These intrinsically middle-class groups established relations with organizations of shanty-town women, principally the Movimiento de Mujeres Populares de la Zona Norte (MOMUPO, Popular Women's Movement of the Northern Zone of Santiago, founded in 1983); MOMUPO declared itself feminist in 1985. Women were very visible in demonstrations against Pinochet during 1983, with International Women's Day (8 March) enjoying a particular focus, but as the political parties began to re-emerge after the beginning of negotiations between regime and opposition, they attempted to co-opt women activists. Thus, the centrist Democratic Alliance and the left Popular Democratic Movement began to permeate groups and political fragmentation ensued. This situation has continued to divide women since the civilian transition in 1989. Integrationists have wanted to engage in conventional politics, independents have repudiated it as futile, socialist feminists stress the class struggle and poor women attempt to maintain their organizational integrity.[63]

Attempts by Mexican feminists to break free from the controlling tentacles of the PRI emerged in the 1970s with campaigns around abortion (persistently rejected by Congress) and the pursuit of contact with both left-wing parties (and since its inception, the PRD), trade unions and other social movements. The Red Nacional de Mujeres (National Women's

Network) was created in 1983 with the purposes of drawing together disparate strands and activities. However, it has been argued that the 'feminist movement lacks the ability to voice common demands, to establish a central axis for its struggles or to settle effectively ideological differences'.[64] In the 1990s, three new fronts – Mujeres en Lucha por la Democracia, contra Violencia and por Derechos (Women Struggling for Democracy, against Violence and for Rights) – have emerged, representing a broader social base (in that they bring together unionists, *pobladores*, political and independent feminists, intellectuals and cultural activists) than was the case in the past and demonstrating greater powers of co-ordination than previously. The fight for abortion continues, as it does in the vast majority of Latin American states. The Mexican state, in the light of its increasing illegitimacy, has sought to regain its credibility and to deflect women's support for the PRD by introducing seemingly progressive policies. Thus, President Salinas pressed for more punitive penalties for rape and promised to establish a specific government agency which would facilitate women's ability to seek legal redress for discrimination and abuse. As in other countries, such policy-making appears to be more on paper than in fact. Perhaps a more realistic and depressing assessment of the status of women in contemporary Mexico may be gauged from consideration of the massacre of 45 people (mainly women and children) in the village of Acteal in the state of Chiapas in December 1997; however, a more positive note was struck by the mobilization of women, of all classes and ethnic origins, across Mexican society who, subsequently, travelled to Chiapas to express their outrage.

The experience and achievements of feminist movements in other countries attest to similar problems as have beset Chilean and Mexican women. The Brazilian movement has divided along partisan and strategic lines; Sonia Alvarez has described it as an 'organisationally complex and ideologically diverse political movement'.[65] She cites key political developments which were significant in the growth of feminism. The Church encouraged poor women to engage in community struggles; women professionals and academics were called upon to advise them and collaborative activities resulted. Left-wing women militants began to organize in shanty towns; the Left's underground organizational network facilitated the spread of feminist debate (although left leaderships were often hostile to

women committing themselves to the so-called double militancy of gender and class struggle). The military regime's protracted transition process opened up a political space which
women were able to take advantage of; women's organizations
were not regarded as threatening and thus escaped severe repression.[66] Alvarez's contention is that Brazilian feminists have
no alternative but to engage with the state and, depending on
the nature of the political landscape and their skill in dealing
with political actors, they may hope to have some impact on
policy formulation and implementation, but that this is inevitably a long-term programme which will involve them in disappointments and retreats as well as successes.

Influencing state policy is one important element of a feminist strategy; another, and a more intractable challenge, is
changing social attitudes towards gender relations. A major
obstacle to women's empowerment has been and remains the
Catholic Church. The Church's role as a bulwark of the dominant political system and as a significant socializing agency has
been a fundamental constant of Latin American politics. It has
been argued that it has played 'a particularly insidious role in
defining and enforcing ideologies of womanhood'.[67] However,
the liberation theology vein which runs through its national
churches and the proactive role many priests and lay people
play in encouraging popular and community organization have
also contributed to the mobilization of women. The Church
thus occupies an ambivalent niche within contemporary Latin
America. There is, however, one area of life about which it is
resolutely unambivalent and that is the question of women's
reproductive control and abortion rights. In most Latin American and Caribbean countries, abortion is illegal, and both the
woman and the person who performs the procedure are liable
to criminal proceedings.[68] The result is that millions of women
undergo backstreet abortions every year, putting their future
reproductive possibilities and their lives at risk.[69] Clearly this
is a particular problem for poor women who cannot afford to
pay private doctors or go abroad for an abortion. The Church
hierarchy – backed by the fundamentalist lobby – resists demands for a relaxation of these draconian restrictions and governments and political parties of all complexions acquiesce.[70]
The Church has constructed the boundaries of public discourse
on the issue of abortion. It endorses the idea of the family as
the cornerstone of the nation, despite the fact that this is not

the reality of many Latin Americans, who engage in diverse forms of personal relationship and household formation. At the Beijing Women's Conference held in 1996, the head of SERNAM made no mention of the word 'gender' in her speech and additionally maintained that homosexual families were 'not part of Chilean reality'. Although the Catholic Church was separated from the Mexican state in 1917, it has recently benefited from a constitutional amendment of 1992 which strengthened freedom of religion. This institutionalized and augmented the Church's political influence over Mexican social life, offering it the means to promote its views concerning women's sexuality, abortion and birth control as well as its homophobia. Marta Lamas argues that the moral climate created by the Church has had a negative impact upon the Mexican feminist movement which has concentrated upon political, social and economic matters and has attempted to sideline questions related to sexuality as well as distancing itself from lesbian activists.[71]

Apart from the literature which is specifically devoted to them, women remain largely invisible in much academic and journalistic writing about contemporary Latin American politics.[72] This reflects the position they continue to occupy within political systems which still hope to exclude and ignore them. The evidence offered in this chapter demonstrates the breadth and diversity of women's political activity, be it based in popular mobilization, incursions into the official male world of party and governmental politics, or feminism. One must, however, ask how important a presence and how influential a lobby women represent. Other issues that must be addressed include the following. Men and women experience different socialization processes, participate differently and pursue different agendas; is it possible for them to work together? If it is, will it lead to changes in gender relations, roles and identities? Rodríguez argues that poor women are challenging the traditional gendered division of labour and that the very 'constraints of being housewives, mothers and daughters become potential forces for transforming their subordination ... powerless women are changing everyday power relations ... they (have) learned to recognise and question power within the household and outside it'.[73] Another consideration is the fact that women are differentiated in terms of class and ethnicity. Alvarez maintains that 'one woman's strategic gender interests (may) threaten another's'.[74] Thus a professional woman – who may be a feminist – needs a servant in order to enable her to pursue her career and her activism, but in employing a poor woman – possibly of indigenous extraction – is she not compounding the latter's oppression? Alvarez concludes that 'the rigid class structures and the elite-based political systems that prevail throughout Latin America present formidable obstacles to the common pursuit of gender-based interests within cross-class political movements'.[75] Poor women and women of colour have to fight class and ethnic barriers as well as struggling for gender empowerment. They are engaged in a far more complex process than are, relatively privileged, middle-class feminists. Is there a common denominator which compels women to political action, a single, determining impulse? Bearing in mind the class and ethnic cleavages which separate them, the answer must be no. This should be taken into account by feminists who often attempt to introduce exclusive strategies and may try to impose them upon poor women. There should be a recognition of first, the existence of what Norma Stoltz Chinchilla has called 'a plurality of social subjects',[76] and second, that women do mobilize in distinct ways, 'some through struggle around practical gender interests . . . and some through an analysis of gender subordination'. Women 'contribute to the construction of an individual and collective gender identity' through the pursuit of multiple courses of action.[77] In the 1990s, important co-ordinating bodies – for example, networks on health and reproductive rights and against violence – have emerged, but the differences between middle-class and popular women continue to impede sustained collaboration. Mobilization around practical gender interests creates greater awareness of strategic interests, 'but this process is halting and contradictory and the creation of a new women's identity remains fractured and incomplete'.[78] How women engage with each other and the strategies they adopt will have short- and long-term consequences for the relationships they enjoy with both the state and democracy.

Notes

1 J. Foweraker, *Theorising Social Movements* (London, Pluto Press, 1995), p. 74.

2 T. P. de Rio Caldeiro, 'Women, Daily Life and Politics', in E. Jelin (ed.), *Women and Social Change in Latin America* (London, Zed Books, 1990), p. 55.

3 P. M. Chuchryk, 'Feminist Anti-Authoritarian Politics: The Role of Women's Organisations in the Chilean Transition to Democracy', in J. S. Jaquette (ed.), *The Women's Movement in Latin America* (Boston, Unwin Hyman, 1989), p. 153.

4 S. E. Alvarez, 'Politicising Gender and Engendering Democracy', in A. Stepan (ed.), *Democratising Brazil. Problems of Transition and Consolidation* (Oxford, Oxford University Press, 1989), p. 210.

5 It should not be forgotten that there was considerable female support for the Pinochet *junta* in Chile organised by Poder Femenino (Feminine Power). Allende's government had not addressed women's citizenship, nor had it improved their position within society. Indeed, Allende and others enunciated a very conservative approach towards women which was disturbingly close to the military's (see Chuchryk, 'Feminist', pp. 160–2 and G. Waylen, 'Rethinking Women's Political Participation and Protest: Chile 1970–90', *Political Studies*, XL, 1992, 306, 309–10).

6 Alvarez, 'Politicising', p. 205.

7 Foweraker, *Theorising*, p. 33.

8 Discussed by J. Schirmer, 'The Seeking of the Truth and the Gendering of Consciousness: The Comadres of El Salvador and the Conavigua Widows of Guatemala', in S. A. Radcliffe and S. Westwood (eds), *'Viva'. Women and Popular Protest in Latin America* (London, Routledge, 1993), pp. 32–49.

9 Waylen, 'Rethinking', 304; M. Fuentes, 'The Recent Chilean Women's Movement', in S. Wierenga (ed.), *Women's Struggles and Strategies* (Brookfield, VT, Gower, 1988), p. 103 and M. E. Valuenzuela, 'The Evolving Roles of Women under Military Rule', in P. W. Drake and I. Jaksic (eds), *The Struggle for Democracy in Chile, 1982–90* (Lincoln, University of Nebraska Press, 1991) discuss the Chilean experience.

10 Waylen, 'Rethinking', 304.

11 J. Fisher, *Out of the Shadows. Women, Resistance and Politics in South America* (London, Latin America Bureau, 1993), p. 117.

12 *Ibid.*, p. 122.

13 *Ibid.*, p. 135.

14 Schirmer, 'Seeking', pp. 52–5.

15 Molyneux's dichotomy defines pragmatic gender interests as those grounded within women's position within the gendered division of labour and their response to perceived immediate needs. Strategic interests derived from an analysis of women's subordination in society and the formulation of strategies aimed at eliminating the sexual division of labour. She maintains that different women place greater emphasis on one or the other of these objectives: 'A theory of interest that has an application to the debate about women's capacity to struggle for and benefit from social change must begin by recognising difference rather than assuming homogeneity' ('Mobilisation Without Emancipation? Women's Interests, State and Revolution in Nicaragua', in D. Slater (ed.), *New Social Movements and the State in Latin America*, Amsterdam, CEDLA, 1985, p. 239).

16 C. Andreas, *When Women Rebel. The Rise of Popular Feminism in Peru* (Westport, CT, Laurence Hill & Co., 1985), pp. 103–7.

17 M. Molyneux, 'The Woman Question in the Age of Perestroika', *New Left Review*, 183 (1990), 48.

18 L. Rodríguez, 'Barrio Women. Between the Urban and the Feminist Movement', *Latin American Perspectives*, 21: 82: 3 (Summer 1994), 37 discusses these problematic gender relations in the context of Quito, Ecuador.

19 C. O. N. Moser, 'Adjustment from Below: Low-Income Women, Time and the Triple Role in Guayaquil, Ecuador', in Radcliffe and Westwood (eds), *Viva*, pp. 188–93.

20 Y. Corcoran-Nantes, 'Women and Popular Urban Social Movements in São Paulo, Brazil', *Bulletin of Latin American Research*, 9: 2 (1990), 258.

21 Fisher, *Out of the Shadows*, pp. 36–42.

22 Waylen, 'Rethinking', 305.

23 Fisher, *Out of the Shadows*, p. 16.

24 *Ibid.*, p. 148.

25 M.-P. García Guadillo, 'Ecología: Women, Environment and Politics in Venezuela', in Radcliffe and Westwood (eds), *'Viva'*, p. 68.

26 J. Benton, 'The Role of Women's Organisations and Groups in Community Development. A Case Study of Bolivia', in J. H. Momsen and V. Kinnaird (eds), *Different Places, Different Voices* (London, Routledge, 1993), pp. 236–8.

27 L. M. Vieira Machado, ' "We Learned to Think Politically": The Influence of the Catholic Church and the Feminist Movement on the Jardim Nordeste Area in São Paulo, Brazil', in Radcliffe and Westwood (eds), *Viva* and Concoran Nantes, 'Women and Popular' discuss the health movement.

28 Vieira Machado ' "We Learned" ', p. 110.

29 García Guadilla, 'Ecología' pp. 66, 71, 85.

30 M. Barrig, 'The Difficult Equilibrium between Bread and Roses: Women's Organisations and the Transition from Dictatorship to Democracy in Peru', in Jaquette (ed.), *The Women's Movement*, p. 119.

31 *Ibid.*, pp. 144–5 and S. A. Radcliffe, ' "Así Es Una Mujer Del Pueblo": Low-Income Women's Organisations under APRA, 1985–1987' (Centre of Latin American Studies, University of Cambridge, Working Paper 43, 1988), pp. 14–15.

32 Andreas, *When Women Rebel*, pp. 114–17.

33 S. E. Alvarez, *Engendering Democracy in Brazil. Women's Movements in Transition Politics* (Princeton, NJ, Princeton University Press, 1990), pp. 205–6.

34 Alvarez, *Engendering*, ch. 7 discusses the PT's reluctance to be drawn into a highly visible position on the subject. During the 1988 Mexican Presidential elections, the PRD also skirted the issue of abortion. The PRI's Carlos Salinas mentioned neither abortion nor birth control, while the Catholic PAN, mindful of its church connections as well as the female vote, also trod the path of careful neutrality (F. Miller, *Latin American Women and the Search for Social Justice* (Hanover and London, University Press of New England, 1991)), pp. 232–3.

35 Fisher, *Out of the Shadows*, p. 151 ff.

36 Valenzuela, 'Evolving', p. 179. She continues: 'Political parties incorporated women's demands in purely formal terms but did not accede to the recomposition of internal political power as women demanded' *(ibid.)*.

37 This is discussed by C. Perelli, 'Putting Conservatism to Good Use: Women and Unorthodox Politics in Uruguay, from Breakdown to Transition', in Jaquette (ed.), *The Women's Movement*, p. 97.

38 Vanguardia Revolucionaria is discussed in Chapter 3, note 40. The relationship between left-wing parties and women is explored in G. Lievesley, 'Stages of Growth? Women Dealing with the State and Each Other in Peru', in S. M. Rai and G. Lievesley (eds), *Women and the State: International Perspectives* (London, Taylor & Francis, 1996), pp. 54–5.

39 Alvarez, *Engendering*, p. 109.

40 Lievesley, 'Stages', p. 55.

41 Waylen, 'Rethinking', 309.

42 E. Jelin, 'Citizenship and Identity: Final Reflections', in Jelin (ed.), *Women*, p. 185.

43 Jelin (ed.), *Women* (chs. 4 and 5) discusses Chile and Bolivia; Fisher, *Out Of the Shadows* (ch. 2) considers the Uruguayan situation whilst Andreas, *When Women Rebel* focuses upon Peruvian women unionists. In Brazil, women constitute more than one-third of the labour force (the largest proportion of employed women in Latin America) but less than 10 per cent of union leaders. Attempts to ensure quotas (the CUT, for example, in 1992 voted that 30 per cent of all leadership posts should be filled by women) have met with male resistance. Despite women's increased presence, their working conditions have not improved. They are still caught in badly paid, part-time, unskilled and temporary employment with inadequate day care and few labour benefits (R. Reichmann, 'Brazil's Denial of Race', *NACLA. Report on the Americas*, XXVIII: 6 May–June 1995, 40–1).

44 S. A. Radcliffe, Multiple Identities and Negotiation Over Gender: Female, Peasant Union Leaders in Peru', *Bulletin of Latin American Research*, 9: 2 (1990).

45 Susan Higuchi's case is discussed by Lievesley, 'Stages', p. 53.

46 Reichmann, 'Brazil's Denial', 41.

47 G. Waylen, 'Democratisation, Feminism and the State in Chile: The Establishment of SERNAM', in Rai and Lievesley (eds), *Women and the State*, p. 110.

48 M. Randall, *Gathering Rage. The Failure of Twentieth Century Revolutions to Develop a Feminist Agenda* (New York, Monthly Review Press, 1992), p. 23.

49 J. M. Bunck, *Fidel Castro and the Quest for a Revolutionary Culture in Cuba* (Philadelphia, Pennsylvania State University Press, 1994), p. 93.

50 *Ibid.*, p. 115.

51 *Ibid.*

52 A. Criquillon, 'The Nicaraguan Women's Movement: Feminist Reflections From Within', in M. Sinclair (ed.), *The New Politics of Survival. Grass Roots Movements in Central America* (New York, Monthly Review Press, 1995), p. 212.

53 Miller, *Latin American Women*, p. 209.

54 Molyneux, 'Mobilisation', p. 251.

55 Criquillon, 'Nicaraguan Women's', p. 225.

56 Criquillon discusses the fraught relations between *independientes* and the AMNLAE. Since 1990, and in a sense facilitated by the dismantling of the Sandinista State, a broad front of women has emerged including Sandinistas, Christians from base communities, radical feminists and lesbians who are working towards the creation of a national project of a civil society. Although they face a hostile political environment, they have managed to co-ordinate with other Central American groups; Nicaraguan women exert most influence and organizational flair and this is due, in part, to their experience of post-1979 politicization. Margaret Randall argues that Cuba failed to develop an authentic critical process, which resulted in dogmatism and the denial of difference (she cites the denial of status to and oppression of homosexuals): 'If the revolutionary party in power had been willing to support a feminist agenda, individual women and men would have felt more fully supported in (their) personal battles to challenge traditional ways of confronting these issues and relating to one another. Since it was unable, or unwilling, change was made – but never *structural* change' (*Gathering*, p. 149). This is an implicit critique of the Cuban government's failure to engage in authentic gender politics.

57 Fuentes, 'Recent', p. 91. E. M. Chaney, *Supermadre. Women in Politics in Latin America* (Austin, University of Texas Press, 1979, ch. 3) discusses what she terms 'the precursors of the emancipation movement' in Chile.

58 S. Chavkin, *Storm Over Chile* (Westport, CT, Lawrence Hill & Co., 1982), p. 197.

59 Chaney, *Supermadre*, pp. 52–6 and pp. 69–73 offers an account of the early Peruvian movement.

60 E. Tuñon Pablos, 'Women's Struggles for Empowerment in Mexico. Accomplishments, Problems and Challenges', in J. M. Bystydzienski (ed.), *Women Transforming Politics. Worldwide Strategies for Empowerment*, Bloomington, Indiana University Press, 1992, pp. 96–7. The Uruguayan women's movement was influenced by the guerrilla war waged by the Tupamaros from the late 1960s (C. Perelli, 'Putting', pp. 99–100).

61 The *Encuentros* are discussed by Miller, *Latin American Women*, p. 215 ff. and N. Saporta Stembach, M. Navaro-Aanguren and S. E. Alvarez, 'Feminisms in Latin America: From Bogotá to San Bernardo', in A. Escobar and S. E. Alvarez (eds), *The Making of Social Movements in Latin America* (Boulder, CO, Westview Press, 1992).

62 Jean Franco, 'The Long March of Feminism', *NACLA. Report on the Americas*, XXXI: 4 (January–February 1998), 10.

63 Chilean feminism is discussed by the following authors: Fuentes, 'Recent', pp. 104–6; Valenzuela, 'Evolving', pp. 171–4; P. M. Chuchryk, 'Subversive Mothers: The Women's Opposition to the Military Regime in Chile', in S. E. M. Charlton, J. Everett and K. Staudt (eds), *Women, the State and Development* (Albany, State University of New York Press, 1989), pp. 145–8 and J. Kirkwood, *Ser Política en Chile: Las Feministas y Los Partidos* (Santiago, FLACSO, 1986).

64 Tuñon Pablos, 'Women's Struggles', p. 103.

65 Alvarez, 'Politicising', p. 133.

66 Alvarez, *Engendering*, p. 266.

67 L. Rayas, 'Criminalizing Abortion. A Crime Against Women', *NACLA. Report on the Americas*, XXXI: 4 (January–February 1998), 22.

68 Abortion is available on demand in Cuba, is totally forbidden in Chile, Colombia and El Salvador and is subject to severe restrictions in other countries (for example it is available to women in Argentina, Bolivia, Costa Rica, Peru and Uruguay but only for health reasons), *ibid.*, 24.

69 It has been estimated that about 75 per cent of all annual maternal deaths in Colombia are the result of botched abortions (Franco, 'Long March', 7).

70 Although things may be changing and the Church may find itself fighting a rearguard action in the future. In 1995, President Fujimori of Peru made contraception available to poor families. At the Beijing Conference on Women, he announced his 'social miracle' which would ensure that by the year 2000, 50 per cent of all social expenditure would be on women. In reality, his neo-liberal programme has intensified women's impoverishment. The World Bank and other international agencies now promote birth control as essential for population control, thus putting pressure upon Latin American governments who seek their financial assistance (*Ibid.*, 9).

71 M. Lamas, 'Scenes From A Mexican Battlefield', *NACLA. Report on the Americas*, XXXI: 4 (January–February 1998).

72 Including the radical model of participatory democracy which frequently exhibits a gender-free perspective. It can be argued that the persistence of gender-based inequalities precludes any chance of real democratization; both models ignore this.

73 Rodríguez, 'Barrio Women', 45.

74 Alvarez, *Engendering*, p. 26.

75 *Ibid.*, p. 27.

76 N. Stoltz Chinchilla, 'Marxism, Feminism and the Struggle for Democracy in Latin America', in Escobar and Alvarez (eds), *Making*, p. 44.

77 *Ibid.*, p. 46.

78 Foweraker, *Theorising*, p. 58.

6

The constraints upon democracy

In this penultimate chapter, I consider some of the socio-economic and political constraints which challenge the possibility of promoting and enhancing democracy in contemporary Latin and Central America. My contention is that they represent obstacles to the democratization and democratic consolidation strategies pursued by both the formal and popular models of democracy. The political trends and processes which I have outlined in earlier chapters are characterized by numerous contradictions and paradoxes. Thus, we are confronted by commitments to expanding democratic political activity, institutional probity, due legal process and modernization on the part of governments which are undermined by creeping authoritarianism, corruption, limited access to political and socio-economic opportunities and growing income differentiation between governing elites and the mass of citizens. Movements for popular empowerment and self-governance are restricted by governmental interference, manipulation by political parties and the socio-economic attrition caused by the consequences of the debt and restructuring policies. Compounding these contradictions are the problems of insurgency, the drugs wars and the way that national states and their economies insert into the global political economy (a huge subject not addressed by the present volume). All of these paradoxes pose serious questions about the legitimacy of the Latin and Central American state, the degree of obligation it should expect from its citizens, the nature of that citizenship and its future prospects (further authoritarianism, incremental militarization even coups, ungovernability?).

I start with a discussion which addresses the political and social consequences of the macro-economic strategies of neo-liberalism which have dominated the 1980s and the 1990s. What follows is not an in-depth economic analysis, which would be both beyond the reach of this author and out of context in a book of this nature; rather I look for the political *implications* of such policies and the political *agenda* which motivates them.[1] The economies of the region have to be understood within the context of the processes of globalization which themselves, I argue, are grounded in the historical relationship between dominant and poor Third World countries, which has been intrinsically one of domination and dependency. The restructuring of the international economy has created a new layer of dependency and a new stage in the unequal power relationship between dominant powers and the Third World.[2] Thus stabilization and adjustment programmes, which have been formulated by international organizations such as the IMF and the multinational banks and the dominant world powers (principally the Group of 7 nations), have resulted in significant transfers of resources between rich and poor nations and, specifically, a decline in the commercial position of Latin and Central America and greater and ever-growing internal inequalities.[3] Leslie Sklair has described the changes in the global political economy which have concentrated upon 'export-led industrialisation fuelled by foreign investment and technology' as a 'reformation of capitalism'.[4] Its principal focus has been a move away from state economic management and import substitution industrialization. This strategy aimed to protect domestic industrial growth through tariff barriers to foreign goods, social security provision and attempts to keep prices, interest and exchange rates under control. The *desarrollista* (developmentalist) state financed state social expenditure and was instrumental – with the aid of the oil bonanza – in underpinning economic booms in Venezuela and Mexico and also, for a period, stimulated economic growth in oil-poor countries. This situation facilitated a growth in the proportion of the economically active population who were able to make regular social security contributions and who, therefore, enabled the state to finance social provision and to use this as a means of creating political support. The 1950s witnessed a restructuring of capitalism as the financial sector came to dominate the industrial. By the 1970s, there was a breakdown in this ISI consensus as neo-liberalism extended its influence and attacked the state's economic role and its commitment to welfare.[5] What followed was the end of protectionism, the deregulation of economies and an accelerated process of opening them up to international trade, thus creating a major role for transnational corporations. Foreign private investment was and is regarded as the panacea for all economic ills and the key to growth. Government, as President Carlos Salinas de Gortari of Mexico once declared, has no business in production; rather, its role is to provide an environment in which private business can operate advantageously and to create a favourable climate for foreign investment.[6]

The onset of the debt crisis, with Mexico's declaration of 1982 that it could not meet its repayment schedule, and the response of the international financial and political community to this created the circumstances which facilitated the 'reformation of capitalism'. I do not intend to examine the causes of the crisis – this has been amply documented elsewhere – nor to discuss the various proposals offered for its resolution; rather I am concentrating upon the political offshoots of the economic programmes imposed in its wake.[7] In 1980 approximately 183 million Latin Americans (about one-third of the total population) lived under the official poverty line; by 1990, the figure had risen to 196 million, or approximately half of the total population, and half of these were living in extreme poverty. Carlos Vilas has argued that 'this 'exclusionary style of development . . . conspires against the integrative principle which is implicit in every definition of democracy'.[8] The high incidence of poverty and massive income differentials within political systems which lay claim to democracy return us to a consideration of the distinction that the liberal pacted model makes between procedural political democracy and substantive socioeconomic democracy, which is itself endorsed by the radical model. It was Tancredo Neves – President-elect of Brazil before his untimely death in 1985 – who coined the term *deuda social*, that is, 'the social debt'. Its implication was that the burden of the debt was extremely unequal, with incomes being 'transferred from the working classes to the most well-off and from Latin America to the developed world'.[9] The economic sacrifice urged upon citizens by governments in order to escape from the debt has not been borne equally by all sectors, but principally by the poor and the middle classes whose real income, purchasing power and social benefits have been drastically reduced. Vilas argues that the 'solutions' introduced by

Latin American governments under the aegis of their rescheduling arrangements with the international banks and the IMF
have meant that the state has effectively abandoned its obligation to address poverty and deprivation.

Civilian, 'democratizing' governments inherited the debt
problem from the military regimes which had created it (with
the exception of states such as Mexico and Venezuela) and
accepted this (arguably illegal) responsibility (admittedly under
extreme pressure from the international community). Governments which tried to redefine the debt situation and were
reticent about going down the restructuring/neo-liberal road
found themselves in difficulty. The example of President Alan
García of Peru was mentioned in Chapter 2. His predecessor,
Fernando Belaúnde, had introduced economic measures such
as acquiescence with IMF edicts, trade liberalization and the
sale of public enterprises which complied with the new orthodoxy. In contrast, García repudiated the IMF arrangement and
announced that Peru would not pay more than 10 per cent of
its export earnings in debt service. He also pursued a demand-
driven expansion of the domestic economy, raising wages and
reducing taxation and interest rates and imposing tariffs and
protectionist controls on capital flows. He believed that economic growth was being obstructed by unemployment and
under-used industrial capacity, as well as the burden of the
debt. His economic nationalism alarmed domestic and foreign
financial interests and his nationalization of the Peruvian banks
in July 1987 in an attempt to regulate speculation was the
final straw. The IMF and private Peruvian domestic capital
reacted angrily and García, finding himself a pariah on the
international stage, was forced to retract and return to the
fold.[10] Similarly, Raúl Alfonsín attempted to resist monetarist
policies and espoused distributive ones after his 1983 election
in Argentina. He was handicapped by the massive and persistent financial crisis he had inherited from the military *junta*
and by the absence of a consensus within political, financial
and military circles, and by 1985 had abandoned any attempts
at economic radicalism. Monica Peralta Ramos considers that
Alfonsín pursued contradictory aims. He wanted to appease
business and at the same time respond to popular socio-
economic demands, and he attempted this in a society where
the military presence remained strong and governmental authority had not yet been consolidated. The fiscal crisis created,

above all, by servicing of the debt prohibited distributive programmes but did not prevent divisions within the business and financial communities about the nature of the economic discourse the government should follow. With the military looking over his shoulder and the absence of a consensus, Alfonsín was set on a projectory of policy confusion and a public perception of political vacillation (thus, he deepened restructuring but at the same time maintained state subsidies for manufacturing), which eventually alienated all support and caused the premature end of his presidency.[11]

The macro-economic strategies which have been introduced since the 1970s in the majority of Latin and Central American states have centred upon the role of the state in economic and financial management, and have had consequential repercussions upon issues of income distribution and service and social security provision.[12] Anti-statism is implicit in monetarist and liberalization programmes. A major shift has occurred, with the transition from state control of commanding heights industries and service provision, to an emphasis upon privatization of the economic and social functions of the state. Privatization has been lauded as a means of modernizing and making more profitable commercial and service transactions. In reality, it has initiated a process of the selling off of national assets cheaply – theoretically to pay a debt which cannot actually be paid and, in fact, to enrich already privileged sectors at home and abroad.[13] The state stills plays a role, but a totally different one; from providing, admittedly limited, support to its citizens, it has been transformed 'into a conduit for further accumulation of wealth by elites'.[14]

The state, in taking responsibility for what had been *private* debts owed by the private sector to international banks, not only saved the former from going bankrupt but then proceeded to offer it incentives to encourage exports. Huge profits have been made by the private sector in the highly speculative business of foreign debt-swap arrangements, which, although subsidized by governments, are not subject to scrutiny and which offer many opportunities for lucrative insider dealing. Debt swap involves foreign institutions and organizations buying the titles to the foreign debt owed to creditor banks for nominal prices, and then selling them on at their real prices in secondary debt markets. One particularly profitable form of debt swap is the practice of buying nationalized industries for far below their market value (a process of asset-stripping of the public sphere), with the state subsidizing domestic or foreign purchasers. The latter can then operate the privatized industry without any degree of public accountability. Let us take two examples from Mexico. In 1990 the Mexican state phone system TELMEX was privatized in an insider deal with the billionaire Carlos Slim, which allowed him to 'create a huge financial base with foreign partners, tender a large international public stock offering and still retain a very profitable controlling interest'.[15] In similar vein, the banking system which had been nationalized in 1982 was reprivatized in 1990 (a decision later declared unconstitutional), with the Central Bank assuming a semi-independent role vis-á-vis the state. This action can be viewed as 'part of a broader effort to remove economic policy from accountability to popular representation'.[16]

Their defenders argue that liberalization and privatization programmes are designed to create greater economic efficiency, to promote economic modernization and to address poverty over the long term. However, even its admirers may admit that liberalization's short-term consequences are extremely negative in terms of both growth and human suffering. Under pressure from the World Bank and the Inter-American Development Bank (who fear that the incidence of rising poverty caused by structural adjustment will lead to political instability), governments have been compelled to introduce programmes directed at reducing poverty and deprivation (such as Mexico's PRONASOL and the Programa de Apoyo a la Pobreza Extrema, or Programme for the Support of Extreme Poverty, introduced in Peru in 1993). These have been essentially vote-catching exercises aimed at creating popular support for governments and presidents alike. Given that they offer short-term, unskilled palliatives to structural un- and under-employment, such programmes can be regarded as being neither productive nor solutions. In Chile, the Pinochet regime adopted a purist approach towards liberalization in that it made no effort to alleviate poverty (the ideological justification being that repression was much cheaper than social provision). The discourse introduced to post-coup Chile was the concept of a limited state, which provided a broad framework which was only concerned with defence, law and order and administrative functions, but this proved to be an untenable and illogical position in that if a free market is to work effectively, it will need increases in employment opportunities and a skilled and mobile workforce in order to maximize profits. A more pragmatic position was taken after 1990, when the civilian Aylwin government engaged in a variety of projects aimed at assisting the poor into jobs, training and community development, as well as restoring some level of job security and a higher minimum wage. None of these measures were radical and the commitment to liberalization, albeit of a slightly watered-down nature, remained central. John Sheahan reports that these more proactive policies did produce results in that between 1990 and 1994, the 'incidence of poverty was cut by nearly a third, from 35 to 24 per cent and that of absolute poverty by half from 14 to 7 per cent'. However, income differentials continued to widen, so that 'one fourth of Chilean households remain in poverty despite improvement in economic conditions'.[17] Chronic, absolute poverty and inequality were not addressed; although the present incumbent of the Chilean presidency, Eduardo Frei, has pledged to eliminate extreme poverty by the year 2000, this will be impossible without structural reform of the economy, which is unlikely, given the resistance of elites to income redistribution and an overhaul of the taxation system.[18] What the poverty eradication programmes have done is to try to stop the poor becoming poorer, but without eliminating their condition of poverty. Such programmes view the poor as marginal to the issues of development and growth, when in fact they should be central to these long-term strategies.

Cardoso and Helwege contend that 'economic poverty reflects political poverty: the poor lack the means to voice their demands'.[19] The deepening of the crisis of structural poverty has been aggravated by the withdrawal of the state from social provision. As liberalization policies are generally judged in terms of their macro-economic performance (that is, their ability to control inflation and their impact upon the competitive edge of their country's export capacity), there has been a tendency in 'official' accounts to neglect estimating the impact of the absence of state provision for individual recipients and for deprived and middle-ranking social sectors (official statistics are notoriously unreliable and also tend to neglect social groups – the underclass, indigenous communities, women single heads of household – which are not regarded as pertinent to national economic performance indicators). Welfare provision is no longer a social right linked to citizenship and its demise has had important repercussions upon the fabric of civil life. I have documented (in Chapters 4 and 5) the types of survival strategies which poor communities have had to develop in order to try to cope with the precariousness of everyday life in the face of state and institutional retreat. These strategies build upon what Abel and Lewis have termed the 'legacy of poverty', which has resulted from 'earlier patterns of distorted development that is now exacerbated by protracted crises of debt rescheduling, capital flight and economic reorganisation'. As earlier chapters have indicated, the local community and the informal sector have replaced the state as the focus of social provision and support; Abel and Lewis have described this as the privatization of welfare, resulting in its 'communalisation' by the poor.[20] If one adheres to a popular-democracy model of Latin American political life, then this may be seen as good coming from adversity, as the expression of self-help and the participatory ethos. However, whether popular mobilization and collective organization are able to provide such support in the long term is a deeply problematic question. Another positive reading is that endorsed, with quite distinct ideological motives, by Hernando de Soto, whose book, *El Otro Sendero* (*The Other Path*), enthusiastically declares the triumph of the free market and promotes what he terms the micro-enterprise (that is, the informal family firm) as the creator of wealth so long as the state does not intervene. His interpretation is that the market can only be a force for good.[21]

The neo-liberal perspective views the replacement of institutionalized social welfare by personal and communal provision as a positive development. The state only steps in – via its poverty eradication programmes – in emergencies; for the rest of the time, informal and community groups provide a safety net and the consequences of restructuring produce an increasingly desperate and available workforce. One must ask what this says about the state's credibility and legitimacy and the sense of responsibility it should feel towards its citizens. I have already discussed the risks that popular groups face in terms of their incorporation and manipulation by the state, political parties and other institutions such as charities which create yet another form of dependency. Poverty eradication programmes practise a policy of 'selective incorporation' which divides communities into the compliant and the recalcitrant, permitting some to enjoy the dubious privilege of access and condemning others to social exclusion.[22] Low-income workers no longer have the right to medical provision (even if it has been historically inadequate, given the dire conditions pertaining in public hospitals) because social security systems have been privatized, and totally overwhelmed state-administered hospitals are closing because finance is no longer available for them. The leaders in the health industry are now large and expensive private hospitals, professional doctors' associations, pharmaceutical companies and their international partners.

One of the main tenets of liberalization is that host governments must do everything in their power to create attractive conditions for foreign investment. One way of doing this has been to reduce the social costs of production, which are wages and safe and secure working conditions, thus stripping the workforce of any vestiges of protection and support provision. The resulting impoverishment of workers has had many and varied outcomes. There has been a marked loss of trade-union presence within the economy (what Barkin, Otiz and Rosen have called the 'relentless cheapening of labour power'[23]). This has been the result of falling real wages, the end of food subsidies, the retraction of formal employment, the disappearance of labour security and the increasing casualization of labour with the advent of flexible and temporary contracts, and the deregulation of working conditions. Trade unions have responded to these developments in a generally defensive manner as they have attempted to protect minimum rights and conditions. Many have entered *convenios de concertación* with government and employers.[24] However, these pacts tend to demand far greater compromise on the part of workers than their partners in the arrangement. This is not to say that all unions have been passive. Ronaldo Munck believes that Uruguayan and Chilean workers have preserved some trade-union freedoms and some element of employment stability more successfully than, say, those in Brazil and Argentina.[25] One must conclude, however, that the juggernaut and all-encompassing nature of liberalization makes traditional union militancy a difficult and possibly disappearing phenomenon. There are exceptions (some of which were discussed in Chapter 4), and there certainly have been processes which have resulted in the ending of strongly entrenched and highly corrupt union hierarchies (for example, the death in 1997 of Fidel Velázquez, who had controlled the Confederación de Trabajadores Mexicanos (CTM,

Confederation of Mexican Workers) since 1941 and who provided the PRI with a docile workforce. His reign had been
increasingly contested by independent unions who challenged
both the CTM and the PRI).

Contemporary economic orthodoxy focuses upon growth
centred in the export-driven economy – transnational firms,
the automobile, computing and other sophisticated industries and *maquiladora* (assembly-line) production – but these
make little contribution to domestic productivity and development. Small businesses, the professional middle classes, farmers,
workers, and the informal sector cannot compete with this
transnationalized economy and, indeed, they are marginalized
from it except in terms of being exploited by it. Small business
cannot compete because of its inability to invest in industrial
plant and new technologies, and its lack of competitive edge
with respect to the increasing volume of imported, cheap manufactured goods. The opening of agriculture to the international
economy and the creation of agro-industrial estates have intensified income differentials and placed insurmountable obstacles
in terms of the modernization of rural production. Small and
subsistence farmers have lost their livelihoods, having no
access to the dollar economy brought in by export crops and receiving no support from the state. In Mexico, the *ejidos* (communally
owned lands, long regarded as one of the greatest legacies of the
Revolution) were privatized during the Salinas administration
and then sold to agro-industrial interests in partnership with
foreign firms. This resulted in loss of employment, with many
reduced to seasonal working or the *maquiladoras*.

Maquiladoras are often concentrated in export zones (most
famously, along the Mexican–US border); assembly-line and
sweatshop production is undertaken in harsh working conditions, the absence of labour rights and protection and authoritarian managements.[26] Governments have not expended much
energy in enforcing labour and environmental regulations as
these would inhibit foreign capital's interests. In 1965, the
Border Industrialisation Programme opened Mexico's northern
border to foreign-owned export-processing plants. By the 1990s,
this sector had become central to the Mexican state's growth
strategy, particularly as oil revenues declined. The *maquiladoras*
have replaced tourism as the second largest source of foreign
exchange. This is because factory owners have to exchange
dollars for *pesos* in order to pay their workforce, enabling the

Central Bank to accumulate a dollar reserve. However, despite claims about the economic success of the *maquiladoras*, their contribution to the rest of the Mexican economy and to sustained growth must be questioned. On the positive side, there is some exposure to new skills and technology, for some, although not the mass, of *maquiladora* workers. However, as Leslie Sklair points out, the acquisition of skills is not recognized by management, who continue to pay extremely low wages.[27]

It is not just the poor who have been adversely affected by liberalization. Public-sector employees and professional groups such as doctors and teachers have seen their powers of collective bargaining eliminated and their contracts ended. Universities have been pressed to drop courses on the arts, humanities and cultural studies, which are judged to be commercially useless. Resource allocation for higher education is being shifted to primary education (notwithstanding the medium-term impact upon the supply of teachers and other professions). Primary education is subject to a process of decentralization, with educational boards (comprising municipal governments, religious institutions, teachers and parents) assuming the role previously filled by the state. Many of these boards are inept managers and lack sufficient funds to ensure educational standards are maintained. Thus schools are closing, and education is increasingly just another commodity which you can enjoy only if you can pay for it. Clearly the poor are the group most damaged by these developments, which are occurring in Peru, Mexico, Argentina, Colombia, Chile and Nicaragua since the demise of the FSLN. These strategies have been endorsed by the World Bank as a means of streamlining admittedly ineffective education systems. One would argue that the 'solution' makes the situation worse, not better, and creates ever-deepening inequality and disadvantage.[28]

I wish to turn now to consider the experience of governments which have attempted to introduce socialist economic programmes, looking first at the constraints under which the FSLN laboured during the 1980s in Nicaragua. When the Sandinistas came to power in 1979, they inherited an economy dominated by subsistence agriculture and dependent upon an external primary-product export trade with a small and unsophisticated industrial sector. The FSLN immediately launched campaigns aimed at attacking urban and rural poverty through literacy and health drives, and also introduced social security and service provision (having inherited a country whose previous incumbent government had personified incompetence, corruption and indifference). Acknowledging the historic exclusion of the rural poor in particular, the government initiated a huge shift of resources towards the countryside as well as generating an approach which privileged the importance (and centrality to the Revolution) of the value of human capital.[29] Its efforts were supported by large injections of foreign assistance, but the beginning of the *contra* war in 1982 increasingly handicapped such development programmes and a downward spiral of economic crisis began. The FSLN attempted to contain inflation by operating a strict policy of wage restraint. It also focused upon winning over the support of the private business sector through credit subsidies and joint ventures, but the former remained suspicious of the government's socialist ambitions. The FSLN was committed to a mixed economy, but what was at dispute was how big a role private-sector elites would play; the government recognized that it needed their input in order to help the country recover from civil war, but wanted to control them politically. The elites were alienated by the expropriation of land, agro-industries, mining and private banks, but they were also divided as to how to respond. The 'considerable variation among the private sector leaders . . . on a series of issues . . . prevented the Nicaraguan bourgeoisie from functioning as a united bloc or pursuing a clear, common agenda'.[30]

As the war accelerated, huge amounts of government expenditure had to be directed to buying arms (and this at a time when export earnings on Nicaragua's main crops, cotton and coffee, dropped as world prices fell[31]). Agricultural production was interrupted and roads and infrastructure destroyed; this economic attrition was accentuated by the enforced transfers of populations as they escaped theatres of war. By the mid-1980s, the economy was carrying a huge budget deficit and the government was unable to satisfy the demands of its supporters (the working class and the poor, who experienced not only the dislocations of war but also food shortages and wage reductions, speculation and hoarding). Thus, the previously marginalized popular classes, urban and rural, who had been intended as the beneficiaries of the Sandinistas' strategy of popular hegemony, were subjected to increasing privation which produced growing disenchantment. By 1988, inflation reached 11,500 per cent

and the FSLN's political position had become extremely tenuous.[32] It had begun to reorient its economic policy from the
mid-1980s and in 1988 introduced its first stabilization programme, with a complete transformation of money system
and a downsizing of state departments and agencies. It initially offered palliatives to low-income groups in the form of
an increase in the minimum wage and price controls, but
these soon disappeared.[33] As the 1990 election approached, the
government cultivated a far closer relationship with private
financial and industrial elites and appeared willing to accept
the prevailing economic orthodoxies of restructuring and liberalization. Its socialist agenda had all but disappeared. The macro-
economic policies pursued by the FSLN government – and the
political sensibilities which underpinned them – can be criticised, and they certainly share responsibility for its 1990 defeat.
However, the fate of the Sandinista Revolution was also fash-
ioned by external circumstances – the fact of the war and the
economic aggression directed by the USA (this, of course, has
been the case in the rest of Latin and Central America, not
least in Cuba). The external dependence which had characterized the Nicaraguan economy before 1979 continued to shape
its relations with the rest of the world after the FSLN's capture of power. Conroy remarks that this dependence 'provided
opponents of the revolution with their greatest element of
economic leverage'.[34] Nicaragua's vulnerability also facilitated
the US government's persistent intervention in its domestic
affairs. Thus, the USA moved to close off export markets for
Nicaraguan goods and to freeze the country's credit and investment possibilities (from both private and international donors).
This policy was complementary to its support for the *contra*
rebels, disinformation campaigns against the FSLN and succour
for its political opponents.

The Cuban Revolution adopted a state socialist economic
model in the 1960s. John Sheahan has suggested that since
1959, the Cubans have made great advances in the war against
poverty and in the promotion of egalitarianism, but these successes have been tempered by their inability to promote economic growth without external dependence and to reduce the
concentration of power – both economic and political – at the
centre of government.[35] Thus the early years of the Revolution
saw the advent of an enduring commitment to mass education
and health, the reduction of child mortality, the raising of life

expectancy, full employment and the shifting of resources to the previously neglected rural sector. The downside was that industrial and agricultural production were highly inefficient, top-heavy, bureaucratic and over-manned. The poor quality of manufactured goods could not satisfy demand, and scarcity and rationing became a constant feature of Cuban life. Nevertheless, Cardoso and Helwege argue that until the 1980s, Cuba avoided the structural poverty associated with all other Latin and Central American societies. Cuba 'succeeded in achieving substantial economic growth along with distributional equity'.[36] This growth was situated within the dependent relationship shaped by Cuba's links with the Soviet Union and the Eastern Bloc and their demise cast the Cuban economy adrift.

When Castro announced the Rectification Campaign in 1986, it was an acknowledgement of the precarious state of the Cuban economy and the need for urgent reform. The government was compelled to introduce extensive adjustment policies in order to respond to shortages of food and consumer goods, the lack of foreign exchange and secure markets and the vulnerability which its continued reliance upon sugar, the price of which had been depressed for years, had created. It also sought to improve industrial management and productivity, accepting that its hierarchical leadership model was a major obstacle to better economic performance (although there has been much resistance by entrenched interests in the party and the state, who feel threatened by such a radical agenda). Experiments with market mechanisms had been conducted since the 1970s. Rectification repudiated recourse to the market, demanding instead a return to the socialist ethos of the 1960s. However, the collapse of the Soviet system and the declaration of the 'Special Period' led to the acceptance of market trade in agriculture and the export sector, to ever-increasing joint ventures with foreign firms and governments and, finally, the pursuit of foreign exchange which has itself resulted in the 'dollarization' of the Cuban economy. Official rhetoric pronounced that the Revolution was in danger and that economic survival must be a priority if the social achievements of the past decades were to be protected. Food self-sufficiency was regarded as crucial; land previously used for export crops (particularly sugar cane) was turned over to production for domestic consumption. Food scarcity and the breakdown of basic service provision became the most pressing concern to individual Cubans. In effect,

Cubans were experiencing similar consequences to those imposed on the rest of Latin America following the fall-out from the debt crisis and its restructuring 'solutions'. The early to mid-1990s saw a growing disenchantment with government, particularly amongst the young. Emblematic of this disillusionment was the *balsero* (raft) crisis of August 1994, when thousands set sail for the US coast, many drowning in the process. The two governments were forced to begin negotiations, which resulted in many *balseros* returning to Cuba under conditions of immunity and the USA imposing restrictions on immigration for the first time since 1959. Although the economic situation appeared to have improved during the late 1990s, it was at considerable political and social cost. The veneer of unity and integrity at the core of the Cuban state had already been threatened by the Ochoa trial of 1987 after which the General – a close friend of Castro's – and a number of other high-ranking officials were executed, ostensibly for drug-trafficking, but apparently as a consequence of political conflict. 'Dollarization' has caused a bifurcation within Cuban society between those who have access to dollars and the majority who do not. This economic apartheid can only create fissures within the country and undermine or even destroy the sense of collective solidarity which has been a linchpin since the mid-1950s. The creation of the dual dollar/peso economy was made possible by the fact that Cuba opened its doors to foreign tourism and its attendant evils – the reappearance of prostitution, gambling and drugs and speculation in land and buildings. What is at stake here is the concept of social equity which the Cuban government has adhered to, however parlous the economic circumstances. If this is jettisoned, then the very real achievements which have been consolidated since 1959 will disappear and the one, continuing experiment in socialism in Latin and Central America will cease to exist.[37] This is the negative view; the positive reading is that Cuba will manage the transition to a more decentralized and participatory political system and that the vision and the social legacy of egalitarianism will continue to provide the cement for Cuban society.

What will be the future trajectories for Latin American economies? One outcome may be the extension of the idea of free-trade areas. The North American Free Trade Agreement (NAFTA) was signed by Mexico, Canada and the USA on 1 January 1994, and was acclaimed by many commentators as the first stage of a process of economic and political integration between North and Latin America (although subsequently only Chile has been singled out as possibly joining in the foreseeable future). Its advocates talk about the creation of a hemispheric trade bloc based upon the free-market principles espoused by the USA, and one which will prove extremely attractive to foreign investors. It is claimed that rather than suffering disadvantage with respect to its northern neighbours, 50 years of ISI and state protectionism have enabled certain manufacturing sectors (such as the automobile industry) and services such as private medical care to attain world-class competitive status.[38] Despite the fact that Mexican manufacturing does not enjoy the same levels of infrastructure and skilled personnel as either the USA or Canada, it does have a huge advantage in the reserves of labour it can draw upon.[39]

Its detractors argue that NAFTA is just another stage in the exploitation of cheap Latin American labour, that it seriously undermines Mexico's autonomy and that it is a clear indication of the absence of democracy in the lives of millions of Mexicans. The precondition for the Mexican economy's 'competitiveness' is that most of its citizens continue to live in abject poverty and to work in unregulated and dangerous conditions. Although some sectors may benefit from the Free Trade Agreement, many more – landless peasants, small farmers, *maquila* workers – will suffer.[40] Added to this is the stagnation which agriculture has suffered for many decades and which has resulted from a lack of investment, technological backwardness and the exclusion of poor peasants from credit facilities and training. It is clear that regional disparities (the gap between the rich northern states and the marginalized south, which is exemplified by the Chiapas rebellion) will intensify as traditional agriculture based in the southern part of the country declines, while the urban, manufacturing and financial conglomerates of the northern and central states draw closer to the USA and the international trade community. As indicated in earlier chapters, the political consequences of this economic divide will be a growing confrontation of the incumbent PRI and its right-wing challenger, the PAN, with the PRD, the Zapatistas and the social movements of the south (although their propensity to create a common programme and strategy may be questioned).

Resistance to the policies imposed by neo-liberalism has proved difficult 'because of the social disarticulation caused by adjustment policies'.[41] Given the global nature of liberalization, it is often difficult to understand its impact upon specific communities and how they try to challenge its detrimental consequences. The El Barzón debtors' movement in Mexico was mentioned in Chapter 4 (note 65). This new social movement has become sufficiently powerful and autonomous to allow it to negotiate independently of the PRI-state (thus bypassing traditional channels of corporate representation and demand-making) with both the IMF and the anti-NAFTA lobby in the USA. The debtors have argued that the 1996 Mexican Supreme Court ruling that the privatization of Mexico's ten largest banks in 1990 was illegal has effectively eliminated any debt which they owe to these banks. They have demanded that the IMF restructure the management of the Mexican debt so as to make it payable, or else they will refuse to make any private debt repayments and will thus close down the national banking system. They have also attacked the Mexican government's policy of bailing out the private banks through loans made from public money (and the close relationship between bankers and the PRI has been a useful piece of publicity), while apparently doing nothing to help small debtors. The interesting aspect of this situation has been that the IMF has taken El Barzón's threats seriously; it accepts that they are in a position to disrupt the Mexican banking system and clearly does not have confidence in the latter's ability to manage the 'flows of private international capital that are the driving force of the new Mexican economy'.[42] Another example of popular resistance is that *maquila* workers (despite the harsh environment they have to contend with) have forged links with US labour unions.[43] Additionally, rural communities are challenging the orthodoxy of export-oriented agro-industry and, with the support of NGOs and activists (and in Mexico, through links with the EZLN), are promoting independent land management and self-reliance.

Liberalization programmes have been justified by critiques of the pre-existing state in Latin America and its profound inefficiency, which cannot be gainsaid.[44] Economic reforms were clearly urgently needed, but the evidence of the last two decades does not suggest that neo-liberalism is the answer. What has occurred is backward development – externally-oriented activity, which has only benefited already wealthy sectors in Latin America and in the prosperous and dominant nations of the world, and consigned the majority of Latin and Central American citizens to ever-greater and intensifying income differentials, and the poor to an existence of intense deprivation. It has been argued that monetarist liberalization 'destroys the state's . . . capacity for rational action':

> When left on its own and without recourse to the state, private enterprise is unable to come up with an adequate development policy: yet it opposes any rational state action that would limit its ability to profit from the state's inefficiency. . . . The situation can only be sustained through an increasingly more repressive orientation of the Latin American states.[45]

Markets are not self-sufficient; they require an institutional framework. In light of this dilemma, Boron argues for the need for 'the construction of new democratic legitimacy'; 'the complete inadequacy of the market's mechanisms to respond to the most basic needs of civil society' necessitates 'a broad and efficient state intervention'.[46] Boron's belief is that the state has been colonized by domestic and foreign business and cannot represent the whole of society. Reform should not mean privatization, but must involve a serious consideration of pressing issues of landownership, income distribution, education, employment and health opportunities. This is a position also argued by Bresser Pereira, Maravall and Przeworski, who contend that the state should co-ordinate the economy in conjunction with the market not take a back seat to it, and that it must use the growth in public savings which will accrue from tax reform and campaigns against corruption to 'stimulate strategic private investments and technological developments, to protect the environment and to ensure health and educational standards'.[47] They accept that the resistance of the internal elite will be considerable, but do not explain how this can be negotiated nor which groups – the Left, social movements – could become the standard-bearers of a revitalized and modernizing state. The adherents of neo-liberalism view the state purely in terms of how it can enhance profitability, but Boron believes that the state must be more than that. Its role is to provide a framework of social justice, to stimulate productive activities and to satisfy the basic needs of its citizens.

Moisés Naim identifies four deficits which undermine attempts to combine liberalization with democratization. Poverty and inequality constitute the social deficit and must be addressed by programmes which reduce inflation, generate employment and improve infrastructure and the provision of services. The second deficit is an institutional one, which is characterized by poor standards of public management and high levels of inefficiency and corruption. Naim believes that a solution is to be found in privatization, which allows the state to rationalize its structures and practice. However, he does not address the relationship between privatization and public responsibility or scrutiny. Latin America also suffers from a democratic deficit which has several elements. One is that the power of the head of state has diminished as it has been challenged by legislatures, the judiciary and provincial governors; another is the growing independent power of the mass media; a third is the constant demand for more democracy and greater participation (which he regards as destabilizing); and the final element is a growing dissatisfaction with traditional politicians and political parties. His final deficit is that domestic investment in both the public and private sectors undermines the region's economic competitiveness. His conclusion is that Latin America must seek to attract ever-more foreign capital and that more, not less, privatization is the solution and democratic demand-making appears to be the culprit.[48]

The major political consequence of the dominance of market solutions to economic problems has been that the state's legitimacy has been threatened, perhaps mortally: 'The crisis has created a marked disenchantment with politics generally, and party politics in particular, as the virtues of citizenship appear more fiction than reality as the promises of democracy [Alfonsín's famous 'con la democracia también se come' – 'democracy also means eating'] fade away.'[49] Disillusionment with politics and governments has certainly intensified as neo-liberalism has established itself as economic orthodoxy, but there are also other reasons for public alienation. The legitimacy of the state is brought into question when popular insurgent movements challenge its authority and repudiate the political and socio-economic order it defends. It is not my intention to offer a history of recent insurgencies (Central America, Colombia, Mexico and Peru), but to make some observations about their consequences and achievements. I also consider the impact counter-insurgency campaigns have upon the nature of citizenship. The militarization of the state which the enormous powers given to the armed forces, police, special forces and intelligence has produced leads one to question how much government is able to control counter-insurgency programmes, and how effective it is in defending human rights and judicial processes. The experience of these recent and contemporary insurgencies suggests a weak state which is subordinate to military imperatives and which does not respond to demands for reform and democracy which popular insurgencies represent. Here, the caveat must be made that contemporary insurgencies do not share similar identities and objectives. Thus, the anti-participatory, authoritarian ethos of SL contrasts sharply with the EZLN's programme, which is committed to radical reform and the democratization of Mexico's political culture.

The insurgent movements in Central America, in Nicaragua (which climaxed in the 1979 Revolution of the FSLN), in El Salvador and Guatemala were initiated in the 1960s by left-wing parties but gained considerable popular endorsement as they addressed issues of autocratic and corrupt governments (which were supported by the USA in diplomatic, financial and military terms), poverty, land hunger, ethnic and gender oppression and the implicit denial of human rights and civil liberties.[50] By the mid-1980s, the civil wars in both El Salvador and Guatemala had reached a stalemate; although the insurgents controlled substantial areas of liberated territory, they were incapable of a direct assault upon the state whilst the latter, despite the huge concentration of military power it had accumulated, was also rent with divisions and power struggles. This impasse offered the possibility of a democratic opening. However, the negotiations which began and which resulted in the 1987 Central American Peace Accords were handicapped by the fact that the military High Commands in both countries, and indeed their US backers, were committed to complete victory, no matter how politically and militarily impossible this was. There was eventually an end to armed struggle in both El Salvador and Guatemala but it was never a consensual peace. Major contradictions include the contested position of ex-guerrillas within mainstream political and electoral activity, the continued abuse of human rights, particularly with respect to indigenous communities, and linked to this the fact that the military continues to enjoy untrammelled power. In Guatemala, the 1985 Constitution 'technically returned the country to the rule of law', but the military preserved its position at the heart of the state, those political elites who had collaborated with the military retained control, and left-wing and other activists continued to live with the risk of repression and 'disappearance'.[51] Decades of war had destroyed infrastructure, disrupted agriculture and displaced huge populations. Popular mobilization and the long years of armed struggle did not result in the resolution of demands for economic change and social justice although, arguably, they succeeded in carving out a place, albeit a constricted one, within the political system. Democratization remains an unresolved issue as the division of power continues to be highly differentiated and exclusive. Carlos Vilas concludes that 'to very large parts of the population, the prospects for democratization are still tied to the prospects for social reform, and to a close relationship between political citizenship and social citizenship'.[52] Such prospects may be viewed in a pessimistic way, given that post-insurgency governments have not attempted to create processes of integration which would give hitherto excluded and marginalized social groups – the rural and urban poor, women and indigenous communities – access to education, social provision, employment and political rights. Rather, they have pursued liberalization, deregulation and privatization, have maintained an elitist political system (what Jonas sees as the embodiment of the pacted democratic model of a 'very minimalist definition of a "political settlement"'[53]), and have singularly failed to address outstanding human rights violations and empower truth commissions, an issue which continues to be a cancer at the heart of all states in Latin and Central America. The end of insurrection has seen the 'propping up (of) a bankrupt social order'.[54]

A protracted guerrilla struggle has been waged in Colombia since the 1960s by the FARC. The origins of the insurrection lay in peasant struggles for legal and labour rights and resistance to the aggressive policies of both government and large landowners, which began in the 1920s and which were particularly intense during *la violencia*. Beset by political discord and schism, the FARC's military presence was somewhat marginal until the early 1980s. However, following a government crackdown on legal opposition, it restructured itself as an army and established strong bases of support in the south and east of the country. It also prospered as a result of its practice of imposing taxes on drug traffickers, which enabled it to operate as a highly prosperous business organization. By the late 1990s, the FARC controlled about two-fifths of Colombian territory, acting as a surrogate police force, judiciary and government and constituting the only source of authority for huge sections of the population. The FARC had responded positively to President Belisario Betancur's initiation of a peace process in 1983. He recognized that the roots of the conflict lay in socio-economic causes and that the guerrillas must be partners in any political solution to the crisis. However, his successor, Virgilio Barco (1986–90), rejected this initiative arguing that the FARC and other guerrilla groups, such as the Ejército de Liberación Nacional, or ELN, National Liberation Army, were beyond the pale of legitimacy and accelerated counterinsurgency operations. In the 1990s, the military and security forces were involved in a very dirty war, during which thousands of peasants, activists, state officials and politicians died or were 'disappeared'. Paramilitary groups established themselves in FARC areas and terrorized populations. Ricardo Vargas Meza has written about the state 'privatizing its war against the guerrillas by delegating its counterinsurgency operations' to these paramilitary groups who appear to be able to act with impunity, outside the jurisdiction of either government or law.[55]

By the late 1990s, the Colombian political system had descended into chaos. Revelations about President Samper's ties to the drug barons, the corruption of public life and the environment of violence in which it operated, the persistent violation of human rights, and governmental disdain for the profound socio-economic and political inequities which give sustenance to the ongoing insurrection, are issues which have destroyed the legitimacy of the state in Colombia. Given the FARC's military strength, it was clear that there could be no armed resolution of the conflict and peace negotiations were once again initiated in 1998. The incoming president, Andrés Pastrana, promised to begin the demilitarization of the South, provided the FARC responded by starting its own disarming. However, a political solution will be impeded by the increasingly confrontational nature of public discourse and the uncontrolled repression which Colombian citizens endure. Future prospects appear bleak, although a glimmer of hope may be found in the Mandate for Peace initiative. This has brought together social movements, local and regional politicians and guerrillas in an effort to broker a peace which would not follow the example of other Latin and Central American countries emerging from periods of military rule or civil war, but would address issues of the resolution of human rights abuses and socio-economic and political exclusion.

The insurrection of SL which began in Peru in 1980 is a political phenomenon distinct from other contemporary insurgencies. Certainly the roots of rebellion were authentic in that Ayacucho, the department in which SL hatched and then launched its insurrection, had endured decades of neglect by the far-distant Lima government and had alarming indicators of social and economic deprivation. The Sendero leadership effectively manipulated the levels of discontent that this engendered, but it also attempted to impose its own elitist, millenarian and inherently anti-democratic vision upon an increasingly recalcitrant peasant community.[56] The impact of the Senderista war had a number of important consequences for Peruvian politics in the 1980s and 1990s. Given that the year of the onset of the insurrection also saw the return to civilian rule, the implications for democracy have been immense. Thus, the Peruvian Left's efforts to compete as a recognized political actor were undermined by the official perception of it as, at least, complicit in Sendero's activities (this was despite the fact that Sendero had declared war on the electoral Left, regarding it as no better than the 'fascist' state, and proceeded to assassinate left-wing politicians, local government officials and community activists). The Belaúnde government (1980–85) initially failed to understand the seriousness of the insurgency (the President famously referring to SL as 'cattle thieves'), but then attempted to eliminate the guerrillas through massive retaliation and ruthlessness (which targeted the civilian population), without any consideration of a 'hearts and minds' approach based upon recognizing the social issues which had produced the war. Throughout the early 1980s, SL was clearly in the lead in terms of its organizational and strategic superiority. However, it progressively alienated its popular support with its authoritarian and repressive proclivities. Peasants were compelled to create their own self-defence groups to protect them from the attentions of both the army and the guerrillas. Again, as in the Colombian case, the situation was further complicated by relationships between both the military and SL with *traficantes* (drug barons).

There was a massive expansion of counter-insurgency between 1983 and 1992, with the military operating a scorched-earth policy which eliminated any respect for individual human rights. The lack of political and judicial control over the armed forces was evident. Alán García's attempts to establish the domination of the civilian state floundered and he allowed the army virtual autonomy in order to engage with Sendero. Sendero extended its operations (possibly in response to the increasing repudiation it experienced in its erstwhile stronghold, Ayacucho) to include Lima and the central highlands. The period following the election of Alberto Fujimori in 1990 saw a dramatic restructuring of the state–Sendero power balance. A retreat was evident in Sendero Luminoso's trajectory. The arrest of Guzmán and other prominent leaders was accompanied by a 'fatal erosion of its social base'.[57] The military high command had evolved more sophisticated strategies, which enabled it to conduct a more successful policy both in terms of operation of the war and the political dimension of it. Its conduct of the counter-insurgency was fortified by Fujimori's election in 1990. He gave precedence to ending the insurgency; it was clear that by 1996, 'the third phase of the civil war was clearly won by the Peruvian state, to the extent that by 1996 the PCP-SL, despite continuing to function, no longer represented "una opción de poder" ("an option of power")'.[58] Degregori argues that Sendero's growth in the 1980s was 'facilitated by a crisis that was not just economic, but also moral and political, particularly in the area of political representation'.[59] Although the Peruvian state appears to have been defeated, although not eliminated, Sendero Luminoso and the socio-economic conditions and political marginalization which fuelled its rebellion still endure, and disillusionment with electoral politics has grown.

The final insurrection to be considered is the newest, that of the EZLN, which began in the southern states of Mexico in January 1994 (although the guerrillas had been based in the region since 1983, establishing a strong rapport with communities). The indigenous – mostly Mayan – population of the state of Chiapas had struggled for decades to force local oligarchs to implement land reform; the latter attempted to prevent peasant organization and militancy with harsh repression which, in turn, spurred the creation of peasant self-defence militias. The Zapatista rebellion has proved to be distinct from the old style of insurrection in that there has been no assault on power; rather, there has been the consolidation of armed civil resistance, the creation of autonomous, alternative local government and a sophisticated dialogue with the rest of the country and international opinion which has emphasized the EZLN's commitment to participatory democracy. The pattern of governmental response has been highly reminiscent of other counter-insurgencies: a growing spiral of army repression, the employment of private armies by landowners, disappearances and massacres. Faced with demands for social justice, free elections and an end to the PRI's domination of the political system, the state has responded with violence and with what has been termed the 'feudalization of power', as local PRI bosses ally with landowners and their paramilitary gangs in an attempt to suppress the mobilization of peasants and indigenous communities.[60] The PRI-state has persistently attempted to sabotage peace negotiations which began shortly after the uprising itself in 1994. The EZLN's challenge to the incumbent system has highlighted the bankruptcy of the latter. While the crisis which has engulfed Mexican politics continues to develop, it is difficult to envisage what kind of political regime will take its place when the PRI's hegemony finally dissolves.

An examination of contemporary insurgencies and the state's response to them provides one example of how the military is at the heart of contemporary political power. Its presence undermines constitutional and judicial processes, inhibits investigation of human rights abuses and obstructs reform. For Felipe Agüero, 'The State is ... split into separate realms of authority: one supported by democratic-electoral legitimacy, the other by the legitimacy which the military grants itself.'[61] A glaring example of this self-legitimization was provided by General Pinochet, who, on his retirement as head of the Chilean army in March 1998, designated himself senator for life and, as such, the recipient of immunity from the crimes his regime had perpetrated. The immunity from prosecution for human rights abuses which Latin American militaries generally enjoy (a right often bestowed by themselves but upheld by civilian governments) has prevented any resolution of collective memories of repression and makes a mockery of the democratic conventions governments claim to adhere to. As Agüero concludes, 'the spectre of intervention still manages to exert a perverse influence on the political process'.[62] The seemingly unrestricted influence of the military creates a culture of appeasement and places considerable constraints upon policy initiatives, as well as being particularly detrimental to the development of left-wing and popular agendas.

I have previously mentioned what I see as the militarization of the state in the context of counter-insurgency practice and the power that military hierarchies wield over elected governments, but one may also speak of the militarization of political culture. Violence penetrates all aspects of public life, whether it be in the countryside, where peasants are caught between drug barons, government forces and guerrillas; in the cities, where street children are routinely executed by vigilantes with the complicity of the police, gay men are subjected to harassment and beatings and political and state office-holders are vulnerable to assassination. The justice system is completely overloaded as well as being compromised in terms of its impartiality. Constitutional rights are ignored and legal citizenship is stripped of significance. The so-called 'faceless courts' in Colombia, which try persons suspected of drug-related activities, have been used to target trade unionists and community activists; as always, the state's definition of 'subversive' is an elastic one. State prisons are overpopulated, with inmates living in appalling conditions; riots and massacres are common. Crime levels are rising but government policies do not address the structural origins of much criminal activity by the poor (such as robbery and looting). Imprisonment is an easy evasion of the state's responsibility to provide basic services and to offer legal protection to its citizens. The poor are jailed, whilst 'elite' crimes – such as fraud, tax evasion, drug money-laundering and the protection of drug cartels from prosecution through corrupt practices – go unheeded.[63]

I began this chapter with a discussion of the social and political consequences of neo-liberal economic policies in contemporary Latin America. One of the major problems recognized by governments is the need to eradicate the drugs trade. Tremendous pressure is exerted upon individual regimes by the USA and international agencies with the aim of encouraging greater persistence and tenacity in their conflict with the *traficantes*.[64] An irony is evident here. It is that the drugs trade is the best advertisement of the free-market imperative in that it makes economic sense for Andean peasants to cultivate the coca leaf. The fusion of 'dirty' and 'clean' money through the repatriation of drug profits and their 'laundering' into legitimate activities have created an international trade with its own structures and division of labour (production and processing in Latin America, transit through Central America and the Caribbean, retail and profit-making in the USA and Europe). The huge profits made do not go to peasants in the Andes but to the businessmen who market it; however, peasant producers can still make a better living out of coca than other crops or other activities in the legal/formal economy. One result of market liberalization has been that work in the drugs industry appears to be a sensible and rational choice for people whose other economic activities have been severely curtailed by government cuts, unemployment and plummeting living standards. As a consequence, peasant organizations have opposed drug-eradication programmes, arguing that not only do they challenge traditional cultural forms but also that they threaten the economic survival of farmers and communities. Drug production fuels the rural economy and, in the absence of any governmental initiative to provide alternatives and support (in terms of investment and training), will continue to do so. A consequence of the drugs trade which must be treated in a non-ironic manner is that it has given sustenance to the justification of an authoritarian current which gained tremendous momentum in the 1990s. This authoritarianism has embedded itself in public life and is responsible for the increasing disillusionment with formal politics which is now visible. The continuing inability to deal with (or disdain for) the resolution of seemingly intractable and ongoing problems of social exclusion, political violence and economic deprivation on the part of elected governments remains a thorn in the side of their presumed dedication to the deepening of democracy.

Notes

1 An accessible (for the non-economist) survey of Latin American economies is provided in E. Cardoso and A. Helwege, *Latin America's Economy. Diversity,*

Trends and Conflicts (Cambridge, MA, MIT Press, 1992). J. A. Morales and G. McMahon (eds), *Economic Policy and the Transition to Democracy* (Cambridge, MA, MIT Press, 1996) analyses specific policies and problems encountered in a number of countries during the 1980s and early 1990s.

2 Atilio Borón has described the debt as a form of 'imperial tribute' *(State, Capitalism and Democracy in Latin America* (Boulder, CO, Lynne Rienner, 1995), p. 177, provoking the thought that the same relationship has been reproduced since the Conquest.

3 L. Lozano, 'Adjustment and Democracy in Latin America', in S. Jonas and E. J. McCaughan (eds), *Latin America Faces the Twenty-First Century. Reconstructing a Social Justice Agenda* (Boulder, CO, Westview Press, 1995), p. 55.

4 L. Sklair, *Assembling for Development. The Maquila Industry in Mexico and the USA* (Boston, Unwin Hyman, 1989), p. 1.

5 ISI is discussed in Chapter 3 note 30. An additional critique of ISI strategies and the obstacles they faced is found in Cardoso and Helwege, *Latin America's Economy*, pp. 84–99.

6 D. Barkin, I. Ortiz and F. Rosen, 'Globalization and Resistance. The Remaking of Mexico', *NACLA. Report on the Americas*, XXX: 4 (January–February 1997), 22.

7 Amongst the most stimulating books on the debt crisis are B. Stallings and R. Kaufman (eds), *Debt and Democracy in Latin America* (Boulder, CO, Westview Press, 1989) and R. Thorp and L. Whitehead (eds), *Latin American Debt and the Adjustment Crisis* (Basingstoke, Macmillan, 1987). S. Branford and B. Kucinski, *The Debt Squads. The US, the Banks and Latin America* (London, Zed Books, 1988) provides a comprehensive account of the institutional relationships between the IMF, the banks, other governments and Latin America and the various negotiation and rescheduling processes of the 1980s. D. Green, *Silent Revolution. The Rise of Market Economics in Latin America* (London, Latin America Bureau, 1995) charts the bankruptcy of ISI and the rise of neo-liberalism. Both the latter two volumes also discuss the social costs and popular resistance to restructuring policies (in chs 3 and 4 respectively).

8 C. M. Vilas, 'Participation, Inequality, and the Whereabouts of Democracy', in C. M. Vilas, D. A. Chalmers, K. Hite, S. B. Martin, K. Piester and M. Segarra (eds), *The New Politics of Inequality in Latin America. Rethinking Participation and Representation* (Oxford, Oxford University Press, 1997), p. 21. Elsewhere, Vilas demonstrates how these figures reversed the downward trend of the previous 20 years in that the percentage of the poor had been reduced from 51 per cent in 1960 to 33 per cent in 1980 ('Neoliberal Social Policy. Managing Poverty', *NACLA. Report on the Americas*, XXIX: 6, May–June 1996, 16). He explains that reduction of poverty was the result of state economic interventionism, with new social sectors joining the labour market and an improved and more equal (although this was highly relative) distribution of income.

9 Vilas, 'Neoliberal', 14.

10 Cardoso and Helwege, *Latin America's Economy*, p. 208. Also J. Crabtree, *Peru Under García. An Opportunity Lost* (Basingstoke, Macmillan, 1992), pp. 39–45.

11 M. Peralta Ramos, 'Economic Policy and Distributional Conflict among Business Groups in Argentina: From Alfonsín to Menem', in E. C. Epstein (ed.), *The New Argentinian Democracy. The Search for a Successful Formula* (Westport, CT, Praeger, 1992).

12 M. González de la Rocha and A. Escobar Latapí (eds), *Social Responses to Mexico's Economic Crisis of the 1980s* (San Diego, University of California Center for US–Mexican Studies, 1991) describes the impact of restructuring upon different social classes. Other references include C. M. Vilas, *Between Earthquakes and*

Volcanoes. Market, State and the Revolutions in Central America (New York, Monthly Review Press, 1995 (ch. 4); B. F. Crisp, 'Lessons from Economic Reform in the Venezuelan Democracy', *Latin American Research Review*, 33: 1 (1998) and D. G. Richards, 'The Political Economy of the Chilean Miracle', *Latin American Research Review*, 32: 1 (1997).

13 S. Rosenfeld and J. L. Marré, 'How Chile's Rich Got Richer', *NACLA. Report on the Americas*, XXX: 6 (May–June 1997) discuss a phenomenon which is true throughout Latin America. There is an ongoing radical redistribution of wealth to entrenched elites through their membership of conglomerates *(grupos)* who have benefited from the selling off of industries, utilities and pension funds; this wealth is spent in ever-more conspicuous consumption, stock-market speculation and capital flight. The super-rich benefit from the absence of an equitable and effective tax system and ineffectual governmental regulation.

14 F. J. Hinkelammert, 'Our Project for the New Society in Latin America: The Regulating Role of the State and Problems of Self-Regulation in the Market', in Jonas and McCaughan (eds), *Latin America*, p. 19.

15 Barkin *et al.*, 'Globalization', 22.

16 *Ibid.*

17 J. Sheahan, 'Effects of Liberalization Programs on Poverty and Inequality: Chile, Mexico and Peru', *Latin American Research Review*, 3: 3 (1997), 19–20.

18 Tax evasion is the norm in Latin America. Taxes are not levied on income but at points of expenditure (sales taxes, customs fees, official transactions). The rich and the very rich evade taxation.

19 Cardoso and Helwege, *Latin America's Economy*, p. 223. Their ch. 9 examines the nature of this poverty, ranging from definitions of who constitute 'the poor', the structure and organization of the informal sector, the physical environment of shanty-town life and the health and deprivation problems experienced by those who are excluded from even the most rudimentary notions of a minimum wage or a minimum food intake.

20 C. Abel and C. M. Lewis (eds), *Welfare, Poverty and Development in Latin America* (Basingstoke, Macmillan, 1993), p. 2.

21 H. de Soto, *El Otro Sendero* (London, Tauris, 1989).

22 Abel and Lewis (eds), *Welfare*, p. 15.

23 Barkin *et al.*, 'Globalization', 25.

24 Such pacts are presented as a means of involving diverse social groups in the processes of decision-making and implicating them as responsible for the decisions made. The reality is that, given the division of economic and political power within the state, these can never be equal partnerships. A comprehensive account of the processes of *concertacíon* is provide by R. Berlins Collier and D. Collier, *Shaping the Political Arena. Critical Junctures, The Labor Movement and Regime Dynamics in Latin America* (Princeton, NJ, Princeton University Press, 1997).

25 R. Munck, 'Workers, Structural Adjustment and Concertación Social in Latin America', *Latin American Perspectives*, 82: 21: 3 (Summer 1994), 95.

26 Useful accounts of the nature of *maquila* production are given in Sklair, *Assembling*, H. Browne, *For Richer, For Poorer. Shaping US–Mexican Integration* (London, Latin America Bureau, 1994) and A. Dwyer, *On the Line. Life on the US–Mexican Border* (London, Latin America Bureau, 1994).

27 Sklair, *Assembling*, p. 208.

28 The future of education is discussed by A. Puiggros, 'World Bank Education Policy. Market Liberalism Meets Ideological Conservatism', *NACLA. Report on*

the Americas, XXIX: 6 (May–June 1996). A case study on the impact of neoliberalism upon Chilean teachers is given in L. Lomnitz and A. Melnick, *Chile's Middle Class. A Struggle for Survival in the Face of Neoliberalism* (Boulder, CO, Lynne Rienner, 1991).

29 For a discussion of the FSLN's social policies see P. Sollis, 'Welfare in Nicaragua: the *Somocista* and *Sandinista* Experiences Compared', in Abel and Lewis (eds), *Welfare*.

30 R. J. Spalding, *Capitalists and Revolution in Nicaragua. Opposition and Accommodation, 1979–93* (Chapel Hill, University of North Carolina Press, 1994), p. 155. Spalding makes the point that the FSLN's economic strategy was just as ambivalent, constantly shifting between socialist rhetoric and pragmatic compromise in an effort to maintain popular support.

31 Cardoso and Helwege, *Latin America's Economy*, p. 214.

32 *Ibid.*, p. 215.

33 Spalding, *Capitalists*, p. 102.

34 M. E. Conroy, 'External Dependence, External Assistance, and Economic Aggression Against Nicaragua', *Latin American Perspectives*, 45: 12: 2 (Spring 1985), 39.

35 J. Sheahan, *Patterns of Development in Latin America. Poverty, Repression and Economic Strategy* (Princeton, NJ, Princeton University Press, 1987), p. 243.

36 Cardoso and Helwege, *Latin America's Economy*, p. 244.

37 'As Cuba finds itself having to administer its own "structural adjustment" and prepare for more . . . cost-effective, less technified basic-needs approaches in its "special period", new pressures will be on the rural household; social welfare and equity will again be at stake' (J. Stubbs, 'Social Equity, Agrarian Transition and Development in Cuba, 1945–90', in Abel and Lewis (eds), *Welfare*, p. 293. The 'Special Period' is examined by D. Parker, 'The Cuban Crisis and the Future of the Revolution: A Latin American Perspective', *Latin American Research Review*, 33: 1 (1998) and F. T. Fitzgerald, *The Cuban Revolution in Crisis. From Managing Socialism to Managing Survival* (New York, Monthly Review Press, 1994).

38 V. Bulmer Thomas, N. Craske and M. Serrano, 'Who Will Benefit?', in Thomas, Craske and Serrano (eds), *Mexico and the North American Free Trade Agreement. Who Will Benefit?* (Basingstoke, Macmillan, 1994), p. 204.

39 The formation of this reserve army of labour has been aided by the imposition of ever-stricter border controls which prevent migrant workers moving north of the Rio Grande, and the privatization of the *ejidos* (Communally owned lands instituted after the Revolution), which have ensured a steady flow of desperate peasants to the cities.

40 K. Appendini, ('Agriculture and Farmers within NAFTA: A Mexican Perspective', in Bulmer Thomas *et al.* (eds), *Mexico*) describes the impact the agreement has had upon differentiation between farmers. Some crops – fruit and vegetables, for example – offer a competitive advantage (in terms of a propitious climate, the leasing of ex-*ejido* lands, low labour costs, the availability of irrigation and a good foreign exchange value), but the majority of small peasant producers cultivate basic food and animal feeds for domestic consumption which are not attractive to the international market.

41 R. Munck, 'After the Transition: Democratic Disenchantment in Latin America', *European Review of Latin American and Caribbean Studies*, 55 (1993), 13.

42 Barkin *et al.*, 'Globalization', 16.

43 Dwyer, *On the Line*, ch. 8 discusses these linkages. The US labour movement is concerned that so-called open trade allows US companies to relocate their activities

to Mexico and then deluge the domestic market with cheap goods, which will have a detrimental impact upon employment and market competitiveness.

44 Proposals with respect to strategies which could reform state structures and practice as well as promoting economic growth and social equity are offered by J. G. Castañeda, *Utopia Unarmed. The Latin American Left After The Cold War* (New York, Vintage Books, 1994), ch. 13.

45 Hinkelammert, 'Our Project', pp. 21, 22.

46 Borón, *State*, p. 172. This would involve a complete rejection of the orthodoxy of the last decades.

47 L. C. Bresser Pereira, J. M. Maravall and A. Przeworski, *Economic Reforms in New Democracies. A Social–Democratic Approach* (Cambridge, Cambridge University Press, 1993), p. 35.

48 M. Naim, 'New Competitive Tigers or Old Populist Nationalisms?', in J. S. Tuchin with B. Romero (eds), *The Consolidation of Democracy in Latin America* (Boulder, CO, Lynne Rienner, 1995).

49 Munck, 'After', 14.

50 The evolution of the insurgencies in El Salvador and Guatemala and the complex political environment in which they operated are analysed with great clarity and insight by J. Dunkerley, *The Long War. Dictatorship and Revolution in El Salvador* (London, Verso, 1982) and S. Jonas, *The Battle for Guatemala. Rebels, Death Squads, and US Power* (Boulder, CO, Westview Press, 1991). The harrowing personal and social costs of these long, immensely brutal conflicts are discussed by J. Didion, *Salvador* (London, Chatto & Windus, 1983) and R. Menchú, *I, Rigoberta Menchú. A Peasant Woman in Guatemala* (London, Verso, 1984). US involvement is dissected in J. Peck (ed.), *The Chomsky Reader* (New York, Pantheon, 1987).

51 S. Jonas, 'Contradictions in Guatemala's "Political Openings"', in S. Jonas and N. Stein (eds), *Democracy in Latin America. Visions and Realities* (New York, Bergin & Garvey, 1990), p. 68. She concludes that peace had resulted in 'the transformation of a national security dictatorship into a national security democracy' (p. 81). In El Salvador in 1993, it was evident that the military resolutely believed in its right to intervene; its attempted coup was defeated by popular mobilization.

52 Vilas, *Between*, p. 183.

53 Jonas, 'Contradictions', p. 241.

54 L. Whitehead, 'The Prospects for a Political Settlement: Most Options have been Foreclosed', in G. Di Palma and L. Whitehead (eds), *The Central American Impasse* (London, Croom Helm, 1986), p. 219.

55 R. Vargas Meza, 'The FARC, the War and the Crisis of the State', *NACLA. Report on the Americas*, XXXI: 5 (March–April 1998). The paramilitaries do not engage in battle with the guerrillas; rather they target the civilian population, unleashing a reign of terror on left-wing activists, trade unionists, human rights groups, base communities and peasant defence forces. It is clear that their activities are facilitated by both the military and the state, and they have close links with the drug cartels. Paramilitary groups have insisted that they participate in any negotiations to which the FARC will be party. The nature of the 'peace' discussed must be a matter of anxiety.

56 An extremely detailed and insightful account of the stages of the Peruvian insurgency is given by G. Gorriti Ellenbogen, *Sendero. Historia de la Guerra Milenaria en el Perú* (Lima, Editorial Apoyo, 1990).

57 L. Taylor, 'Counter-insurgency, the PCP-Sendero Luminoso and the civil war in Peru, 1980–1996', *Bulletin of Latin American Research*, 17: 1 (1998).

58 *Ibid.*, 52.

59 C. I. Degregori, 'Shining Path and Counterinsurgency Strategy Since the Arrest of Abimael Guzmán', in J. S. Tulchin and G. Bland (eds), *Peru in Crisis: Dictatorship or Democracy?* (Boulder, CO, Lynne Rienner, 1994), p. 82.

60 L. Hernández Navarro, 'The Escalation of the War in Chiapas', *NACLA. Report on the Americas*, XXXI: 5 (March–April 1998), 8.

61 F. Agüero, 'The Military and the Limits to Democratization in South America', in S. Mainwaring, G. O'Donnell and J. S. Valenzuela (eds), *Issues in Democratic Consolidation. The New South American Democracies in Comparative Perspective* (Bloomington, University of Notre Dame Press, 1992), p. 155.

62 *Ibid.*, p. 154. It is not always just a spectre. There were four military risings in Argentina during the Alfonsín presidency. He had initially attempted to curtail the military's autonomy by imposing limits on expenditure and bringing civilians into the National Defence Council and the Ministry of Defence. The 1988 National Defence Law took security functions away from military control and attempted to institutionalize military subordination to the civilian state. However, these were superficial measures which were not implemented effectively; the new democracy's weakness and the military's growing assertiveness were apparent (a major impulse was to lay the demoralization which had followed the Malvinas defeat to rest). In the 1990s, Carlos Menem actively courted the High Command, contributing to the increasingly authoritarian political culture. For a discussion of the risings, see D. Pion-Berlin and E. López, 'A House Divided: Crisis, Cleavage and Conflict in the Argentine Army', in E. C. Epstein (ed.), *The New Argentine Democracy. The Search for a Successful Formula* (Westport, CT, Praeger, 1992).

63 The epidemic of crime and the chaos which prevails in Venezuelan prisons is described by M. Ungar, 'Prison Mayhem. Venezuela's Explosive Penitentiary Crisis', *NACLA. Report on the Americas*, XXX: 2 (September–October 1996). The identification of the poor as the perpetrators of crime has been called the 'apartheid of justice' (P. S. Pinheiro, 'Democracies without Citizenship', *NACLA. Report on the Americas*, XXX: 2 (September–October 1996), 22). Class and wealth are projected as the signifiers of who are and who are not criminals. This effectively despoils the citizenship of the poor, the homeless and the politically marginalized.

64 D. Mabry (ed.), *The Latin American Narcotics Trade and US National Security* (New York, Greenwood Press, 1989) and E. Joyce and C. Malamud, *Latin America and the Multinational Drug Trade* (London, Macmillan, 1998).

Conclusion

The title of this book poses the question of whether it is possible to entertain the idea of a 'new politics' in contemporary Latin and Central America. Such a category would encompass the varied resistance, defence and empowerment strategies pursued by poor, marginalized and victimized communities, as well as those sectors who campaign for respect for citizenship rights in their attempts to have an impact upon the 'old politics' of exclusionary and authoritarian institutions and processes which has been dominant throughout this century. Within the context of the two perspectives upon democratic theory and practice which provide the backbone of this work, the central issue is if the liberal, pacted model remains central to political discourse or whether it has been substantially challenged and forced to adapt by the radical participatory model. The latter view concerning the nature of a desirable political culture is widely held by diverse groups, including the democratized Left, the women's organizations demanding gender equality, indigenous groups calling for an end to racial discrimination, housing and community groups, small businesses, CEBs, radical unionists, and gay and lesbian activists mobilizing around the need for society to acknowledge the existence of different sexualities and gender identities. Many have recognized the need to work together in their campaigns for social justice. Thus, the guerrillas of the Mexican EZLN have introduced the concept of a social Left based upon a partnership with the PRD, other radical parties, the liberation Church and a broad range of social movements. Such a coalition would have a national political agenda rather than the individual, fragmented ones that popular movements have typically pursued. One of the Zapatista leaders, Comandante Marcos, in a talk to members of the debtors' organization, El Barzón, in July 1996, stated that 'If we had to give our support, that force would be civil society, a force independent of the political parties, or which, including them, was greater than the egotism of their leaderships, more inclusive than particular sectarianisms.'[1]

Some writers have wanted to broaden the definition of what constitutes popular mobilization. Thus, Vilas contends that 'the popular' represents 'the intersection of economic exploitation, political oppression, and poverty' and 'a self-identification of subordination and oppression (labor, ethnic, gender . . .) in the face of a domination that is articulated by exploitation (insufficient income, meager wages, denial of a dignified life or prospects for the future) and is expressed institutionally through insecurity, arbitrariness, and socially biased coercion.'[2] Taken together, these concerns translate into 'opposition to established power' and its resistance to change. I have demonstrated the difficulties such a wide coalition has in orchestrating its activities and co-ordinating the pressures it has hoped to exert upon incumbent governments and embedded conservative institutions such as the military, the hierarchy of the Catholic Church and business elites, all of which identify these participatory impulses as contesting their vested interests, both ideological and socio-economic. Vilas contrasts the dichotomy between the endorsement of formal democratic and constitutional rights by the contemporary state and the exclusion from the freedoms and opportunities offered by citizenship of the poor, women, the young and ethnic groups; he believes that contemporary political systems continue to work on behalf of 'men, . . . whites or mestizos, . . . those who have stable jobs, . . . adults'.[3]

Another contradiction revolves around the different views the pacted and radical models of democracy possess upon whether the latter should be procedural or substantial, and the manner in which the relationship between political institutions and social demands is articulated, that is, the interaction of the state and civil society. Lucy Taylor, in her study of citizenship in Chile and Argentina, distinguishes between the constitutional definition of citizenship – which is likely to posit it as one of unrestricted equality – and the way that that is translated into political and socio-economic practice and the relationships between government and governed – which may provide a more differentiated and constrained picture. She identifies a neo-liberal model of citizenship which fragments society into individuals, and as a result offers a reinterpretation of sovereignty: 'Instead of power residing in the political arena and being expressed through a universalized political identity, power is located in the social arena and is expressed through an individualized, social identity.'[4] If this definition is accepted, then, 'politics become irrelevant', as neither the state nor society has any responsibility for the actions of sovereign individuals, and 'the mechanism of participation is the market and it is through the identity of producer, and most especially consumer, that the citizen exercises her sovereignty'.[5] The participatory model of citizenship is completely opposed to this view in that it argues that citizens should involve themselves fully in the political community, recognizing that a collective interest and collective responsibilities exist and matter. Participation is seen as the hallmark of a thriving democracy.

My presentation of the characteristics of existing political regimes in Chapter 2 suggested that the nature of the 'democracy' they project has many flaws and limitations and that many are undergoing considerable tensions and crises. The literature on formal transitions from military to civilian regimes, which took much of its inspiration from the way in which consolidated systems such as the Mexican and Venezuelan had evolved, tended to emphasize (albeit with some reservations) the importance of electoral arrangements, competition between political parties, elite interactions and the restricted nature of political and socio-economic agendas and programmes. There was an implicit acceptance of the need for strong executives and, thus, the existence of weak legislative and judicial branches of government as well as a recognition of the inability of civilian authorities to exercise control over the military. In sum, this paradigm was concerned with the rules of democracy and its limited outcomes rather than being committed to broadening and deepening that democracy in order to improve the living conditions and expectations of the broad sectors of society.

Latin American political systems exhibit these features as elements of what Guillermo O'Donnell has termed 'delegative democracy'.[6] This combines traditional *hacer política* (patron–client networks and the dependency cultures they create, the importance of populist political leaders and the absence of coherent political programmes) with the dominance of executive power within government, and the continuation of military veto over legislation and of immunity from prosecution for past and present crimes against citizens. Together, these suggest a trend towards mounting authoritarianism with, as its concomitant, a decline in an already weak democratic culture. These factors have facilitated the emergence of political mavericks such as Fujimori, Collor de Mello and Menem at the national and all lower levels of government, contribute to the disappearance of strong partisan identification, and encourage the disintegration of the linkages of loyalty and legitimacy between state and citizens. Political parties – of both left, right and centre – have proved resistant to internal democratization, frequently fail to offer voters real choices at elections and their chronic factionalism allows presidents to take the upper hand. Hoskin states that 'Most Latin American parties are organizationally weak, shallowly rooted in civil society, ideologically bankrupt, nonaccountable to their electorates, and increasingly less relevant than technocrats in the formation of economic policy.'[7]

The situation is further compounded by the mounting incidence of corruption, linked to elite enrichment through the privatization of state resources as a consequence of the near universal endorsement of neo-liberal 'reforms'. Free-market neo-liberalism has opened up new possibilities for corrupt behaviour penetrating all levels of the state, from presidents downwards. Judicial systems have been brought into grave disrepute because of their inept handling of charges of corruption against state officials. The impeachments of Presidents Carlos Andrés Pérez of Venezuela and Fernando Collor de Mello of Brazil, both in 1993, are evidence that an independent legal system can still operate. Nevertheless, the ability of other presidents, such as Salinas de Gortari of Mexico and García of Peru, to avoid justice, and the prevalence of the massive collusion of state officials and elected politicians in insider dealing and drug trafficking, are serious constraints upon the functioning of a democratic system.

Their adherents contend that contemporary political systems may be far from perfect, but that they do ensure the stability which greater democracy and participation would endanger. I contest this view, believing that there is increasing disenchantment on the part of large sectors of societies and the risk of ungovernability which will stimulate greater authoritarianism and the possibility of military intervention. How can such an eventuality be prevented? In his discussion of Mexican politics, Garrido argues for the following necessary changes. The first would be the decentralization of power to regional and local government, which would be underpinned by ending the power of local and regional bosses within both party and state bureaucracies. Implicit in this process would be a reduction in executive power and an increase in legislative influence over policy-making, and ensuring the accountability of public officials. Opposition parties should be brought into decision-making, as should popular organizations. Attempts by the PRI–state to manipulate the latter through the formation of corporatist relations should be abandoned. Corruption should be rooted out both in terms of fraudulent elections and patronage and malpractice within the state. The PRI should accept the fact that it could be defeated at the national level and still survive as a political force.[8] Obviously, some of these suggestions focus exclusively upon Mexico, but the majority could be applied to other Latin and Central American states. All are eminently sensible, but a belief that they will be adopted by incumbent regimes appears very optimistic. The political will to initiate such a root-and-branch approach to deepening democracy just does not exist within political elites.

A fundamental constraint upon even piecemeal reform of these political systems is the pre-eminence of neo-liberal economic strategies. Neo-liberalism does not need representative and responsible participatory processes; as described in the previous chapter, it is inherently anti-popular. Governments accede to the demands of domestic and international finance capital and continue to receive its support only so long as they maintain the political stability which it requires. Business looks to the short-term profit, not long-term investment, in either development projects or democracy. It is mistrustful of government, alarmed by popular mobilization and resolutely opposed to reform of the financial and fiscal sytems, taxation, income distribution and employment practices. Catherine Conaghan maintains that in the Andean countries, domestic capital remains sceptical 'about the ability of politicians and technocrats to engineer a stable investment climate and policy predictability'; this scepticism might lead it to speculate about the stability military rule might provide.[9] Given that, one may wonder how long the neo-liberal project can endure before it provokes widespread and sustained social discontent; such an outcome in some countries might be more rather than less likely. However, the resilience of the 'old politics' and its inability to adapt to changing circumstances and to some degree reinvent itself, should not be forgotten.

Under the aegis of neo-liberalism and in the shadow of the question of debt repayment, the state's boundaries have been transformed, but to the benefit of the rich and privileged, and in the context of a political economy which connects with global processes, institutions and actors rather than making domestic development its priority. Indeed, its vulnerability to international recession, the impact of protectionist policies introduced in the North and the exigencies of the debt will combine to undermine any future attempts by the Latin American state to turn away from neo-liberalism in favour of a more distribution-oriented and inclusionary political economy. The poor, the working and middle classes continue to suffer as income distribution has become even more skewed and the trajectory and focus of economic decision-making has narrowed. They have also been adversely affected by the reformulation of the state's role as it has denied its obligation to provide services, security and modernization and, in their place, has concentrated upon regulating debt repayments and selling off the national family silver to a burgeoning elite which appears to harbour no instincts leading it to social responsibility.

These political and economic circumstances suggest that the development of democratic fatigue to which I referred in the early chapters of this book will continue and become more pervasive. Ronaldo Munck has talked of the phenomenon of *desgaste* both in physical terms (the wear and tear of daily life, the disintegration of productive plant and infrastructure and the detrimental consequences to the wellbeing and psychological health of human beings) and in the political and cultural sense. Economic restructuring, the dismantling of the state's social role and the fragmentation of political alignments has, arguably, also resulted in a 'destructuring of social and political identities'.[10] 'Democracy' has not satisfied people's expectations, has not ensured security, safety from harassment, individual freedoms or social improvement. Disappointment with these failures can and may result in the perceived attractiveness of populist, authoritarian options. It can also undermine efforts to produce radical political alternatives by the Left or popular organizations within civil society. At the very least, and this is clearly evident in Latin America today, it may lead to the demobilization of that civil society and, as Munck suggests, 'the withdrawal from the public arena to the private is a poor basis on which to build a democratic citizenship and stable political institutions'.[11]

If Munck's sober reading of the implications of the present political economy in Latin and Central America is correct, the opportunity for the development of an agenda which challenges the domination of the limited form of pacted democracy and aspires to restructure political cultures along radical, participatory lines appears very limited. The transformation of the state and its submission to the market has had profound repercussions upon the ability of popular movements to have an impact upon politics. Hinkelammert contends that if the state uses its power positively, it is in a position to 'universalize the actions of the popular organizations', but 'Without this universalization, resistance becomes as fragmented as is human activity within the market, and it consequently reproduces the destructive effects of the market without being able to correct them.'[12] My analysis of the niches that the democratized Left, new social movements and women's organizations occupy within contemporary political cultures attests to the persistent fragmentation that they endure and to the immense difficulties involved in achieving a coherent and co-ordinated programme of action. They operate within a hostile environment and under the shadow of structural constraints which are compounded by their own internal problems and differences. This, however, is the universe in which they *must* operate; popular sectors and social movements and all those groups concerned with a participatory conception of democracy have to deal with the present political system in the best way they can.

Thus, with respect to the women's movement, Sonia Alvarez discusses a double strategy of inside and outside the state. Women must pressurize government to adopt 'gender-specific policy outputs', exploiting political differences between politicians, ministries and bureaucrats, as well as concentrating upon consolidating the momentum of independent women's activism.[13] For Shirin Rai, democratization presents ambiguous possibilities for women. The liberal discourse on citizenship rights is highly individual and repudiates political intervention in the private sphere. The possession of individual rights is vital, but women – as with all social groups who feel excluded from the exercise of power – also have to accept that they have to negotiate with the state for their enjoyment of these rights. It will not give them freely. Such negotiations can only be accomplished in a collective manner and, thus, must be sustained by a participatory ethos grounded in the recognition of *society* which the neo-liberal outlook denies.[14] We can consider the role of the Left in a similar fashion. Left-wing parties have had to come to terms with three separate, although connected, spheres of action. The first is that they must accept democratic principles in their own organizations and their dealings with other actors; the second is that, having decided to participate in electoral regimes, they must still attempt to create a distinctive personality and strategies which do not betray the interests of their constituencies; and the last is that they must support rather than try to direct the diverse expressions of popular democracy. For Jorge Castañeda, 'the first democratic order of battle for the left [is] to encourage every conceivable expression of civil society, every social movement, every form of self-management that Latin American reality generates'. As discussed in Chapter 3, he believes that the best opportunity for such an expression is in municipal politics, that politics which is closest to local communities and movements.[15]

The difficult and tenuous condition of the 'new politics' is addressed by Chalmers, Martin and Piester, who introduce the concept of 'associative networks' of social movements to the debate. They contrast this idea with previous analyses, which have described popular mobilization in terms of its incorporation by populist regimes, the class-based model of it long endorsed by the Left and the liberal perspective which regards it as a problem rather than a contribution to democracy. The authors embrace the notion of this mobilization as the result of multiple and constantly changing interactions between a diverse range of social actors, whose involvements alter under the pressure of regime shifts, the history of particular communities and individual circumstances. The result, they imply, is a flexible relationship between the popular sectors and the state, which also involves NGOs and government consultative bodies, as well as foreign agencies, and which finds itself in a process of constant reconfiguration. Not all members of the popular sector are involved in this process, but the consequence is that one sees 'A highly differentiated and rapidly shifting set of popular groups struggling, and sometimes succeeding, to form a cluster of organizations equipped to recognize, analyze, debate, and bring pressure to bear on issues.'[16] Popular organizations enter such networks with disadvantages in terms of their access to resourcing, information and influence, and their outcomes are always going to be unpredictable. No matter how organized and militant, the popular sectors will not necessarily be taken seriously by the state. However, their activism is ongoing and is impelled by the ideal of social justice. The pursuit of political, economic and social equity will be multifaceted, with different actors committed to both particular and common objectives, and the accomplishment of justice and participation 'will be [effected] if at all, *by many individuals and organizations operating in many different arenas*'.[17]

As I finish writing this book in late 1998, prognostications for the future of Latin and Central America are mixed. Generally the region is ignored by the North unless crises occur; currently these include the political and legal debates concerning the proposed extradition of ex-General Pinochet from London to Spain, which has revived discussion about the legacy of military regimes and the abdication of civilian governments in response to the social and human need for injustices, violations and massacres to be both recognized and vindicated. Another issue is the aftermath of Hurricane Mitch within Central America which, apart from highlighting the tremendous poverty of these societies (without, of course, explaining the historical causes of this), has brought the debt debate back into fashion (as if, somehow, it had disappeared from the consciousness of the North). I began this book with the Mexican Zapatistas and I would wish to end it with them. The EZLN, amid intensifying levels of state violence, has proposed a countrywide rebel plebiscite in 1999 which would hope to expose the emptiness of the PRI – State's defensive and repressive stance. What this says is that the forces which are dedicated to a new, equitable and participatory formulation of Latin American politics may still be subordinate, but that they will continue to challenge inept, invidious and profoundly anti-democratic systems.

Notes

1 D. I. Barkin, I. Ortiz and F. Rosen, 'Globalization and Resistance. The Remaking of Mexico', *NACLA. Report on the Americas*, XXX: 4 (January–February 1997), 27.

2 C. M. Vilas, 'Participation, Inequality, and the Whereabouts of Democracy', in C. M. Vilas, D. A. Chalmers, K. Hite, S. B. Martin, K. Piester and M. Segarra (eds), *The New Politics of Inequality in Latin America. Rethinking Participation and Representation* (Oxford, Oxford University Press, 1997), p. 6.

3 *Ibid.*, p. 8.

4 L. Taylor, *Citizenship, Participation and Democracy. Changing Dynamics in Chile and Argentina* (Basingstoke, Macmillan, 1998), p. 25.

5 *Ibid.*, p. 26.

6 G. O'Donnell, 'Delegative Democracy', *Journal of Democracy*, 5: 1 (1994).

7 G. Hoskin, 'Democratisation in Latin America', *Latin American Research Review*, 32: 3 (1997), 215.

8 L. J. Garrido, 'The Crisis of Presidencialismo', in W. A. Cornelius, J. Gentleman and P. H. Smith (eds), *Mexico's Alternative Political Futures* (San Diego, University of California Center for US–Mexican Studies, 1990).

9 C. M. Conaghan, 'Capitalists, Technocrats and Politicians: Economic Policy-making and Democracy in the Central Andes', in S. Mainwaring, G. O'Donnell and S. Valenzuela (eds), *Issues in Democratic Consolidation: The New South American Democracies in Comparative Perspective* (Indiana, University of Notre Dame Press, 1992), p. 234.

10 R. Munck, 'After the Transition: Democratic Disenchantment in Latin America', *European Review of Latin American and Caribbean Studies*, 55 (December 1993), 17.

11 *Ibid.*, 15.

12 F. J. Hinkelammert, 'Our Project for the New Society in Latin America: The Regulating Role of the State and Problems of Self-Regulation in the Market', in S. Jonas and E. J. McCaughan (eds), *Latin America faces the Twenty First Century. Reconstructing a Social Justice Agenda* (Boulder, CO, Westview Press, 1995), p. 23.

13 S. Alvarez, *Engendering Democracy in Brazil. Women's Movements in Transition Politics* (Princeton, NJ, Princeton University Press, 1990), p. 213.

14 S. M. Rai, 'Gender and Democratization: Or What Does Democracy Mean for Women in the Third World?', *Democratization*, 1: 2 (1994), 226.

15 J. G. Castañeda, *Utopia Unarmed. The Latin American Left After The Cold War* (New York, Vintage Books, 1994), p. 372.

16 D. A. Chalmers, S. B. Martin and K. Piester, 'Associative Networks: New Structures of Representation for the Popular Sectors?', in Vilas *et al.* (eds), *The New Politics*, p. 571.

17 *Ibid.*, p. 582 (original emphasis).

Bibliography

Abel, C., and C. M. Lewis (eds), *Welfare, Poverty and Development in Latin America*, Basingstoke, Macmillan, 1993.

Adler Hellman, J., 'Mexican Popular Movements, Clientelism and the Process of Democratisation', *Latin American Perspectives*, 81: 21 (Spring 1994).

Afshar, H. (ed.), *Women and Politics in the Third World*, London, Routledge, 1996.

Agüero, F., 'The Military and the Limits to Democratization in South America', in S. Mainwaring, G. O'Donnell and J. S. Valenzuela (eds), *Issues in Democratic Consolidation. The New South American Democracies in Comparative Perspective*, Notre Dame, IN, University of Notre Dame Press, 1992.

Alecio, R., 'Uncovering the Truth: Political Violence and Indigenous Organisations', in M. Sinclair (ed.), *The New Politics of Survival. Grassroots Movements in Central America*, New York, Monthly Review Press, 1995.

Alvarez, S. E., 'Politicising Gender and Engendering Democracy', in A. Stepan (ed.), *Democratising Brazil. Problems of Transition and Consolidation*, Oxford, Oxford University Press, 1989.

Alvarez, S. E., *Engendering Democracy in Brazil. Women's Movements in Transition Politics*, Princeton, NJ, Princeton University Press, 1990.

Andreas, C., *When Women Rebel. The Rise of Popular Feminism in Peru*, Westport, CT, Laurence Hill & Co., 1985.

Angell, A., 'Why is the Transition to Democracy Proving So Difficult in Chile?', *Bulletin of Latin American Research*, 5: 1 (1980).

Appendini, K., 'Agriculture and Farmers within NAFTA: A Mexican Perspective', in V. Bulmer-Thomas, N. Craske and M. Serrano (eds), *Mexico and the North American Free Trade Agreement. Who Will Benefit?*, Basingstoke, Macmillan, 1994.

Archetti, E. P., P. Cammack and B. Roberts (eds), *Latin America*, London, Macmillan, 1987.

Arrate, J., and P. Hidalgo, *Pasión y Razón del Socialismo Chileno*, Santiago, Las Ediciones del Ornitorrinco, 1989.

Assies, W., G. Burgwal and T. Salman, *Structures of Power, Movements of Resistance. An Introduction to the Theories of Urban Movements in Latin America*, Amsterdam, CEDLA, 1990.

Azicri, M., 'Twenty-Six Years of Cuban Revolutionary Politics: An Appraisal', in S. Jonas and N. Stein (eds), *Democracy in Latin America. Visions and Reality*, New York, Bergin & Garvey, 1990.

Bachrach, P., and M. S. Baratz, 'Two Faces of Power', *American Political Science Review*, LVI: 4 (December 1962).

Bachrach, P., and M. S. Baratz, 'Decisions and Non-Decisions: An Analytical Framework', *American Political Science Review*, LVII: 3 (September 1963).

Ballón, E. (ed.), *Movimientos Sociales y Democracia: La Fundación de un Nuevo Orden*, Lima, Centro de Estudios y Promoción del Desarrollo, 1986.

Ballón, E., 'El proceso de constitución del movimiento popular peruano', in D. Camacho and R. Menjívar (eds), *Los movimientos populares en América latina*, Mexico, SigloVeintiuno Editores, 1989.

Banck, G., and A. M. Doimo, 'Between Utopia and Strategy: A Case Study of a Brazilian Urban Social Movement', in G. Banck and K. Koonings (eds), *Social Change in Contemporary Brazil*, Amsterdam, CEDLA, 1988.

Banck, G., and K. Koonings (eds), *Social Change in Contemporary Brazil*, Amsterdam, CEDLA, 1988.

Barkin, D. I., I. Ortiz and F. Rosen, 'Globalization and Resistance. The Remaking of Mexico', *NACLA. Report on the Americas*, XXX: 4 (January–February 1997).

Barricada Internacional, 'The São Paulo Forum. Looking for Alternatives', Managua, Nicaragua, XII: 352 (August 1992).

Barrig, M., 'The Difficult Equilibrium between Bread and Roses: Women's Organisations and the Transition from Dictatorship to Democracy in Peru', in J. S. Jaquette (ed.), *The Women's Movement in Latin America*, Boston, Unwin Hyman, 1989.

Barros, R., 'The Left and Democracy', *Telos*, 68 (1986).

Bascuñan Edwards, C., *La Izquierda sin Allende*, Santiago, Editorial Planeta Espejo de Chile, 1990.

Bell, D., *The End of Ideology: On the Exhaustion of Political Ideas in the Fifties*, New York, Free Press, 1965.

Benton, J., 'The Role of Women's Organisations and Groups in Community Development. A Case Study of Bolivia', in J. H. Momsen and V. Kinnaird (eds), *Different Places, Different Voices*, London, Routledge, 1993.

Berlins Collier, R., and D. Collier, *Shaping the Political Arena. Critical Junctures, the Labor Movement and Regime Dynamics in Latin America*, Princeton, NJ, Princeton University Press, 1997.

Bernales, E., *Crisis Política: Solución Electoral?*, Lima, Centro de Estudios y Promoción del Desarrollo, 1980.

Blanco, J. A., 'Cuba: Utopia and Reality Thirty Years Later', in Centro de Estudios Sobre América (ed.), *The Cuban Revolution Into the 1990s. Cuban Perspectives*, Boulder, CO, Westview Press, 1992.

Boeninger, E., 'The Chilean Road to Democracy', *Foreign Affairs*, 64 (1985–86).

Booth, D., and B. Sorj (eds), *Military Reformism and Social Classes: The Peruvian Experience, 1968–80*, London, Macmillan, 1982.

Borón, A., *State, Capitalism and Democracy in Latin America*, Boulder, CO, Lynne Rienner, 1995.

Branford, S., and B. Kucinski, *The Debt Squads. The US, the Banks and Latin America*, London, Zed Books, 1988.

Branford, S., and B. Kucinski, *Brazil: Carnival of the Oppressed. Lula and the Brazilian Workers' Party*, London, Latin America Bureau, 1995.

Brenner, P., and P. Kornbluh, 'Clinton's Cuba Calculus', *NACLA. Report on the Americas*, XXIX: 2 (September–October 1995).

Brentlinger, J., *The Best of What We Are. Reflections on the Nicaraguan Revolution*, Amherst, University of Massachusetts Press, 1995.

Bresser Pereira, L. C., J. M. Maravall and A. Przeworski, *Economic Reforms in New Democracies. A Social-Democratic Approach*, Cambridge, Cambridge University Press, 1993.

Brown, D., 'Sandinismo and the Problem of Democratic Hegemony', *Latin American Perspectives*, 65: 17: 2 (Spring 1990).

Browne, H., *For Richer, For Poorer. Shaping US–Mexican Integration*, London, Latin America Bureau, 1994.

Bulmer-Thomas, V., N. Craske and M. Serrano, 'Who Will Benefit?', in V. Bulmer-Thomes, N. Craske and M. Serrano (eds), *Mexico and the North American Free Trade Agreement. Who Will Benefit?*, Basingstoke, Macmillan, 1994.

Bulmer-Thomas, V., N. Craske and M. Serrano (eds), *Mexico and the North American Free Trade Agreement. Who Will Benefit?*, Basingstoke, Macmillan, 1994.

Bunck, J. M., *Fidel Castro and the Quest for a Revolutionary Culture in Cuba*, Philadelphia, Pennsylvania State University Press, 1994.

Burbach, R., and O. Nuñéz, *Fire in the Andes. Forging a Revolutionary Agenda*, London, Verso, 1987.

Bystydzienski, J. M. (ed.), *Women Transforming Politics. Worldwide Strategies for Empowerment*, Bloomington, Indiana University Press, 1992.

Camacho, D., 'Latin America: A Society in Motion', in P. Wignaraya (ed.), *New Social Movements in the South*, London, Zed Books, 1993.

Camacho, D., and R. Menjívar (eds), *Los movimientos populares en América latina*, Mexico, SigloVeintiuno Editores, 1989.

Cammack, P., 'Democratisation: A Review of the Issues', *Bulletin of Latin American Research*, 4: 2 (1985).

Cardoso, E., and A. Helwege, *Latin America's Economy. Diversity, Trends and Conflicts*, Cambridge, MA, MIT Press, 1992.

Carr, B., 'The Mexican Left, the Popular Movements and the Politics of Austerity, 1982–85', in B. Carr and R. Anzaldúa Montoya, *The Mexican Left, the Popular Movements and the Politics of Austerity*, San Diego, University of California Center for US–Mexican Studies, 1986.

Carr, B., 'The Left and its Potential Role in Political Change', in W. A. Cornelius, J. Gentleman and P. H. Smith (eds), *Mexico's Alternative Political Futures*, San Diego, University of California Center for US–Mexican Studies, 1990.

Carr, B., 'Mexico: The Perils of Unity and the Challenge of Modernization', in B. Carr and S. Ellner (eds), *The Latin American Left. From the Fall of Allende to Perestroika*, Boulder, CO, Westview Press, 1993.

Carr, B., and R. Anzaldúa Montoya, *The Mexican Left, the Popular Movements and the Politics of Austerity*, San Diego, University of California Center for US–Mexican Studies, 1986.

Carr, B., and S. Ellner (eds), *The Latin American Left. From the Fall of Allende to Perestroika*, Boulder, CO, Westview Press, 1993.

Carranza Valdés, J., 'The Current Situation in Cuba and the Process of Change', *Latin American Perspectives*, 69: 18: 2 (Spring 1991).

Castañeda, J. G., *Utopia Unarmed. The Latin American Left After The Cold War*, New York, Vintage Books, 1994.

Castañeda, J. G., *Compañero. The Life and Death of Che Guevara*, London, Bloomsbury, 1997.

Castells, M., *The City and the Grassroots*, London, Edward Arnold, 1983.

Cavarozzi, M., 'Patterns of Elite Negotiations and Confrontations in Argentina and Chile', in J. Higley and R. Gunther (eds), *Elites and Democratic Consolidation in Latin America and Southern Europe*, Cambridge, Cambridge University Press, 1992.

Cavarozzi, M., and O. Landis, 'Political Parties Under Alfonsín and Menem: the Effects of State Shrinking and the Devaluation of Democratic Politics', in E. C. Epstein (ed.), *The New Argentinian Democracy. The Search for a Successful Formula*, Westport, CT, Praeger, 1992.

Centro de Estudios Sobre América (ed.), *The Cuban Revolution Into the 1990s. Cuban Perspectives*, Boulder, CO, Westview Press, 1992.

Chalmers, D. A., M. do Carmo Campello de Souza and A. A. Borón (eds), *The Right and Democracy in Latin America*, New York, Praeger, 1992.

Chalmers, D. A., S. B. Martin and K. Piester, 'Associative Networks: New Structures of Representation for the Popular Sectors?', in C. M. Vilas, D. A. Chalmers, K. Hite, S. B. Martin, K. Piester and M. Segarra (eds), *The New Politics of Inequality in Latin America. Rethinking Participation and Representation*, Oxford, Oxford University Press, 1997.

Chaney, E. M., *Supermadre. Women in Politics in Latin America*, Austin, University of Texas Press, 1979.

Charlton, S. E. M., J. Everett and K. Staudt (eds), *Women, the State and Development*, Albany, State University of New York Press, 1989.

Chavkin, S., *Storm Over Chile*, Westport, CT, Lawrence Hill & Co., 1982.

Chilcote, R. H., 'Post-Marxism. The Retreat from Class in Latin America', *Latin American Perspectives*, 65: 17: 2 (Spring 1990).

Chilcote, R., S. Hadjiyannis, F. A. López III, D. Nataf and E. Sammis, *Transitions from Dictatorship to Democracy*, London, Taylor & Francis, 1990.

Chuchryk, P. M., 'Subversive Mothers: The Women's Opposition to the Military Regime in Chile', in S. E. M. Charlton, J. Everett and K. Staudt (eds), *Women, the State and Development*, Albany, State University of New York Press, 1989.

Chuchryk, P. M., 'Feminist Anti-Authoritarian Politics: The Role of Women's Organisations in the Chilean Transition to Democracy', in J. S. Jaquette (ed.), *The Women's Movement in Latin America*, Boston, Unwin Hyman, 1989.

Collier, D., *Squatters and Oligarchs: Authoritarian Rule and Policy Change in Peru*, Baltimore, MD, Johns Hopkins University Press, 1976.

Conaghan, C. M., 'Capitalists, Technocrats and Politicians: Economic Policy Making and Democracy in the Central Andes', in S. Mainwaring, G. O'Donnell and S. Valenzuela (eds), *Issues in Democratic Consolidation: The New South American Democracies in Comparative Perspective*, Notre Dame, IN, University of Notre Dame Press, 1992.

Conroy, M. E., 'External Dependence, External Assistance, and Economic Aggression Against Nicaragua', *Latin American Perspectives*, 45: 12: 2 (Spring 1985).

Coppedge, M., *Strong Parties and Lame Ducks. Presidential Partyarchy and Factionalism in Venezuela*, Stanford, CA, Stanford University Press, 1994.

Corcoran-Nantes, Y., 'Women and Popular Urban Social Movements in São Paulo, Brazil', *Bulletin of Latin American Research*, 9: 2 (1990).

Cornelius, W. A., J. Gentleman and P. H. Smith (eds), *Mexico's Alternative Political Futures*, San Diego, University of California Center for US–Mexican Studies, 1990.

Cornelius, W. A., J. Gentleman and P. H. Smith, 'Overview: The Dynamics of Political Change in Mexico', in W. A. Cornelius, J. Gentleman and P. H. Smith (eds), *Mexico's Alternative Political Futures*, San Diego, University of California Center for US–Mexican Studies, 1990.

Corradi, J. E., P. Weiss Fagan and M. A. Garretón (eds), *Fear At the Edge. State Terror and Resistance in Latin America*, Berkeley, University of California Press, 1992.

Corragio, J. L., and G. Irvin, 'Revolution and Democracy in Nicaragua', *Latin American Perspectives*, 45: 12: 2 (Spring 1985).

Cotler, J., 'Military Interventions and "Transfer of Power to Civilians" in Peru', in G. O'Donnell, P. Schmitter and L. Whitehead (eds), *Transitions from Authoritarian Rule: Prospects for Democracy*, Baltimore, MD, Johns Hopkins University Press, 1986.

Cotler, J., 'Los partidos políticos y la democracia en el Perú', in L. Pásara and J. Parodi (eds), *Democracia, Sociedad y Gobierno en el Perú*, Lima, Centro de Estudios de Democracia y Sociedad, 1987.

Crabtree, J., *Peru under García: An Opportunity Lost*, Basingstoke, Macmillan, 1992.

Crick, B., *In Defence of Politics*, Harmondsworth, Penguin, 1964.

Criquillon, A., 'The Nicaraguan Women's Movement: Feminist Reflections from Within', in M. Sinclair (ed.), *The New Politics of Survival. Grassroots Movements in Central America*, New York, Monthly Review Press, 1995.

Crisp, B. F., 'Lessons from Economic Reform in the Venezuelan Democracy', *Latin American Research Review*, 33: 1 (1998).

Dahl, R. A., *Who Governs? Democracy and Power in an American City*, London, Yale University Press, 1961.

Debray, R., *The Revolution on Trial*, Harmondsworth, Penguin, 1978, vol. 1.

Degregori, C. I., 'Shining Path and Counterinsurgency Strategy Since the Arrest of Abimael Guzmán', in J. S. Tulchin and G. Bland (eds), *Peru in Crisis: Dictatorship or Democracy?*, Boulder, CO, Lynne Rienner, 1994.

Delgardo, G., 'Ethnic Politics and the Popular Movement', in S. Jonas and E. J. McCaughan (eds), *Latin America Faces the Twenty First*

Century. Reconstructing a Social Justice Agenda, Boulder, CO, Westview Press, 1995.

De Mesquita Neto, P., 'Interview with Lula', *NACLA. Report on the Americas*, XXXI: 1 (July–August 1997).

De Rio Caldeiro, T. P., 'Women, Daily Life and Politics', in E. Jelin (ed.), *Women and Social Change in Latin America*, London, Zed Books, 1990.

De Soto, H., *El Otro Sendero*, London, Tauris, 1989.

Didion, J., *Salvador*, London, Chatto & Windus, 1983.

Dietz, H. A., 'Elites in an Unconsolidated Democracy: Peru During the 1980s', in J. Higley and R. Gunther (eds), *Elites and Democratic Consolidation in Latin America and Southern Europe*, Cambridge, Cambridge University Press, 1992.

Dietz, H. A., 'Peru Since 1990', *Latin American Research Review*, 33: 2 (1998).

Di Palma, G., and L. Whitehead (eds), *The Central American Impasse*, London, Croom Helm, 1986.

Drake, P. W., and I. Jaksic (eds), *The Struggle for Democracy in Chile, 1982–90*, Lincoln, University of Nebraska Press, 1991.

Dunkerley, J., *The Long War. Dictatorship and Revolution in El Salvador*, London, Verso, 1982.

Dunkerley, J., 'Beyond Utopia: The State of the Left in Latin America', *New Left Review*, 206 (July–August 1994).

Dwyer, A., *On the Line. Life on the US–Mexican Border*, London, Latin America Bureau, 1994.

Eckstein, S., *Power and Popular Protest: Latin American Social Movements*, Berkeley, University of California Press, 1989.

Elizondo, J. R., *Las Crisis de las Izquierdas en América Latina*, Caracas, Editorial Nueva Sociedad, 1990.

Ellner, S., *Venezuela's Movimiento al Socialismo. From Guerrilla Defeat to Innovative Politics*, Durham, NC and London, Duke University Press, 1988.

Ellner, S., 'The Changing Status of the Latin American Left in the Recent Past', in B. Carr and S. Ellner (eds), *The Latin American Left. From the Fall of Allende to Perestroika*, Boulder, CO, Westview Press, 1993.

Ellner, S., 'The Venezuelan Left: From Years of Prosperity to Economic Crisis', in B. Carr and S. Ellner (eds), *The Latin American Left. From the Fall of Allende to Perestroika*, Boulder, CO, Westview Press, 1993.

Ellner, S., 'Recent Venezuelan Political Studies: A Return to Third World Realities', *Latin American Research Review*, 32: 2 (1997).

Ellner, S., 'The Politics of Privatization', *NACLA. Report on the Americas*, XXXI: 3 (November–December 1997).

Epstein, E. C. (ed.), *The New Argentinian Democracy. The Search for a Successful Formula*, Westport, CT, Praeger, 1992.

Escobar, A., and S. Alvarez (eds), *The Making of Social Movements in Latin America*, Boulder, CO, Westview Press, 1992.

Ethier, D., *Democratic Transition and Consolidation in Southern Europe, Latin America and Southeast Asia*, London, Macmillan, 1990.

Evers, T., 'Identity: The Hidden Side of New Social Movements in Latin America', in D. Slater (ed.), *New Social Movements and the State in Latin America*, Amsterdam, CEDLA, 1985.

Faúndez, J., *Marxism and Democracy in Chile. From 1932 to the Fall of Allende*, New Haven, CT, Yale University Press, 1988.

Fisher, J., *Out of the Shadows. Women, Resistance and Politics in South America*, London, Latin America Bureau, 1993.

Fitzgerald, F. T., *The Cuban Revolution in Crisis. From Managing Socialism to Managing Survival*, New York, Monthly Review Press, 1994.

Foweraker, J., 'Popular Movements and the Transformation of the System', in W. A. Cornelius, J. Gentleman and P. H. Smith (eds), *Mexico's Alternative Political Futures*, San Diego, University of California Center for US–Mexican Studies, 1990.

Foweraker, J., *Theorising Social Movements*, London, Pluto Press, 1995.

Fox, E., (ed.), *Media and Politics in Latin America. The Struggle for Democracy*, London, Sage, 1988.

Franco, J., 'The Long March of Feminism', *NACLA. Report on the Americas*, XXX1: 4 (January–February 1998).

Fruhling, H., 'Resistance to Fear in Chile: The Experience of the Vicaría de Solidaridad', in J. E. Corradi, P. Weiss-Fagan and M. Garréton (eds), *Fear at the Edge. State Terror and Resistance in Latin America*, Berkeley, University of California Press, 1992.

Fuentes, S. M., 'The Recent Chilean Women's Movement', in S. Wierenga (ed.), *Women's Struggles and Strategies*, Brookfield, VT, Gower, 1988.

Fukuyama, F., *The End of History and the Last Man*, Harmondsworth, Penguin, 1992.

Furci, C., *The Chilean Communist Party and the Road to Socialism*, London, Zed Books, 1984.

García Guadillo, M.-P., 'Ecología: Women, Environment and Politics in Venezuela', in S. A. Radcliffe and S. Westwood (eds), *'Viva'. Women and Popular Protest in Latin America*, London, Routledge, 1993.

Garretón, M. A., *The Chilean Political Process*, Boston, Unwin Hyman, 1989.

Garrido, L. J., 'The Crisis of Presidencialismo', in W. A. Cornelius, J. Gentleman and P. H. Smith (eds), *Mexico's Alternative Political Futures*, San Diego, University of California Center for US–Mexican Studies, 1990.

Gilbert, A., and J. Gugler, *Cities, Poverty and Development. Urbanisation in the Third World*, Oxford, Oxford University Press, 1982.

Gillespie, C. G., *Negotiating Democracy: Politicians and Generals in Uruguay*, Cambridge, Cambridge University Press, 1991.

Gillespie, C. G., 'The Role of Civilian–Military Pacts in Elite Settlements and Elite Convergency: Democratic Consolidation in Uruguay', in J. Higley and R. Gunther (eds), *Elites and Democratic Consolidation in Latin America and Southern Europe*, Cambridge, Cambridge University Press, 1992.

González de la Rocha, M., and A. Escobar Latapí (eds), *Social Responses to Mexico's Economic Crisis of the 1980s*, San Diego, University of California Center for US–Mexican Studies, 1991.

Gorman, S. (ed.), *Post-Revolutionary Peru. The Politics of Transformation*, Boulder, CO, Westview Press, 1982.

Gorriti Ellenbogen, G., *Sendero. Historia de la Guerra Milenaria en el Perú*, Lima, Editorial Apoyo, 1990.

Gott, R., *Rural Guerrillas in Latin America*, Harmondsworth, Penguin, 1970.

Green, D., *Silent Revolution. The Rise of Market Economics in Latin America*, London, Latin America Bureau, 1995.

Habel, J., *Cuba*, London, Verso, 1991.

Haber, P., 'Cárdenas, Salinas and the Urban Popular Movement', in N. Harvey (ed.), *Mexico – Dilemmas of Transition*, London, Institute of Latin American Studies and British Academy Press, 1993.

Hagopian, F., 'The Compromised Consolidation: The Political Class in the Brazilian Transition', in S. Mainwaring, G. O'Donnell and J. S. Valenzuela (eds), *Issues in Democratic Consolidation. The New South American Democracies in Comparative Perspective*, Notre Dame, IN, University of Notre Dame Press, 1992.

Hall, A., 'Non-Governmental Organisations and Development in Brazil under Dictatorship and Democracy', in C. Abel and C. M. Lewis (eds), *Welfare, Poverty and Development in Latin America*, Basingstoke, Macmillan, 1993.

Handal, S. J., 'A Proposal for El Salvador', in S. J. Handal and C. M. Vilas, *The Socialist Option in Central America*, New York, Monthly Review Press, 1993.

Handal, S. J., and C. M. Vilas, *The Socialist Option in Central America*, New York, Monthly Review Press, 1993.

Harris, R. L., *Marxism, Socialism and Democracy in Latin America*, Boulder, CO, Westview Press, 1992.

Hartlyn, J., and S. A. Morley, *Latin American Political Economy*, Boulder, CO, Westview Press, 1993.

Harvey, N., 'The Difficult Transition: Neoliberalism and Neocorporatism in Mexico', in N. Harvey (ed.), *Mexico. Dilemmas of Transition*, London, Institute of Latin American Studies and British Academic Press, 1993.

Harvey, N. (ed.), *Mexico. Dilemmas of Transition*, London, Institute of Latin American Studies and British Academic Press, 1993.

Haworth, N., 'Radicalisation and the Left in Peru, 1976–90', in B. Carr and S. Ellner (eds), *The Latin American Left. From the Fall of Allende to Perestroika*, Boulder, CO, Westview Press, 1993.

Hellinger, D. C., *Venezuela. Tarnished Democracy*, Boulder, CO, Westview Press, 1991.

Hernández Navarro, L., 'The Escalation of the War in Chiapas', *NACLA. Report on the Americas*, XXXI: 5 (March–April 1998).

Hernández, R., and H. Dilla, 'Political Culture and Popular Participation in Cuba', *Latin American Perspectives*, 69: 18: 2 (Spring 1991).

Hernández, R., and H. Dilla, 'Political Culture and Popular Participation', in Centro de Estudios Sobre América (ed.), *The Cuban Revolution Into the 1990s. Cuban Perspectives*, Boulder, CO, Westview Press, 1992.

Higley, J., and R. Gunther (ed.), *Elites and Democratic Consolidation in Latin America and Southern Europe*, Cambridge, Cambridge University Press, 1992.

Hinkelammert, F. J., 'Our Project for the New Society in Latin America: The Regulating Role of the State and Problems of Self-Regulation in the Market', in S. Jonas and E. J. McCaughan (eds), *Latin America faces the Twenty-First Century. Reconstructing a Social Justice Agenda*, Boulder, CO, Westview Press, 1995.

Hoskin, G., 'Democratisation in Latin America', *Latin American Research Review*, 32: 3 (1997).

Huntington, S. P., 'Postindustrial Politics: How Benign Will It Be?', *Comparative Politics*, 163 (January 1974).

Huntington, S. P., 'Will More Countries Become Democratic?', *Political Science Quarterly*, 99 (1984).

Huntington, S. P., 'The Modest Meaning of Democracy', in R. A. Pastor (ed.), *Democracy in the Americas: Stopping the Pendulum*, New York, Holmes & Meier, 1989.

Jaquette, J. S. (ed.), *The Women's Movement in Latin America*, Boston, Unwin Hyman, 1989.

Jelin, E. (ed.), *Women and Social Change in Latin America*, London, Zed Books, 1990.

Jelin, E. (ed.), 'Citizenship and Identity: Final Reflections', in E. Jelin (ed.), *Women and Social Change in Latin America*, London, Zed Books, 1990.

Jonas, S., *The Battle for Guatemala. Rebels, Death Squads, and US Power*, Boulder, CO, Westview Press, 1991.

Jonas, S., 'Contradictions in Guatemala's "Political Openings"', in S. Jonas and N. Stein (eds), *Democracy in Latin America. Visions and Reality*, New York, Bergin & Garvey, 1990.

Jonas, S., 'Left Establishes its Presence in Guatemalan Elections', *NACLA. Report on the Americas*, XXIX: 4 (January–February 1996).

Jonas, S., and E. J. McCaughan (eds), *Latin America Faces the Twenty-First Century. Reconstructing a Social Justice Agenda*, Boulder, CO, Westview Press, 1995.

Jonas, S., and N. Stein (eds), *Democracy in Latin America. Visions and Reality*, New York, Bergin & Garvey, 1990.

Joyce, E., and C. Malamud (eds), *Latin America and the Multinational Drug Trade*, London, Macmillan, 1998.

Karl, T. L., 'Petroleum and Political Pacts: The Transition to Democracy in Venezuela', *Latin American Research Review*, 22: 1 (1987).

Karl, T. L., and P. Schmitter, 'Modes of Transition in Latin America, Southern and Eastern Europe', *International Social Science Journal*, 128 (May 1991).

Kaufman, R., and B. Stallings, *Debt and Democracy in Latin America*, Boulder, CO, Westview Press, 1989.

Kaufman, R., and B. Stallings, 'Debt and Democracy in the 1980s: The Latin American Experience', in R. Kaufman and B. Stallings, *Debt and Democracy in Latin America*, Boulder, CO, Westview Press, 1989.

Kaufman Purcell, S., and R. Roett (eds), *Brazil Under Cardoso*, Boulder, CO, Lynne Rienner, 1997.

Keck, M. E., *The Workers' Party and Democratisation in Brazil*, New Haven, CT, Yale University Press, 1992.

Keck, M., 'Brazil's PT: Socialism as Radical Democracy', *NACLA. Report on the Americas*, XXV: 5 (May 1992).

Kirkwood, J., *Ser Política en Chile: Las Feministas y Los Partidos*, Santiago, FLACSO, 1986.

Klesner, J. L., 'Political Change in Mexico: Institutions and Identity', *Latin American Research Review*, 32: 2 (1997).

Knight, A., 'Mexico's Elite Settlement: Conjuncture and Consequences', in J. Higley and R. Gunther (eds), *Elites and Democratic Consolidation in Latin America and Southern Europe*, Cambridge, Cambridge University Press, 1992.

Kopinak, K., 'Workers in Mexico', *Latin American Perspectives*, 84: 22: 1 (Winter 1995).

Laclau, E., and C. Mouffe, *Hegemony and Socialist Strategy. Towards a Radical Democratic Politics*, London, Verso, 1985.

Lamas, M., 'Scenes From A Mexican Battlefield', *NACLA. Report on the Americas*, XXXI: 4 (January–February 1998).

Lauer, M., *El Reformismo Burgués*, Lima, Mosca Azul Editores, 1978.

Lehmann, D., *Democracy and Development in Latin America*, Cambridge, Polity Press, 1990.

Levine, D. H., and S. Mainwaring, 'Religion and Popular Protest in Latin America: Contrasting Experiences', in S. Eckstein, *Power and Popular Protest. Latin American Social Movements*, Berkeley, University of California Press, 1989.

Lewis, O., *Five Families: Mexican Case Studies in the Culture of Poverty*, New York, Basic Books, 1959.

Lievesley, G., 'Stages of Growth? Women Dealing with the State and Each Other in Peru', in S. M. Rai and G. Lievesley (eds), *Women and the State: International Perspectives*, London, Taylor & Francis, 1996.

Lijphart, A., *Democracy in Plural Societies. A Comparative Exploration*, New Haven, CT, Yale University Press, 1977.

Little, W., 'Democracy in Latin America: Problems and Prospects', *Democratization*, 1: 2 (Summer 1994).

Loaeza, S., 'The Role of the Right in Political Change in Mexico, 1982–1988', in D. A. Chalmers, M. do Carmo Campello de Souza and A. A. Borón (eds), *The Right and Democracy in Latin America*, New York, Praeger, 1992.

Lomnitz, L., and A. Melnick, *Chile's Middle Class. A Struggle for Survival in the Face of Neoliberalism*, Boulder, CO, Lynne Rienner, 1991.

López, G. A., and M. Stohl (eds), *Liberalization and Redemocratization in Latin America*, Westport, CT, Greenwood Press, 1987.

Loveman, B., 'The Political Left in Chile, 1970–90', in B. Carr and S. Ellner (eds), *The Latin American Left. From the Fall of Allende to Perestroika*, Boulder, CO, Westview Press, 1993.

Lozano, L., 'Adjustment and Democracy in Latin America', in S. Jonas and E. J. McCaughan (eds), *Latin America Faces the Twenty-First Century. Reconstructing a Social Justice Agenda*, Boulder, CO, Westview Press, 1995.

Luciak, I. A., *The Sandinista Legacy. Lessons from a Political Economy in Transition*, Gainesville, University Press of Florida, 1995.

Lumsden, I., *Machos, Maricones and Gays. Cuba and Homosexuality*, Philadelphia, PA, Temple University Press, 1996.

Mabry, D. (ed.), *The Latin American Narcotics Trade and US National Security*, New York, Greenwood Press, 1989.

Macdonald, L., 'A Mixed Blessing. The NGO Boom in Latin America', *NACLA. Report on the Americas*, XXVIII: 5 (March–April 1995).

MacEwan, A., 'Transitions from Authoritarian Rule', *Latin American Perspectives*, 15: 58: 3 (Summer 1988).

Mainwaring, S., 'Transitions to Democracy and Democratic Consolidation: Theoretical and Comparative Issues', in S. Mainwaring, G. O'Donnell and J. S. Valenzuela (eds), *Issues in Democratic Consolidation. The New South American Democracies in Comparative Perspective*, Notre Dame, IN, University of Notre Dame Press, 1992.

Mainwaring, S., G. O'Donnell and J. S. Valenzuela (eds), *Issues in Democratic Consolidation. The New South American Democracies in Comparative Perspective*, Notre Dame, IN, University of Notre Dame Press, 1992.

Martínez Heredia, F., 'Cuban Socialism: Prospects and Challenges', *Latin American Perspectives*, 69: 18: 2 (Spring 1991).

Mauceri, P., *Militares, Insurgencia y Democrátización en el Perú, 1980–88*, Lima, Instituto de Estudios Peruanos, 1989.

Mauceri, P., 'State Reform, Coalitions and the Neoliberal Autogolpe in Peru', *Latin American Research Review*, 20: 1 (1995).

McClintock, C., and A. Lowenthal (eds), *The Peruvian Experiment Reconsidered*, Princeton, NJ, Princeton University Press, 1983.

Menchú, R., *I, Rigoberta Menchú. A Peasant Woman in Guatemala*, London, Verso, 1984.

Meyer, L., 'Democracy from Three Latin American Perspectives', in R. A. Pastor (ed.), *Democracy in the Americas: Stopping the Pendulum*, New York, Holmes & Meier, 1989.

Mignone, E. F., 'The Catholic Church and the Argentine Democratic Transition', in E. C. Epstein (ed.), *The New Argentinian Democracy. The Search for a Successful Formula*, Westport, CT, Praeger, 1992.

Miller, F., *Latin American Women and the Search for Social Justice*, Hanover, NH and London, University Press of New England, 1991.

Mohanty, C. T., A. Russo and L. Torres (eds), *Third World Women and the Politics of Feminism*, Indiana, Indiana University Press, 1991.

Molyneux, M., 'Mobilisation Without Emancipation? Women's Interests, State and Revolution in Nicaragua', in D. Slater (ed.), *New Social Movements and the State in Latin America*, Amsterdam, CEDLA, 1985.

Molyneux, M., 'The Woman Question in the Age of Perestroika', *New Left Review*, 183 (1990).

Momsen, J. H., and V. Kinnaird (eds), *Different Places, Different Voices*, London, Routledge, 1993.

Morales, J. A., and G. McMahon (eds), *Economic Policy and the Transition to Democracy*, Cambridge, MA, MIT Press, 1996.

Moreira Alves, M. H., 'Cultures of Fear, Cultures of Resistance', in J. E. Corradi, P. Weiss – Fagan and M. A. Garretón (eds), *Fear at the Edge. State Terror and Resistance in Latin America*, Berkeley, University of California Press, 1992.

Moreira Alves, M. H., 'Something Old, Something New: Brazil's Partido de Trabalhadores', in B. Carr and S. Ellner (eds), *The Latin American Left. From the Fall of Allende to Perestroika*, Boulder, CO, Westview Press, 1993.

Moser, C. O. N., 'Adjustment from Below: Low-Income Women, Time and the Triple Role in Guayaquil, Ecuador', in S. A. Radcliffe and S. Westwood (eds), *'Viva'. Women and Popular Protest in Latin America*, London, Routledge, 1993.

Munck, R., *Latin America. The Transition to Democracy*, London, Zed Books, 1989.

Munck, R., 'Farewell to Socialism? A Comment on Recent Debates', *Latin American Perspectives*, 65: 17: 2 (Spring 1990).

Munck, R., 'After the Transition: Democratic Disenchantment in Latin America', *European Review of Latin American and Caribbean Studies*, 55 (December 1993).

Munck, R., 'Workers, Structural Adjustment and Concertación Social in Latin America', *Latin American Perspectives*, 82: 21: 3 (Summer 1994).

Naim, M., 'New Competitive Tigers or Old Populist Nationalisms?', in J. S. Tulchin with B. Romero (eds), *The Consolidation of Democracy in Latin America*, Boulder, CO, Lynne Rienner, 1995.

Nef, J., 'The Trend Towards Democratisation and Redemocratisation in Latin America', *Latin American Research Review*, XXIII: 3 (1988).

Nieto, J., *Izquierda y Democracia en el Perú, 1975–80*, Lima, Centro de Estudios y Promoción del Desarrollo, 1983.

Norden, D. L., 'Democracy and Military Control in Venezuela: From Subordination to Insurrection', *Latin American Research Review*, 33: 2 (1998).

Novaro, M., 'Shifting Alliances, Party Politics in Argentina', *NACLA. Report on the Americas*, XXXI: 6 (May–June 1998).

Nylen, W. R., 'The Workers' Party in Rural Brazil', *NACLA. Report on the Americas*, XXIX: 1 (July–August 1995).

O'Brien, P., and P. Cammack (eds), *Generals in Retreat*, Manchester, Manchester University Press, 1985.

O'Donnell, G., 'Transitions, Continuities and Paradoxes', in S. Mainwaring, G. O'Donnell and J. S. Valenzuela (eds), *Issues in Democratic Consolidation. The New South American Democracies in Comparative Perspective*, Notre Dame, IN, University of Notre Dame Press, 1992.

O'Donnell, G., 'Delegative Democracy', *Journal of Democracy*, 5: 1 (1994).

O'Donnell, G., P. Schmitter and L. Whitehead (eds), *Transitions from Authoritarian Rule: Prospects for Democracy*, Baltimore, MD, Johns Hopkins University Press, 1986.

Ost, D., 'Is Latin America the Future of Eastern Europe?', *Problems of Communism*, XLI: 3 (May–June 1992).

Oxhorn, P., 'The Popular Sector Response to an Authoritarian Regime: Shantytown Organizations and the Military Coup', *Latin American Perspectives*, 68: 18: 1 (Winter 1991).

Oxhorn, P., *Organising Civil Society. The Popular Sectors and the Struggle for Democracy in Chile*, Philadelphia, Pennsylvania State University Press, 1995.

Pankhurst, D., and J. Pearce, 'Feminist Perspectives on Democratisation in the South: Engendering or Adding Women In?', in H. Afshar (ed.), *Women and Politics in the Third World*, London, Routledge, 1996.

Paredes, P., 'Las luchas del movimiento obrero y popular bajo el Belaundismo', *Sociedad y Política*, 12 (1981).

Parker, D., 'The Cuban Crisis and the Future of the Revolution: A Latin American Perspective', *Latin American Research Review*, 33: 1 (1998).

Pásara, L., 'La "Libanización" en democracia', in L. Pásara and J. Parodi (eds), *Democracia, Sociedad y Gobierno en el Perú*, Lima, Centro de Estudios de Democracia y Sociedad, 1988.

Pásara, L., and J. Parodi (eds), *Democracia, Sociedad y Gobierno en el Perú*, Lima, Centro de Estudios de Democracia y Sociedad, 1988.

Pastor, R.A. (ed.), *Democracy in the Americas: Stopping the Pendulum*, New York, Holmes & Meier, 1989.

Patterson, H., and C. Roulston, 'The Sandinistas in Opposition', *Journal of Communist Studies*, 8: 4 (December 1992).

Pease García, H., *Democracia y Precariedad Bajo el Populismo Aprista*, Lima, Centro de Estudios y Promoción del Desarrollo, 1988.

Peck, J. (ed.), *The Chomsky Reader*, New York, Pantheon, 1987.

Peeler, J. A., *Latin American Democracies. Colombia, Costa Rica and Venezuela*, Chapel Hill, University of North Carolina Press, 1985.

Peeler, J. A., 'Elite Settlement and Democratic Consolidation: Colombia, Costa Rica and Venezuela', in J. Higley and R. Gunther (eds), *Elites and Democratic Consolidation in Latin America and Southern Europe*, Cambridge, Cambridge University Press, 1992.

Peeler, J. A., *Building Democracy in Latin America*, Boulder, CO, Westview Press, 1998.

Peralta Ramos, M., 'Economic Policy and Distributional Conflict among Business Groups in Argentina: From Alfonsín to Menem', in E. C. Epstein (ed.), *The New Argentinian Democracy. The Search for A Successful Formula*, Westport, CT, Praeger, 1992.

Perelli, C., 'Putting Conservatism to Good Use: Women and Unorthodox Politics in Uruguay, from Breakdown to Transition', in J. S. Jaquette (ed.), *The Women's Movement in Latin America*, Boston, Unwin Hyman, 1989.

Petras, J., 'State, Regime and the Democratization Muddle', *Latin American Studies Association Forum*, 18: 4 (1988).

Petras, J., 'The Redemocratisation Process', in S. Jonas and N. Stein (eds), *Democracy in Latin America. Visions and Reality*, New York, Bergin & Garvey, 1990.

Petras, J., and F. I. Leiva, *Democracy and Poverty in Chile. The Limits to Electoral Politics*, Boulder, CO, Westview Press, 1994.

Petras, J., and M. Morley, *Latin America in the Time of Cholera: Electoral Politics, Market Economics and Permanent Crisis*, New York, Routledge, 1992.

Petras, J., and M. Morley, 'Aylwin's Chile: The Nature of Latin American "Democratic" Transition', in J. Petras and M. Morley, *Latin America* in the Time of Cholera: Electoral Politics, Market Economics and Permanent Crisis, New York, Routledge, 1992.

Petras, J., and S. Vieux, 'The Transition to Authoritarian Electoral Regimes in Latin America', Latin American Perspectives, 83: 21: 4 (Autumn 1994).

Pinheiro, P. S., 'Democracies without Citizenship', NACLA. Report on the Americas, XXX: 2 (September–October 1996).

Pion-Berlin, D., and E. López, 'A House Divided: Crisis, Cleavage and Conflict in the Argentine Army', in E. C. Epstein (ed.), The New Argentinian Democracy. The Search for a Successful Formula, Westport, CT, Praeger, 1992.

Pollack, B., and H. Rosenkranz, Revolutionary Social Democracy – The Chilean Socialist Party, London, Pinter, 1986.

Portantiero, P., 'Foundations of a New Politics', NACLA. Report on the Americas, XXV: 5 (May 1992).

Przeworski, A., 'Some Problems in the Study of the Transition to Democracy', in G. O'Donnell, P. Schmitter and L. Whitehead (eds), Transitions from Authoritarian Rule: Prospects for Democracy, Baltimore, MD, Johns Hopkins University Press, 1986.

Puiggros, A., 'World Bank Education Policy. Market Liberalism Meets Ideological Conservatism', NACLA. Report on the Americas, XXIX: 6 (May–June 1996).

Quandt, M., 'Nicaragua: Unbinding the Ties that Bind', NACLA. Report on the Americas, XXVI: 4 (February 1993).

Quandt, M., 'Unbinding the Ties that Bind: The FSLN and the Popular Organisations', in M. Sinclair (ed.), The New Politics of Survival. Grassroots Movements in Central America, New York, Monthly Review Press, 1995.

Radcliffe, S. A., ' "Así Es Una Mujer Del Pueblo": Low-Income Women's Organisations under APRA, 1985–1987', Centre of Latin American Studies, University of Cambridge, Working Paper 43 (1988).

Radcliffe, S. A., 'Multiple Identities and Negotiation Over Gender: Female, Peasant Union Leaders in Peru', Bulletin of Latin American Research, 9: 2 (1990).

Radcliffe, S. A., and S. Westwood (eds), 'Viva'. Women and Popular Protest in Latin America, London, Routledge, 1993.

Rai, S. M., 'Gender and Democratization: Or What Does Democracy Mean for Women in the Third World?', Democratization, 1: 2 (1994).

Rai, S. M., and G. Lievesley (eds), Women and the State: International Perspectives, London, Taylor & Francis, 1996.

Randall, M., Gathering Rage. The Failure of Twentieth Century Revolutions to Develop a Feminist Agenda, New York, Monthly Review Press, 1992.

Rayas, L., 'Criminalizing Abortion. A Crime Against Women', NACLA. Report on the Americas, XXXI: 4 (January–February 1998).

Reichmann, R., 'Brazil's Denial of Race', NACLA. Report on the Americas, XXVIII: 6 (May–June 1995).

Remmer, K., 'Redemocratisation and the Impact of Authoritarian Rule in Latin America', Comparative Politics (April 1985).

Richards, D. G., 'The Political Economy of the Chilean Miracle', *Latin American Research Review*, 32: 1 (1997).

Roberts, B., 'The Poor in the City. Urban Careers and the Strategies of the Poor', in E. P. Archetti, P. Cammack and B. Roberts (eds), *Latin America*, London, Macmillan, 1987.

Rochabrun, G., 'Crisis, Democracy and the Left in Peru', *Latin American Perspectives*, 15: 3 (Summer 1988).

Rochabrun, G., 'Deciphering the Enigmas of Alberto Fujimori', *NACLA. Report on the Americas*, XXIX: 1 (July–August 1996).

Rodriguez, I. J., 'The CUT: New Unionism at a Crossroads', *NACLA. Report on the Americas*, XXVIII: 6 (May–June 1995).

Rodriguez, L., 'Barrio Women Between the Urban and the Feminist Movement', *Latin American Perspectives*, 21: 82: 3 (Summer 1994).

Roett, R., 'Politics at Century's End', in S. Kantmen Purcell and R. Roett (eds), *Brazil Under Cardoso*, Boulder, CO, Lynne Rienner, 1997.

Rosenfeld, S., and J. L. Marré, 'How Chile's Rich Got Richer', *NACLA. Report on the Americas*, XXX: 6 (May–June 1997).

Rospigliosi, F., 'Democracy's Bleak Prospects', in J. S. Tulchin and G. Bland (eds), *Peru in Crisis. Dictatorship or Democracy?*, Boulder, CO, Lynne Rienner, 1994.

Rowe, W., and V. Schelling, *Memory and Modernity. Popular Culture in Latin America*, London, Verso, 1991.

Ruccio, D. F., 'State, Class and Transition in Nicaragua', *Latin American Perspectives*, 57: 15: 2 (Spring 1988).

Rustow, D., 'Transitions to Democracy: Towards a Dynamic Model', *Comparative Politics*, 2: 3 (April 1970).

Salman, T., 'The Diffident Movement: Generation and Gender in the Vicissitudes of the Chilean Shantytown Organisations, 1973–1990', *Latin American Perspectives*, 21: 82: 3 (Summer 1994).

Saporta Stembach, N., M. Navaro-Aanguren and S. E. Alvarez, 'Feminisms in Latin America: From Bogotá to San Bernardo', in A. Escobar and S. E. Alvarez (eds), *The Making of Social Movements in Latin America*, Boulder, CO, Westview Press, 1992.

Schirmer, J., 'The Seeking of the Truth and the Gendering of Consciousness: The Comadres of El Salvador and the Conavigua Widows of Guatemala', in S. A. Radcliffe and S. Westwood (eds), *'Viva'. Women and Popular Protest in Latin America*, London, Routledge, 1993.

Schmitter, P., 'Transitology: The Science or the Art of Democratization', in J. S. Tulchin and G. Bland (eds), *Peru in Crisis. Dictatorship or Democracy?*, Boulder, CO, Lynne Rienner, 1994.

Schneider, C., 'Mobilisation at the Grassroots. Shantytowns and Resistance in Authoritarian Chile', *Latin American Perspectives*, 18: 67: 1 (Winter 1991).

Senzek, A., 'The Entrepreneurs Who Became Radicals', *NACLA. Report on the Americas*, XX: 4 (January–February 1997).

Serolnikov, S., 'When Looting Becomes a Right. Urban Poverty and Food Riots in Argentina', *Latin American Perspectives*, 82: 21: 3 (Summer 1994).

Serra, L., 'Democracy in Times of War and Socialist Crisis. Reflections Stemming from the Sandinista Revolution', *Latin American Perspectives*, 77: 20: 2 (Spring 1993).

Sheahan, J., *Patterns of Development in Latin America. Poverty, Repression and Economic Strategy*, Princeton, NJ, Princeton University Press, 1987.

Sheahan, J., 'Effects of Liberalization Programs on Poverty and Inequality: Chile, Mexico and Peru', *Latin American Research Review*, 3: 3 (1997).

Sinclair, M. (ed.), *The New Politics of Survival. Grassroots Movements in Central America*, New York, Monthly Review Press, 1995.

Skidmore, T., 'The Future of Democracy: An Analytical Summary', in R. A. Pastor (ed.), *Democracy in the Americas: Stopping the Pendulum*, New York, Holmes & Meier, 1989.

Skidmore, T. E. (ed.), *Television, Politics and the Transition to Democracy in Latin America*, Baltimore, MD, Johns Hopkins University Press, 1993.

Sklair, L., *Assembling for Development. The Maquila Industry in Mexico and the USA*, Boston, Unwin Hyman, 1989.

Slater, D. (ed.), *New Social Movements and the State in Latin America*, Amsterdam, CEDLA, 1985.

Slater, D., 'Social Movements and Recasting of the Political', in D. Slater (ed.), *New Social Movements and the State in Latin America*, Amsterdam, CEDLA, 1985.

Slater, D., 'Power and Social Movements in the Other Occident: Latin America in an International Context', *Latin American Perspectives*, 81: 21: 2 (Spring 1994).

Sollis, P., 'Welfare in Nicaragua: the *Somocista* and *Sandinista* Experiences Compared', in C. Abel and C. Lewis (eds), *Welfare, Poverty and Development in Latin America*, Basingstoke, Macmillan, 1993.

Spalding, R. J., *Capitalists and Revolution in Nicaragua. Opposition and Accommodation, 1979–93*, Chapel Hill, University of North Carolina Press, 1994.

Stallings, B., and R. Kaufman (eds), *Debt and Democracy in Latin America*, Boulder, CO, Westview Press, 1989.

Stepan, A. (ed.), *Democratising Brazil. Problems of Transition and Consolidation*, Oxford, Oxford University Press, 1989.

Stokes, S., *Cultures in Conflict. Social Movements and the State in Peru*, Berkeley, University of California Press, 1995.

Stokes, S., 'Democracy and the Limits of Popular Sovereignty in South America', in J. S. Tulchin with B. Romero (eds), *The Consolidation of Democracy in Latin America*, Boulder, CO, Lynne Rienner, 1995.

Stolovich, L., 'Uruguay: The Paradoxes and Perplexities of an Uncommon Left', in S. Jonas and E. J. McCaughan (eds), *Latin America Faces the Twenty-First Century. Reconstructing a Social Justice Agenda*, Boulder, CO, Westview Press, 1994.

Stoltz Chinchilla, N., 'Marxism, Feminism and the Struggle for Democracy in Latin America', in A. Escobar and S. E. Alvarez (eds), *The Making of Social Movements in Latin America*, Boulder, CO, Westview Press, 1992.

Stubbs, J., 'Social Equity, Agrarian Transition and Development in Cuba, 1945–90', in C. Abel and C. Lewis (eds), *Welfare, Poverty and Development in Latin America*, Basingstoke, Macmillan, 1993.

Suárez Hernández, G., 'Political Leadership in Cuba', in Centro de Estudios Sobre América (ed.), *The Cuban Revolution Into the 1990s. Cuban Perspectives*, Boulder, CO, Westview Press, 1992.

Taylor, L., 'Counter-insurgency, the PCP–Sendero Luminoso and the Civil War in Peru, 1980–1996', *Bulletin of Latin American Research*, 17: 1 (1998).

Taylor, L., *Citizenship, Participation and Democracy. Changing Dynamics in Chile and Argentina*, Basingstoke, Macmillan, 1998.

Thorp, R., and L. Whitehead (eds), *Latin American Debt and the Adjustment Crisis*, Basingstoke, Macmillan, 1987.

Tovar Samanez, T., *Movimiento popular y paros nacional – historia del movimiento popular, 1976–80*, Lima, DESCO Biblioteca Popular 5, 1982.

Tulchin, J. S., and G. Bland (eds), *Peru in Crisis. Dictatorship or Democracy?*, Boulder, CO, Lynne Rienner, 1994.

Tulchin, J. S., with B. Romero (eds), *The Consolidation of Democracy in Latin America*, Boulder, CO, Lynne Rienner, 1995.

Tuñon Pablos, E., 'Women's Struggles for Empowerment in Mexico. Accomplishments, Problems and Challenges', in J. M. Bystydzienski (ed.), *Women Transforming Politics. Worldwide Strategies for Empowerment*, Bloomington, Indiana University Press, 1992.

Ungar, M., 'Prison Mayhem: Venezuela's Explosive Penitentiary Crisis', *NACLA. Report on the Americas*, XXX: 2 (September–October 1996).

Valenzuela, J. S., and A. Valenzuela (eds), *Military Rule in Chile*, Baltimore, MD, Johns Hopkins University Press, 1986.

Valenzuela, M. E., 'The Evolving Roles of Women under Military Rule', in P. W. Drake and I. Jaksic (eds), *The Struggle for Democracy in Chile, 1982–90*, Lincoln, University of Nebraska Press, 1991.

Vargas Meza, R., 'The FARC, the War and the Crisis of the State', *NACLA. Report on the Americas*, XXXI: 5 (March–April 1998).

Vasconi, T. A., 'Democracy and Socialism in South America', *Latin American Perspectives*, 65: 17: 2 (Spring 1990).

Vasconi, T. A., and E. Peraza Martell, 'Social Democracy and Latin America', *Latin American Perspectives*, XXVII: 20: 1 (Winter 1993).

Vieira Machado, L. M., ' "We Learned to Think Politically": The Influence of the Catholic Church and the Feminist Movement on the Jardim Nordeste Area in São Paulo, Brazil', in S. A. Radcliffe and S. Westwood (eds), *'Viva'. Women and Popular Protest in Latin America*, London, Routledge, 1993.

Vilas, C. M., *The Sandinista Revolution*, New York, Monthly Review Press, 1986.

Vilas, C. M., 'What Future for Socialism?', *NACLA. Report on the Americas*, XXV: 5 (May 1992).

Vilas, C. M., 'The Hour of Civil Society', *NACLA. Report on the Americas*, XXVII: 2 (September–October 1993).

Vilas, C. M., *Between Earthquakes and Volcanoes. Market, State and the Revolutions in Central America*, New York, Monthly Review Press, 1995.

Vilas, C. M., 'Neoliberal Social Policy. Managing Poverty', *NACLA. Report on the Americas*, XXIX: 6 (May–June 1996).

Vilas, C. M., 'Participation, Inequality, and the Whereabouts of Democracy', in C. M. Vilas, D. A. Chalmers, K. Hite, S. B. Martin, K. Piester and M. Segarra (eds), *The New Politics of Inequality in Latin America. Rethinking Participation and Representation*, Oxford, Oxford University Press, 1997.

Vilas, C. M., D. A. Chalmers, K. Hite, S. B. Martin, K. Piester and M. Segarra (eds), *The New Politics of Inequality in Latin America. Rethinking Participation and Representation*, Oxford, Oxford University Press, 1997.

Volk, S., ' "Democracy" Versus "Democracy" ', *NACLA. Report on the Americas*, XXX: 4 (January–February 1997).

Waylen, G., 'Rethinking Women's Political Participation and Protest: Chile 1970–90', *Political Studies*, XL (1992).

Waylen, G., 'Democratisation, Feminism and the State in Chile: The Establishment of SERNAM', in S. M. Rai and G. Lievesley (eds), *Women and the State. International Perspectives*, London, Taylor & Francis, 1996.

Whitehead, L., 'The Prospects for a Political Settlement: Most Options have been Foreclosed', in G. Di Palma and L. Whitehead (eds), *The Central American Impasse*, London, Croom Helm, 1986.

Whitehead, L., 'The Consolidation of Fragile Democracies: A Discussion with Illustrations', in R. A. Pastor (ed.), *Democracy in the Americas: Stopping the Pendulum*, New York, Holmes & Meier, 1989.

Whitehead, L., 'The Alternatives to Liberal Democracy: A Latin American Perspective', *Political Studies*, XL (1992).

Wierenga, S. (ed.), *Women's Struggles and Strategies*, Brookfield, VT, Gower, 1988.

Wignaraya, P. (ed.), *New Social Movements in the South*, London, Zed Books, 1993.

Woy-Hazleton, S., 'The Return of Partisan Politics in Peru', in S. Gorman (ed.), *Post-Revolutionary Peru. The Politics of Transformation*, Boulder, CO, Westview Press, 1982.

Index

Note: 'n.' after a page reference indicates the number of a note on that page